Praise for *Software Testing with Visual Studio 2010*

"Jeff Levinson has written a remarkable book. Remarkable because it distills a massive amount of information into a clear, readable book that will teach you how to best use the Visual Studio 2010 Testing Tools. Remarkable because it shows not just how to use the strengths of the tools, but also how to work around any of their weaknesses. Remarkable because Jeff walks you through the implementation strategies that can bring real business value, not just to the testing team, but also to test the entire organization. If you are implementing the test tools, this book belongs on your desk. My dog-eared and marked-up copy sits on mine."

—*Steven Borg, Owner, Northwest Cadence*

"Testing—and testers—don't get enough respect. By providing a great mix of the what, why, and how of testing with Visual Studio 2010, this book will help change that. More important, it will help make the software we use better."

—*David Chappell, Principal, Chappell & Associates*

"Jeff has once again written a great book, filled with nice nuggets of testing wisdom. A great addition to your testing and ALM library for anyone using Visual Studio 2010 and Team Foundation Server 2010."

—*Mickey Gousset, Microsoft ALM MVP and Senior Technical Developer, Infront Consulting Group*

"Jeff's book is by far the most in-depth investigation of the Test features in Visual Studio ALM I have seen. His insight and experience help the readers understand the impact of poor testing and how they can improve the quality of their software. I particularly liked the obvious real-world understanding of the realities of software testing when applied in practice and the effort by the author to show the readers the ways around those realities."

—*Martin Hinshelwood, Visual Studio ALM MVP and Visual Studio ALM Ranger*

"Software Testing defines much more than the usage of a testing tool; it shows the practical way in which we test at Microsoft Corporation. Additionally, this book provides the definitive process to using Microsoft Test Manager with the rigor that we test here at Microsoft."

—*Randy Miller, ALM Architect, Microsoft*

"Jeff provides the rare combination of deep, insider knowledge of Microsoft's 2010 testing tools coupled with pragmatic details about how to plan, manage, and execute testing in the real world."

—Mark Mydland, Director of Test, Visual Studio
Ultimate, Microsoft

"With Jeff's extensive knowledge with Microsoft's ALM offering, this book will get you started on the right track with all the new testing capabilities offered by the Visual Studio 2010 suite. Whether you are a new or veteran tester, the personal insights the author brings to the testing topic are very interesting and useful...."

—Etienne Tremblay, Microsoft ALM MVP

Software Testing with Visual Studio® 2010

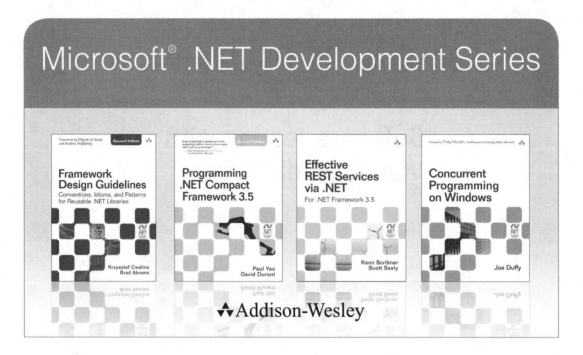

Software Testing with Visual Studio® 2010

■ Jeff Levinson

✦✦ Addison-Wesley

Upper Saddle River, NJ • Boston • Indianapolis • San Francisco
New York • Toronto • Montreal • London • Munich • Paris
Madrid • Cape Town • Sydney • Tokyo • Singapore • Mexico City

The publisher offers excellent discounts on this book when ordered in quantity for bulk purchases or special sales, which may include electronic versions and/or custom covers and content particular to your business, training goals, marketing focus, and branding interests. For more information, please contact:

U.S. Corporate and Government Sales
(800) 382-3419
corpsales@pearsontechgroup.com

For sales outside the United States, please contact:

International Sales
international@pearson.com

Visit us on the Web: informit.com/aw

Library of Congress Cataloging-in-Publication Data:

Levinson, Jeff.
  Software testing with Visual studio 2010 / Jeff Levinson.
     p. cm.
  Includes index.
  ISBN 978-0-321-73448-8 (pbk. : alk. paper) 1. Computer software—Testing—Automation. 2. Microsoft Visual studio. I. Title.
  QA76.76.T48L48 2010
  005.1'4—dc22
                              2010038104

ISBN-13: 978-0-321-73448-8
ISBN-10: 0-321-73448-3
Text printed in the United States on recycled paper at RR Donnelley Crawfordsville in Crawfordsville, Indiana.

Second Printing April 2011

To my wife, Tami, and my daughter, Caitlin, who supported
me and had to deal with me for the last year.
And my new son, Sean: I hope you start sleeping through the night soon.

Contents at a Glance

Foreword   xvii
Preface   xxi
Acknowledgments   xxix
About the Author   xxxi

1   **State of Testing**   1
2   **Software Quality and Testing Overview**   13
3   **Planning Your Testing**   29
4   **Executing Manual Tests**   71
5   **Resolving Bugs**   107
6   **Automating Test Cases**   135
7   **Executing Automated Test Cases**   183
8   **Lab Management**   209
9   **Reporting and Metrics**   239

Contents

Foreword   xvii

Preface   xxi

Acknowledgments   xxix

About the Author   xxxi

1   **State of Testing   1**

Software Testing Challenges   1

The Need for Testers   3

A Different Approach   5

Fixing Communication   5

Increasing Project Visibility   6

What Are the Tools Designed to Do?   7

Metrics   10

Citations   12

2   **Software Quality and Testing Overview   13**

Software Quality   13

Requirements   14

Business Value   14

Expectations   15

Nonfunctional Requirements   15

Where Do You Build Quality?   17

Process and Quality   19

Software Testing   19

    The Testing Mindset   20

    Software Testing Strategies   21

    Types of Software Testing   22

    Test Management   27

    After the Product Is Shipped or Deployed   27

3   Planning Your Testing   29

Microsoft Test Manager   30

    Test Plans   36

    Properties   38

    Contents   43

    Adding Suites and Test Cases to Your Plan   46

Testing Configurations   48

    Managing Test Configurations   49

    Assigning Test Configurations   51

Assigning Testers   53

Test Case Planning Workflow   55

    Analysis and Initial Design   56

    Construction   61

    User Acceptance Testing   62

Common Scenarios   64

    Scheduling and Tracking Test Case Creation and Execution   64

    Feature Driven Development   65

    Moving from One Iteration to Another   67

    Handling Different Test Configurations   68

4   Executing Manual Tests   71

Using the Test Case Work Item Type   72

    Shared Steps   75

    Data Driven Test Cases (Test Parameters)   77

Running Your First Tests   79

    Test Runner   80

Examining Test Results   92

   Test Run Results   93

   Detailed Test Results   95

Exploratory Testing with MTM   101

5 Resolving Bugs   107

A Bug's Life   107

   Customer Reported Bug   110

   Test Team Reported Bug   110

   Triaging the Bug   110

   Reactivations   111

Bug Differences and Modifications   111

The Generated Bug   116

How a Developer Uses IntelliTrace   120

Fixing the Bug   122

   Associated Changesets   124

   Associated Work Items   124

   Impacted Tests   125

Setting the Build Quality   125

Assigning a New Build   127

Verifying That the Bug Is Fixed   129

Dealing with Impacted Tests   131

6 Automating Test Cases   135

To Automate or Not to Automate   136

The Automated Testing Framework   139

Creating an Automated Test from a Manual Test   141

   Examining a Generated Web Application Coded UI Test   142

Adding Validations   157

Adding Additional Recorded Steps   164

Parameterized Coded UI Tests   166

   Handling Issues Due to Inconsistency   168

   Resolving the Data Inconsistency   169

Handling Dynamic Values   172

   Other Tips   177

Combining Multiple Tests   178

Associating Coded UI Tests and Test Cases   178

7   Executing Automated Test Cases   183

Executing Automated Tests Through Visual Studio   183

   Local Execution   184

   Local Execution with Remote Collection   184

   Remote Execution   185

Executing Automated Tests from the Command Line   190

Executing Automated Tests in MTM   191

   Creating an Automated Build   191

   Setting Up the Physical Environment   193

   Running a Coded UI Test Through MTM   196

Executing Automated Tests with Team Build   202

Automated Testing Gotchas   205

   Custom Dialogs   205

   Cleaning Up Your Tests   207

8   Lab Management   209

Managing Virtual Environments Through MTM   210

Finishing Virtual Environment Configuration   217

Automated Test Settings   221

   Lab Management Workflow   222

Executing a Lab Build   231

Running Automated Tests Through MTM   233

Manual Tests in a Virtual Environment   234

9   Reporting and Metrics   239

Understanding the Reporting Structure   240

Built-In Reports   242

   Bug Status   244

   Bug Trends   245

   Reactivations   246

Build Quality Indicators 246

Build Success over Time 248

Build Summary 249

Stories Overview 250

Test Case Readiness 251

Test Plan Progress 252

Excel Services Reports (Dashboards) 253

Reporting with Microsoft Excel 254

Creating a Generated Report 255

The Testing Measures 256

Metrics 268

What to Measure 271

First-Time Defect Rate 273

Bug Reactivations 276

General Bug Counts 277

Index 283

Foreword

OUR PRODUCT TEAM LIKES TO SAY that when we started building Visual Studio Test Professional 2010 we wanted to deliver world peace as a feature. To make our ship date, we reduced our aspirations to making peace between software developers and software testers.

Even with this drastic reduction in scope, we faced a daunting task. Our profession often creates substantial separation, organizationally and sometimes physically, between those responsible for creating and maintaining software and those responsible for validating that the software meets the needs of businesses and customers. Because of the separation developers and testers often communicate by throwing information "over the wall," which results in poor communication of issues (bugs); in uncertainty about what features, bug fixes, and improvements development has added to a particular build; and in mistrust between the development and test organizations. All of which, in turn, contribute to the quality issues, schedule delays, and outright project cancellations that continue to plague our industry. Many of the QA tools currently available in the market exacerbate the communication problems by managing the planning, testing, and tracking of the test effort independently from the tools used to track planning and development.

As we began to dig into the source of the communication breakdowns, we found, somewhat to our surprise, that manual black-box style testing accounts for approximately 70 percent of all testing in our industry. To succeed with this style of testing, testers develop deep domain knowledge around the products they test but spend less time cultivating their knowledge of the deep technical and architectural aspects of the system. To manage their testing efforts, these testers relied largely on Microsoft Word, Microsoft Excel, handwritten notes, and whiteboards. Worse, testers had no tool support for running tests and therefore spent significant portions of the day on time-consuming and often menial tasks such as deploying software, writing bug reports, and finding clear steps to reproduce bugs.

As a software development company, Microsoft clearly recognizes the importance of allowing all members of software development teams, developers, testers, architects, project and program managers, and business analysts to participate fully in the development process. We built Microsoft Visual Studio Test Professional 2010 and the Lab Management capability of Microsoft Team Foundation Server 2010 to help eliminate the friction between developers and testers by providing self-documenting builds that include tests impacted by developers' changes, single-click actionable bugs that eliminate the "No Repro" problem, and work item-based test planning and management that enables visibility and traceability by all project stakeholders. To streamline the test effort and increase the effectiveness of testing, we added streamlined virtual build, deploy and test, fast forward for manual testing, and the capability to generate an automated Coded UI test based on a previously completed manual test.

During development, we relied heavily on feedback and advice from a number of external sources who could provide both industry perspective and feedback based on extensive personal experience. In that capacity, Jeff Levinson helped to shape Microsoft's test offering and TFS's Lab Management capability in just about every way possible. Jeff participated in every formal design review, special interest group, technology preview, and beta program that existed. Beyond the formal interactions, Jeff spent days and weeks of his "free time" installing, using, and testing our product followed by hours spent with me and other members of the team providing feedback, pushing for improvements, and making suggestions. I can't say that all Jeff's feedback made it into the final product, but our product is better for his effort.

As much as I would like to believe that Jeff spent all this time and effort just to make my life easier, I know that Jeff's real motivation came from his passion for helping teams to build quality software. In his book, Jeff brings a pragmatic approach, years of experience, and a clear understanding of how the entire development team must work together to build truly great software. The combination of Jeff's insider knowledge and deep understanding of Microsoft Visual Studio Test Professional 2010 with his proven approach to software testing create a roadmap that can help any team to build high-quality software while avoiding the pitfalls and friction that so often lead to "death marches," missed deadlines, and unsatisfied customers.

Mark Mydland
Director of Test, Microsoft

Preface

AS A PROCESS IMPROVEMENT professional, I have experienced many team challenges. Big challenges. It is not unusual to see teams that seem so perfectly compatible start in excitement only to fizzle in different directions and end up not working together. Products suffer, customers suffer, and ultimately relationships suffer. When Microsoft introduced a new set of tools to help ensure quality applications and bring teams together in an evolutionary way, I was at first skeptical, but not now.

From one company to the next, one organization to the next, or even within a given team, the same problems arise. Granted, the circumstances can make basic problems much more challenging, but you can consistently identify the following issues:

- Challenged or poor communication between developers and testers
- Constant churning with precious little progress due to fixing the same things over and over again
- Organizational structures that sabotage quality work and the capability to productively manage resources
- Management that focuses on the shipping date with no consideration of the long-term cost of poor quality
- Lack of proven toolsets to maximize productivity and efficiency of teams

Enter Microsoft Test Manager. Now there is this single point at which teams can coalesce: quality. Microsoft Test Manager offers the following proposition: Do you want to build a better quality product with less rework, less divisiveness in a shorter period of time? If so, what are you willing to do to achieve this goal? The response seems simple enough:

- Incorporate a basic process with some good old-fashioned common sense.
- Use common tools.
- Share data.

In my experience, there is one obvious set of tools: Team Foundation Server, Visual Studio, and Microsoft Test Manager. Using these tools has been proven to break down barriers, get teams talking, and deliver the promises of the preceding proposition. It is my goal to demonstrate how to accomplish this to as many people as possible. With the tools that Microsoft provides, the level of effort required to use them is minimal and the benefits are huge. Will the tools work for everyone? Well, with the wide variety of tools and platforms that individuals need to test against, I can't make any promises. But if, for the most part, the platforms and languages you test against are somewhat commonplace, you can reap benefits from using this tool suite.

It's funny how we see the process differently depending on our role on a project. I have served in many roles (some better than others). As a developer, I couldn't stand testers because they always broke my code because they didn't know how to use the application. As a tester, I couldn't stand developers because they didn't know how to code. As an architect, I looked on much of the process as a necessary evil. As a process improvement expert, I realized (even though this may be patently obvious) that without testers I couldn't get the metrics I needed to make a difference. As an author, I hope to communicate that by bringing testers and developers together to work *cooperatively* we can make positive changes across the board in a fun and cooperative environment. We can accomplish this by objectively assessing and learning about these unique and valuable new tools from Microsoft.

Thank you for reading this book, and I hope it helps you improve the quality of your software. If you have questions, errata, suggestions, additions, or disagreements with anything you read, please drop me a note at jeffstuff@jtlevinson.com.

Who Should Read This Book?

This book is primarily for software testers or people who test software as one of their primary job roles—from the professional tester or developer to the business analyst who needs to verify software for end users.

The testing process with Microsoft Test Professional 2010 and Visual Studio 2010 Ultimate is structured in a way that the tester can perform manual testing, and the *developer* can automate the tests. For this reason, developers can also find this book useful because considerable resources are dedicated to the developer's role in the testing process. Further, much of this book covers best practices for developers and testers working together. Chapter 6, "Automating Test Cases," and Chapter 7, "Executing Automated Test Cases," are especially relevant to the topic.

For those new, or relatively new, testers Chapter 2, "Software Quality and Testing Overview" provides a solid introduction to the goals of testing, approaches to testing, and considerations when testing. This is designed to be a primer and can be skipped by those already familiar with testing processes.

Test and development managers, in particular those looking for a better understanding of the overall process or those wanting to leverage the reporting offered in Team Foundation Server, can also benefit from reading this book. Understanding reporting is often a conduit for discovering that a seemingly insurmountable problem can actually be fixed. Add to that mix the capability to quantify metrics and improve them over time, and you have a powerful tool for managers. Chapter 1, "State of Testing," Chapter 3, "Planning Your Testing," and Chapter 9, "Reporting and Metrics," are most applicable to managers.

I hope you find this book helpful in your organization and as a guide for your testing teams.

What This Book Does Not Cover

One topic not covered is the virtualization infrastructure required to run Lab Management. The lab infrastructure requires a network administrator and people familiar with virtualization technologies including hardware and software. It would have been too complicated to include everything and would have been beyond the scope of this book. This includes information such as

System Center Virtual Machine Manager and Hyper-V. Setup of the Test Agent, Test Controller, and Build Hosts are discussed because these are items the testing or development team will probably need to deal with at some point—especially if teams switch back and forth between user interface testing and unit testing.

Additionally, you will not find information on load testing, stress testing, and Web performance testing, and only minimal information on unit testing is available. The information on unit testing is presented from the perspective of how a tester or developer might execute these automated tests and relate them to requirements. You will not find any in-depth discussions on the philosophy of unit testing or specific unit testing techniques.

About the Application Used in This Book

The application used throughout this book (and in the exercises) is the BlogEngine.NET application because it is a popular real-world application used by many individuals. It is also open source with a thriving community behind it. BlogEngine.NET was created by Al Nyveldt and Mads Kristensen. You can get more information about it from dotnetblogengine.net and download the original version of this application at blogengine.codeplex.com.

The version used in this book has been modified somewhat because it was ported to Visual Studio 2010 and converted to a Web Application for use with Team Build. You can download the source from here: informit.com/title/9780321734488. This download includes a readme file describing how to set up the application so that you can follow along with the examples. Aside from these modifications, no other material modifications have been made to the source code. The Database project and the MSDeploy project were added to support the different capabilities of the tools demonstrated.

Other software is required to follow these examples. You must have either Visual Studio Ultimate or Premium to create Coded UI tests. You must also have Microsoft Test Professional or Visual Studio Ultimate to get Microsoft Test Manager. Although not a tested configuration, you might run these examples with Microsoft's all-up Lab Management virtual machine. This virtual machine can be downloaded here: www.microsoft.com/downloads/details.aspx?FamilyID=592e874d-8fcd-4665-8e55-7da0d44b0dee&displaylang=en.

How This Book Is Organized

This book is structured to not only be used as a reference but also as a step-by-step guide for a process. The book guides you through the testing process as it would occur on an application. The book starts with a discussion of problems the industry faces and quickly moves to development methodologies and the role of testers. From there, you learn how to plan the testing process using Microsoft Test Manager to write first-draft Test Cases and execute those Test Cases. During the course of execution, bugs can be filed, and developers can fix those bugs. Testers can verify the fix and then determine which Test Cases to automate. Developers automate the Test Cases and then they can be executed by developers and testers in a physical or a virtual environment. Finally, the book ends with a discussion of reporting and metrics and offers some ideas that you can apply to your processes to improve quality.

- Chapter 1, "State of Testing"—This chapter provides an introduction to the problems facing software development teams today from a quality perspective. It covers the cost of poor quality, legal actions because of poor quality, and other commonly known but frequently ignored issues. It also discusses the author's philosophy of software testing and the goals of this book. Finally, it covers some of the basic software development methodologies and where software testing fits in with these methodologies. This chapter provides an overview of the Microsoft technology stack and end-to-end process flow.

- Chapter 2, "Software Quality and Testing Overview"—This chapter presents an introduction to software testing. This includes why we need to do software testing, what the goals of software testing are, different types of software testing and software testing techniques. It provides a foundational view of the tester's world.

- Chapter 3, "Planning Your Testing"—First, you must plan for testing. This chapter shows you how to use the tools in Microsoft Test Manager (MTM). It also details how to navigate MTM, create test settings, and structure Test Cases. It explains how to manage the testing process using the Test Case work item type and requirements.

- Chapter 4, "Executing Manual Tests"—This is your introduction to executing tests with Microsoft Test Manager and Test Runner. You learn how to create Test Cases, reuse test steps, execute manual tests, and file bugs. When teams first start using MTM, this is what they do on a day-to-day basis. This chapter also covers exploratory testing.

- Chapter 5, "Resolving Bugs"—When you file a bug, the process and lifecycle of the bug is critical to reducing rework and driving reporting. This chapter discusses the Bug work item type, some customizations you might want to make to it, and how it serves as a communication mechanism for testers and developers. You are also introduced to how developers can use the Bug work item type to fix software correctly the first time and then how testers can verify that fix. This chapter introduces Test Impact Analysis.

- Chapter 6, "Automating Test Cases"—This is largely a developer-focused chapter on creating automated Test Cases. These Test Cases can be manual (recorded by testers) or automated (unit sting and other types of tests). One key item in this chapter is associating any type of automated test with a requirement. The features in this chapter require Visual Studio 2010 Premium or Ultimate.

- Chapter 7, "Executing Automated Test Cases "—After automating the Test Cases, teams need to execute those automated tests. This chapter describes all possible ways to execute an automated test. This is both a developer-focused chapter (using Visual Studio to execute the tests) and a tester-focused chapter (using Microsoft Test Manager to execute the tests). You also learn how to execute tests as part of the build process.

- Chapter 8, "Lab Management"—This chapter focuses on the Lab Management features of Microsoft Test Professional 2010 and Visual Studio 2010 Ultimate. You learn how to use the virtualization platform to test applications and how to snapshot environments to help developers reproduce bugs. This chapter also focuses on both developers and testers: Developers learn how to set up the code to be deployed in a lab environment and executed through the build process. Testers learn how to execute both manual and automated tests in a virtual environment and file actionable bugs.

- Chapter 9, "Reporting and Metrics"—This chapter covers reporting and metrics. By following the processes in this book, a team has detailed metrics by which they can determine the quality of their product and where the testing process can be improved. You explore the built-in reports provided by TFS but also how to do custom reporting on the data cube to get detailed information about your testing endeavors. This also serves as a brief guide to what type of customizations you can make to the Test Case work item type to capture more detailed information.

Acknowledgments

WRITING THIS BOOK HAS been a labor of love over the last year, and there is no way I could have done it alone. Writing about beta software requires cooperation from the teams at Microsoft, and in this case I got more than I could have imagined. The number of people who provided input is long. If I have left anyone out, my apologies. First a special thanks to Mark Mydland, Ram Cherala, and Euan Garden—all of them put up with me for what seemed like hours on end. Long before starting the book, I pestered them on the philosophy of testing and their approaches to it and tools to implement it. I learned a lot from all of them. Other members of the testing team helped with everything from technical aspects to the understanding of specific decisions made during the creation of Microsoft Test Manager, Lab Management, and the Coded UI features. Many thanks to Naysawn Nadiri, David "Dr. Will" Williamson, Dominic Hopton, Pradeep Narayan, Ravi Shanker, Chris Patterson, Anutthara Bharadwaj, Daryush Laqab, Shay Mandel, Vinod Malhotra, Gautam Goenka, Vijay Machiraju, and Mathew Aniyan.

One other group of individuals helped as well, whether they knew it—the Application Lifecycle Management (ALM) Most Valuable Professionals (MVPs). They put up with hundreds of e-mails and provided responses that helped shape my approach to using the testing tools. Many were supportive during the writing process. I am honored to be included in this exceptionally talented and knowledgeable group of people.

On a personal note, my wife Tami and daughter Caitlin have had to put up with an absentee husband and father for the last several months. Needless to say I could not have done this without their love and support.

My four reviewers deserve a big thank-you. Mario Cardinal, Etienne Tremblay, and Mike Vincent are fellow ALM MVPs who thoroughly vetted my content not once but twice. The book is better for their input. And to Anutthara Bharadwaj (a member of the test team), even after a long plane flight with no power and bad service, she provided excellent feedback and comments and continued to teach me even after I thought I "knew it all." Thank you, Anu, for putting up with me.

I want to call out Mike Vincent specifically here for not only his help but his contributions. Mike was the last reviewer of this book. During the production of this book many ideas were discussed as to what this book should be about and what it should cover. Late in the process we decided that Chapter 2 should be added to provide an introduction for those just coming into the testing space. I did not have time at that point in the schedule to write this chapter. In came Mike to the rescue. Chapter 2 was contributed by Mike and helps round out the book in a way that makes it better than it was before. Thanks Mike!

For Brian Keller, a senior technical evangelist with Visual Studio, I can only say "Thank you." I am just in awe of his ability to quickly read, distill, and correct information or add the tiny details that were missed. And to Sam Guckenheimer for helping iron out the most difficult part of any technical book—the direction.

And to my co-workers at Northwest Cadence who were supportive of the entire process from beginning to end and through the days, weeks, and months of the writing process.

Most important, thanks to my editor Joan Murray and assistant editor Olivia Basegio, without whom this book would not have been possible. As with any endeavor, it isn't the big stuff that trips you up; it's the small stuff. And to the rest of the team at Addison-Wesley from San Dee Phillips my copy editor to Andrew Beaster who shepherded the book through production twice, thank you for sticking with it!

About the Author

Jeff Levinson has 16 years of experience in software development in many different roles—developer, tester, architect, project manager, and scrum master at several large companies. Jeff is currently a Senior Application Lifecycle Management (ALM) Consultant for Northwest Cadence, which is a company that specializes in Team Foundation Server, Visual Studio, methodologies, and process improvement. In his day-to-day work, Jeff helps teams, organizations, and companies adopt more efficient processes, improve quality, and reduce costs associated with software development. Jeff is a frequent speaker at industry events and writes a twice-monthly column for *Visual Studio Magazine* Online. This is his fourth book on software development. His other books are *Building Client/Server Applications with VB.NET* (Apress 2003), *Pro Visual Studio Team System 2005* (Apress 2006), and *Pro Visual Studio Team System with Team Edition for Database Professionals* (Apress 2007). Jeff has a master's degree in software engineering from Carnegie Mellon University and is an MCP, MCAD, MCSD, MCDBA, and MCT.

Jeff currently lives in Washington State with his wife and two children.

▪ 1 ▪

State of Testing

THIS CHAPTER ANSWERS SOME questions about the current crop of challenges and problems that plague the software testing process in organizations today. It offers some new ideas and approaches to testing. It can also give you a slightly different view on how you can accomplish testing with the Microsoft Visual Studio 2010 testing tools. Following this is a series of examples of major failures in testing as a reason for why we, as an industry, need to change our approach to testing. The chapter concludes with the technical capabilities of the Microsoft Visual Studio 2010 and Microsoft Test Professional 2010 tools and how they fit into the software development process.

Software Testing Challenges

I recently started working with a company and was discussing some of the issues the group manager was facing. I remarked that the software did not seem to be tested. He asked what led me to this conclusion. The answer was an apparent lack of testers, lack of comprehensive Test Cases, and upper management being frustrated with the cost of rework. In reply the manager said that the software is tested—by the developers but that they did not have dedicated testing resources. This was obviously a red flag, and the conversation quickly moved to the challenges we face today with software quality assurance and testing. The biggest issues he mentioned were getting all the people associated with software development working together, using a good, consistent process, and having clear testable requirements.

These are some problems you may be facing:

- Your organization doesn't test and you want to start testing.
- Testing leads to finger pointing, which kills morale.
- Projects are late because bugs are found late in the process.
- Developers use one set of tools, and testers use another, and the tools do not integrate.
- The team is always finding and fixing bugs, but the customers continue to find critical bugs.

These items generally all relate to each other. Here are a few quick examples of what these items lead to. Organizations, even though they realize the importance of testing, don't test. They don't hire the resources or have the wrong roles testing the software—namely they rely on the developers to test the software. This invariably leads to customers finding many bugs, which leads to a large amount of rework.

In organizations in which testing does take place, there seems to be a lot of blame to go around. Testers blame developers for not coding something right. Developers blame testers for not using the software correctly. Customers always question why there are so many bugs and why the developers and testers aren't working together better.

Project schedule slips in waterfall processes are frequently built into the process. If you use a process that batches everything from one phase to the next (analysis to architecture to development to testing to release), when bugs are found in testing the team has a short time to find and fix the problem. Because this is not possible in many cases, and the goal is frequently a zero defect release, the schedule slips.

Tooling is frequently a problem both from a usage and an economic standpoint—especially when those tools don't integrate. Consider a situation in which developers use one Integrated Development Environment (IDE) and they work on requirements entered in another system, and the testers work in yet another system and none of the systems talk to each other. Not only is the organization paying for two or three sets of licenses, but also the users (developers and testers) need to be trained on two or three different systems. This situation also contributes to throwing things over the wall in a disconnected fashion, which impacts speed, communication, discoverability, and accuracy.

Finally, many teams strive for a zero defect release, which is a laudable goal. In reality, this is not usually a necessity. Rather, finding and fixing the right bugs is the key to a successful release. For example, fixing normal path bugs first can lead to customers finding fewer bugs because they don't use the alternative paths of features as often. Second, the more bugs you find and fix, the higher the cost is to find and fix each bug. At what point is this cost no longer worth it? Many organizations don't take into account this financial consideration when analyzing bugs. (This book does not cover the economic factors involved in finding and fixing bugs, but which bugs to fix is discussed.)

These issues all negatively impact development teams, products, and ultimately organizations. But there are better ways to approach this process, and better, more integrated tools with which to approach it.

The Need for Testers

If you are reading this book, you know that software is not tested as well as it should be, but it is helpful to step back and put it in perspective. Poor software quality costs the United States' economy approximately $59,500,000,000 (yes, that's 59.5 billion and not a typo) every year (NIST 2002). This is because of lost productivity and resources. Although this is a large number, it doesn't actually put the problem in perspective. Here are a few practical instances of poor testing and the consequences that resulted. When organizations ask themselves what the cost of poor quality is, this data should help answer this question.

In March 2008, Waste Management, Inc., sued SAP for a complete failure of a $100 million software installation.[1] Waste Management stated that SAP could not run even the most basic processes.

In March 2004, the Ohio State Attorney General sued PeopleSoft for $510 million over a failed installation of the PeopleSoft software at Cleveland State University.[2] It was stated, among other items, that the software was "unstable" and that it had to install "hundreds of fixes."

In January 2002, Cigna Corporation, a major provider of health-related services, installed a new set of tools from Siebel Systems and Computer Science Corporation. It went live, had numerous failures, and Cigna concluded that "the new system had not been tested well...."[3] This led to the loss of major corporate customers and numerous customer complaints.

In January 2005, it was reported that the FBI's Virtual Case File system built by Science Applications International Corporation and which cost $170 million was being canceled. According to the *Washington Post*, there were hundreds of problem reports, and many basic functions had not even been tested at that time—and this was one month before delivery.[4]

And only the high profile failures are actually reported. Many hundreds or thousands of other project failures occur every year that no one ever hears about. And although some companies can afford huge losses such as those mentioned here, many cannot. And in particular, smaller companies cannot afford even a small number of failures because they do not have the same resources available as larger companies do.

These are just a handful of the hundreds of incidents that have made headlines in the last several years. And these aren't unusual. Numerous other issues have occurred because adequate testing of software was not performed. But none of these incidents had to occur. Yes, it is true that almost no software system is 100% bug free; the law of diminishing returns does apply here. If you had an infinite amount of money and time, you could theoretically make a system bug free, but most organizations don't have that type of time or money.

It can probably (with a high degree of certainty) be stated that testing alone was not the downfall of all these projects. Fluid requirements, project management issues, and other items most likely contributed to the problems. But testing being identified as a key area of concern is notable.

Even more disturbing is a study by Coleman Parkes Research presented at a quality conference in London November 5, 2007, where it was noted that the "testing budget was the first to be squeezed if difficulties are encountered" and 47% of respondents to the survey believed testing was a necessary evil.[5]

A Different Approach

Microsoft created a set of testing tools and reports that are tightly integrated into the software development process as a way to solve these problems. Microsoft Visual Studio 2010 and Microsoft Test Manager incorporate integrated, traceable Test Cases with tight feedback loops resulting in actionable bugs. Microsoft's mantra for this release was "no more no repro." The goal was to eliminate things like the constant re-opening of supposedly fixed bugs and constant rework related to features being completed but failing testing in ways that the features should not fail. They did this through increasing communication (both the quantity and quality) between all team members and by providing visibility to decision makers. The information is exposed to the stakeholders in a way that they can judge the quality of the software and make timely business decisions based on this information. Leveraging the power of Team Foundation Server as a central hub for all information related to a feature enables developers and testers to communicate efficiently in a collaborative, rather than adversarial, environment.

Fixing Communication

In many organizations the relationship between developers and testers is not the best. This has been viewed as a natural by-product of the work that testers do; they try to find defects in the developers' work. This is a situation that needs to change, and it is a change you can make relatively easily. Developers need to produce code with fewer defects (contrary to popular belief, bugs in functionality are not the sole province of the developer; they are usually nurtured in the requirements phase) and testers need to provide better information to developers to help them run down bugs in the application.

Part of this is solved simply by testers having access (at least in a read-only mode) to what the developers are doing. Testers can see the documents the developers are working off of and can trace the requirements to the code.

Another part of the solution is that as testers write Test Cases, developers have access to the Test Cases, so *they can run them before they submit code for testing*. This is huge. Too many times testers complain of "stupid" bugs. (That is, they clicked a button and the application crashed.) These types of bugs are completely unacceptable—there is just no excuse for them. With developers running the Test Cases first, the testers should rarely find bugs in the Test Cases they run. (And by extension the users won't find bugs either.)

The other half of the communication issue is the quality of the bug reports; they are inadequate to use in fixing a bug. Some bug reports contain a one-line description with a note saying, "fix it." Okay, I admit that filling out bug reports is tedious and boring; however, if testers don't provide enough information, they can't complain when the bug isn't fixed.

This is a key barrier that Microsoft Visual Studio 2010 breaks down. Visual Studio, combined with Team Foundation Server, enables developers and testers to communicate through a common medium and in a common language in a collaborative environment—they are all working off the same information.

Increasing Project Visibility

Although this isn't a book on project management, it is always amazing to see that the only people who are ever surprised about the status of a project are the customers. Why? Teams do not report information in a way that the business can make effective decisions. Clear information about the status of a project is not reported either. This lack of information paints a rosy picture for the customers, and the day after the release when they start using the software and everything starts breaking, the customers become extremely dissatisfied, upset, and confused. They want to know how the team could release such buggy software. And if the team didn't know, how come they didn't know? At what point in the process did everything go wrong?

This is why transparency is such a key part of software development, and projects that aren't transparent don't succeed. This is another key scenario that Team Foundation Server and Visual Studio 2010 address.

What Are the Tools Designed to Do?

Up to this point you have learned about what the tools were designed to do and how they can help improve your process. Now let's walk through a scenario and discuss the technical capabilities of the tools.

This scenario shows a process flow and some of the technical capabilities (see Figure 1-1). Granted, you need to actually use the features properly for all this to work correctly, but it doesn't require a team to go out of its way to get these benefits from the testing tools. Other options haven't been specifically called out in this flow but are covered in Chapter 8, "Lab Management." This also meets a vast number of needs not met by other tools currently available. Look at a few of the highlights.

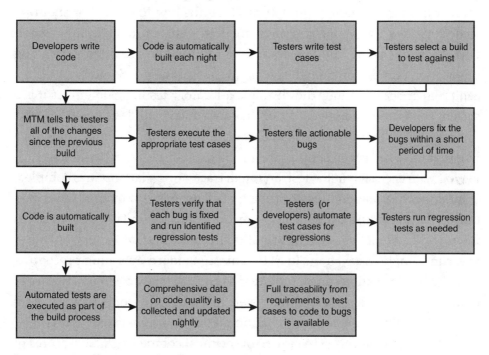

FIGURE 1-1: Development and testing process flow

Automatedbuilds are critical for capturing metrics and using other features of the testing tools such as Test Impact Analysis (TIA). In addition, automated builds quickly help find and identify the cause of build breaks with minimal impact. On top of this, a build is built on Windows Workflow 4.0

(yes, you can still use MSBuild, so no investments are lost) that makes controlling the build, deployment, and testing process easy, and you can easily customize the build process.

Microsoft Test Manager (MTM) (through the automated build) automatically notifies the testers of changes between different builds. Instead of the testers asking the developers what changed between each build, they will know. That lets them focus their testing efforts on new features and reduces the back and forth between testers and developers; therefore, the testers can work more efficiently.

Whether testers file bugs with full information is often a point of contention between the testing and development teams. It evokes comments like, "It works on my machine," and "I can't get the bug to occur," or shouting something like "What did you do to break it?" This is not an optimal situation. The issue stems from the amount of information provided with a bug report. Sometimes not enough information is provided. Sometimes testers can't remember what they did during exploratory testing. Sometimes it is a system configuration issue. Most of that goes away with MTM and VS 2010. Imagine this scenario: The testers execute a test and find a bug. They file a bug that includes screen shots of the problem; a time-stamped video recording log with each step in the test; an IntelliTrace™ log that provides complete debugging information (a historical log of all actions and methods executed during the test run); a list of all tests performed before and after the bug was found; and complete system information from the system on which the test was run. Sounds crazy, huh? In MTM this is standard operating procedure. And other information can be provided as well; that is, developers can work more efficiently, and it is easier for testers to file bugs (testers can work more efficiently) without the testers having to fill out comprehensive reports.

Test Impact Analysis (TIA) is one of the most compelling new features of Visual Studio. The problem that TIA solves is this: Testers have hundreds (if not thousands) of Test Cases as they get close to the release of the product. But lots of last-minute changes are made to code. How do you know that bugs aren't introduced? The only way to verify that bugs haven't been introduced is to run regression tests. But who has time to run hundreds or thousands of regression tests? How do you know which code changes require which tests to be rerun to verify that there are no regression bugs with a given change? The short answer today is that testing teams spend a large amount of time maintaining matrices that record, as best as possible, this information. But by using Visual Studio, you have the potential for a whole different story. TIA can inform you that tests have been successfully run previously but that a code change was made on a portion of code exercised by the Test Case. In this way TIA can cut down the guessing about which tests to run and the number of tests that need to be run to verify that no regression bugs exist. (For example, testers can work more efficiently.) Chapter 4, "Executing Manual Tests," covers TIA in more depth.

Automating functional Test Cases in VS 2010 requires a little bit of work but, depending on the scenario, you do not need any coding skill to do it. Testers can perform this automation, but Microsoft's current vision is that developers would help with the automation of Test Cases (or the testing team would include Software Developers in Test). After a Test Case has been automated, testers can run full suites of automated tests while they perform other work (functional or Unit Tests); therefore, testers can work more efficiently.

MAINTAINING AUTOMATED TESTS

Automated tests have overhead. Microsoft has tried to reduce this overhead by making the automation code more "intelligent" (see Chapter 6, "Automating Test Cases"). The functionality is great but it should be used to achieve specific goals because otherwise the maintenance associated with user interfaces that change significantly over time can quickly become overwhelming.

Comprehensive data collection and reporting is a hallmark of TFS. The reporting capabilities far outstrip anything else available in terms of the amount, quality, and reporting mechanisms available to you. Instantly knowing how many Test Cases you have, how many have been executed, how many have been successful, and how much code they have covered is a tool that every manager should have. Knowing the quality of the code and not just guessing it is critical to a successful release. You can achieve this only with TFS; managers can work more efficiently with better information.

To build on top of the data collected, the traceability features of TFS are second to none for a simple reason: No other testing tools seamlessly integrate with the source code repository or work item tracking. You can argue that other tools have the same features, but this is accomplished mostly through integrations between different systems. They are not built from the ground up to integrate and report on the data, and TFS is built for that purpose.

You might have noticed the not-so-subtle benefit of all this tooling: simple efficiency. The tools are simple to use; they collect most of the information in the background; and they provide the maximum amount of benefit with the least amount of work. Now that isn't to say that the tools are not powerful and not extensible; they are both. The majority of organizations can gain the advantages previously outlined with process change and a small amount of training. More advanced capabilities require a little more work but are available to you. Think of the issues that you have right now. Will any of the preceding features help reduce these issues? If yes, keep reading.

Metrics

In the past, metrics was a dirty word (and maybe still is). Metrics meant a heavy process with developers constantly noting in detail every little step they took. Looking at methodologies such as the Personal Software Process (PSP) or Team Software Process (TSP) that are based on comprehensive metrics, you can see why this is the case. Many organizations took metrics to the extreme, which was the wrong thing to do. Metrics, used properly, do not add a large amount of overhead to a development process and produce tangible benefits.

No organization can determine quality without metrics, so what metrics are important to improving quality? Table 1-1 summarizes the metrics that you should be looking for and *why you should be interested in them*. These metrics are a large focus of Chapter 9, "Reporting and Metrics."

TABLE 1-1: Critical Metrics

Metric	Description
Total bug count	This number simply puts all the other numbers in perspective, such as the percentage of bugs found in a given step or iteration.
Bug count per phase	The goal is to reduce the number of bugs as you proceed along the development path. Teams need to show that the time they put into defect reduction pays off.
Bug count per feature (bug density map)	If certain features experience more defects than other features, it is a good indicator that the team might need to work proactively to find defects before the users do.
Code coverage	Having a lot of tests is not helpful if those tests cover only 10% of the total application. The goal of every team may be different, but strive for approximately 70% to 80% coverage.
Regression bugs	Knowing when bugs reoccur is a good indication of overall regression testing issues. You can also use this to detect fragile areas of code that might need to be made more maintainable.
Defect root cause	Knowing the most common root causes of defects gives you the ability to proactively work to eliminate certain categories of defects.
Defect cost	This is a somewhat nebulous and misleading metric. You do not need to try to hit a cost per defect mark or anything like that. Teams need to determine how much time in manpower (user, analyst, developer, tester) it takes to fix a bug and what the business impact of the bug is (monetary impact if possible). This feeds back into the ROI of a good prevention program, which Chapter 9 discusses.

These are the basic metrics that will be focused on. You can use other metrics, but these are the most prescriptive in trying to improve process and release a quality product.

In addition to determining quality, metrics also measure the effectiveness of any process, but this is especially true with processes involving quality. A quality program without metrics is not useful. One of the key features of the

Team Foundation Server is the capability to capture information and output it in a variety of ways. These include dashboards via Microsoft Office Share-Point Server (MOSS) and Excel Services, SQL Server Reporting Services (SSRS), and through Excel with its capability to report off of a data cube.

SUMMARY

This chapter covered some of the problems that you or your organization may face due to inadequate testing, poor communication between developers and testers, and low project visibility. The impact of testing (good or bad) is not adequately quantified, but you have seen some examples of extremely high profile and expensive cases of the testing process not working correctly. And you have also seen how Microsoft is working to build tools that help to directly improve the role of testers in the software development process. In the next chapter you get your first look at these tools and the process starting with planning your testing efforts with Microsoft Test Manager.

Citations

National Institute of Standards and Technology. (2002). Planning Report 02-3, "The Economic Impacts of Inadequate Infrastructure for Software Testing." U.S. Department of Commerce.

1. http://www.intelligententerprise.com/channels/enterprise_applications/showArticle. jhtml?articleID=207000273&cid=nl_ie_week
2. http://www.computerweekly.com/Articles/2004/03/29/201438/peoplesoft-sued-over-faulty-installation.htm
3. http://wps.prenhall.com/bp_laudon_essbus_7/48/12303/3149749.cw/content/index.html
4. http://www.washingtonpost.com/wp-dyn/content/article/2006/08/17/ AR2006081701485.html
5. http://www.techcentral.ie/article.aspx?id=11470

2

Software Quality and Testing Overview

T HIS CHAPTER IS A QUICK SYNOPSIS of the fundamentals of software quality and testing. For those of you who are developers or new to testing, this is a crash course (but by no means complete) in testing software. If you are an experienced software testing professional, I suggest skimming through the chapter. By the end of this chapter, you should have a good understanding of software quality, the goals of each type of software testing, and various testing techniques, and how they can be applied depending on the overall Software Development Lifecycle (SDLC) process in use.

Software Quality

A solid understanding of software quality is necessary to be effective at software testing. So, just what is software quality and who is responsible for it? A definition in Steve McConnell's *Code Complete* divides software into two pieces: internal and external quality characteristics. External quality characteristics are those parts of a product that face its users, whereas internal quality characteristics are those that do not.

Overall software quality is determined and influenced from several perspectives. Everyone has their own view influenced by how they interact with the product or solution. At the core quality means the software meets the requirements for which it is created, it has business value, it meets or exceeds expectations, and it meets the nonfunctional requirements defined and expected .

Requirements

Quality starts with the definition of good requirements. If a stakeholder or customer writes a list of requirements, is that good enough? Probably not because fully understanding such a list typically requires extensive domain knowledge. Good requirements should specify the desired functionality and how to validate that the functionality has been achieved. Creating and understanding good requirements usually evolves through interaction of the stakeholders, project management, development, and test during project definition and frequent reviews and adjustments as development progresses. Be careful, however, that the requirements do not go into how to achieve the functionality. That is the responsibility of the development team. As requirements are agreed upon, it is then the development team's responsibility to deliver working software that meets these requirements.

Business Value

High-quality software must have business value for those who will use it, whether for internal use, commercial sale, social, entertainment, web, or embedded use. A software solution or product is not high quality unless it adds value for both the consumer and the manufacturer. Both a luxury car and an entry-level car will get you from point A to point B. But the luxury car offers features and capabilities that go beyond the essentials of transportation: usability, safety, comfort, reliability, and so on. Quality encompasses added value plus attention to detail.

Development teams with a quality focus know that a "quality" application must do more than simply provide correct results without crashing. Does the application meet or exceed stakeholder and user requirements and expectations? Is it usable? Secure? Scalable? Reliable? Easily maintained? Easily extended?

Expectations

From the user's perspective, a software product must provide a level of user satisfaction for accomplishing its intended purpose. This is probably the most important external quality characteristic. Fundamentally all users want the same thing: "I just want it to work!" So, first and foremost, quality means that it must work.

An application user interface is subjective, but there are some specifics you should think about concerning qualities of a good user experience. Consider the implicit cost of keystrokes, mouse travel and clicks, shifts in eye focus, and the resulting brain power required to run the UI. Some keys are easier to press than others. Keeping your hands on the keyboard is most efficient. There is context shift to access the number pad, shifted keys, combined keys (key binding), and symbol keys. Mouse travel and clicks can become expensive with options scattered all over the screen. A user may have to drill down several layers in a menu hierarchy to select a desired operation—moving your eyes away from the actual task you are working on to navigate the application. All this effort with awkward user interfaces diverts your focused concentration away at a substantial cost in overall productivity, increased stress and tension, and likely creates a negative emotional response.

Watch customers carefully. Make use of frequent inspect and adopt cycles throughout the development cycle to make sure you get the user interface refined for your users.

Nonfunctional Requirements

In addition to requirements for specific behavior or functional requirements, nonfunctional requirements deal with the operation or qualities of a system: how a system is expected to behave. These are sometimes known as the "ilities" for the suffix many of the words share. You can see an extensive list at http://en.wikipedia.org/wiki/Ilities. A few important nonfunctional requirements for just about all solutions include usability, reliability, performance, security, and maintainability. To the extent reasonably possible, you should try to identify specific metrics to measure, which Chapter 9, "Reporting and Metrics," discusses in more detail.

Usability

Usability is probably the most difficult to specifically measure. Requirements might be expressed about how difficult it will be to learn and operate the system. The requirements are often expressed in learning time or similar metrics.

Reliability

Reliability deals with the capability of a system or component to perform its required functions under stated conditions for a specified period of time without failure. The measurement is often expressed in mean time between failures (MTBF). The definition of a failure must be clear. You may require a specific measure of up-time or have specific service level agreements (SLAs) that you are contractually committed to. Performance is characterized by the amount of useful work accomplished by a system compared to the time and resources used. You may need to support a specific maximum number of users without degradation of response returning data or serving up a new web page.

Security

Security is the degree of protection against damage, loss, unauthorized access, and criminal activity. This is another difficult area to measure because you need to consider so many parameters. Assume that attackers are out there. How do you know that the user of the system is who they say they are and only give them access to authorized functions? How can you protect your system from attack? Think about network attacks, machine attacks, and even attacks from within your own systems.

Maintainability

Maintainability is the ease with which a product can be maintained to correct defects, meet new requirements, make future maintenance easier, or cope with a changed environment. Although maintainability is undisputedly considered one of the fundamental quality attributes of software systems, it is difficult to find a sound and accepted definition or even a common understanding of what maintainability actually is. One good metric related to maintainability is regression bugs. If simple changes cause high numbers of regression bugs, then it's a good bet that the system will be difficult to maintain.

Where Do You Build Quality?

Building quality from the beginning of a project or trying to bolt it on at the end has an impact on both overall quality and total cost. Pay now or pay later. As many managers are fond of saying, "you can't test quality in."

At the End of the Project?

Can you build software quality at the end of the project? This is putting the burden on system testing. In spite of how many may answer this question, in practice you see a lot of organizations that tend to work this way. Critical decisions are pushed back on the project timeline with the expectation that it will be discovered and corrected in testing. Waiting until the eleventh hour to validate quality through testing inevitably extends both the schedule and budget. Good testing can identify potential problem areas and bugs, but this is only part of the overall quality equation.

In the Middle of the Project?

How about building quality in the middle of the project? This focuses on quality engineering practices, also a necessary component of quality. Here you run the risk of building a technically good product, but the ultimate result is a failure because the requirements missed the target. Poor problem domain analysis—and thus poor requirements—can lead to unplanned and costly reworking.

At the Beginning of the Project?

What if you start building quality at the beginning of the project? This is where you can proactively plan and design with a focus on quality. Good requirements, good architectural planning, continuous attention to technical excellence and good design, and involving tests from beginning to end is your best investment for building in quality.

Quality Is a Team Effort

Everyone plays a part in building quality; stakeholders, project management, business analysis, architecture, development, testing, and operations. Agile practices embody the concept of building quality from the beginning. Agile methodologies stress frequent inspections and adoptions by frequently delivering increments of working software, usually every few weeks. Requirements can change, even late in development. Agile processes embrace change for the competitive advantage of the customer. Even if you are not doing pure agile development, consider implementing these practices to improve quality.

Definition of Done

A key concept from agile methodologies is having a well understood and agreed upon definition of done. A clear definition of done applied to each increment of delivered working software is a rich embodiment of quality. So what should a good definition of done include? Consider the following:

- Designed
- Refactored
- Coded
- Code reviewed
- Design reviewed
- Unit tested
- Functional tested
- User Acceptance tested
- Integration tested
- Regression tested
- Performance tested
- Security tested

Adhering to a good definition of done goes a long way to lowering both the cost of producing software and the total cost of ownership. Consider the cost of a defect. As shown in Figure 2-1, a defect discovered and corrected during development is vastly less expensive than a defect released to production.

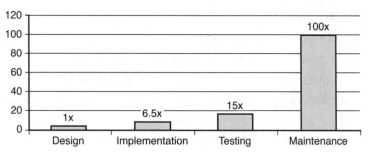

Phase/Stage of the S/W Development in Which the Defect is Found

Source: IBM Systems Sciences Institute

FIGURE 2-1: The cost of a defect in the software development lifecycle

Process and Quality

Product quality also reflects the process behind the product. In the software world, a high-quality SDLC process can keep development organizations from losing time reworking, refactoring, and rewriting software. These organizations can produce more innovative and creative products because they have more time to think about adding value and quality details.

Visual Studio 2010 Application Lifecycle Management (ALM) provides a great end-to-end platform for process implementation.

Businesses that value quality become more responsive and innovative, increase their competitive differentiation, and greatly reduce their total cost of development and ownership. Quality enables responsiveness and innovation; quality is a differentiator in the marketplace between leaders and followers; and quality is (almost) free.

Software Testing

Software Testing helps you assure throughout the development process that your software projects actually conform to the established quality objectives. A primary purpose of testing is to detect software dysfunction and failures so that defects may be discovered and corrected; preferably as early in the develop/deploy cycle as possible.

The Testing Mindset

Good testers are kind of like bull dogs. They bite into a system to be tested and don't let go. Professional testers approach an application with the attitude that the product is already broken: It has defects and it is their job to discover them. Although developers and designers typically look at the expected paths for an application to work correctly, testers look for edge and corner cases in which things can go wrong. They assume the product or system inherently has flaws and it is their job to find them. This approach makes for good testing.

Developing an application's expected paths is certainly important, that is, the purpose, requirement, and user story being satisfied. It's also often times the relatively easy part of development. But a truly great application is resilient; it anticipates things that can go wrong and handles them gracefully. This is where the testers' bull-dog mindset adds value. The testers take nothing at face value. Testers always ask the question "Why?" They seek to drive out the edge-and-corner cases and discover the unexpected paths that must be controlled well to drive quality and a great user experience.

Sometimes this attitude can cause conflict with developers and designers. But you want developers and designers that can be testers, too! You can have developers and testers work as a paired team for a period of time to broaden the team's approach to quality and help to tear down the old traditional wall between development and testing.

AGILE TESTING

Testing and QA is a key component of agile development. The widespread adoption of agile methods has brought the need for effective testing into the limelight, and agile projects have transformed the role of testers. With SCRUM, development teams are cross-functional and self-organizing, so QA is integrated into the development team. Although everyone on the team contributes to what needs to be worked on, the QA function (and mindset) is crucial from the beginning to end of each sprint and to the project as a whole.

For a more in-depth look at agile testing see *Agile Testing: A Practical Guide for Testers and Agile Teams* by Lisa Crispin and Janet Gregory. Addison-Wesley. (Jan 9, 2009)

EDGE-AND-CORNER CASES

An edge case (or boundary case) is a problem or situation that occurs only at or just beyond the maximum or minimum limits of an operating parameter. For example, consider a field which accepts a number—the program may be expecting a range between 0 and 100 but a tester may enter a value such as 2,147,483,648 which happens to be one number higher than the maximum size of a signed integer. If the developer is putting the value into an int, the test will fail. An edge case can be expected or unexpected. The process of planning for and gracefully addressing edge cases can be a significant task part of development.

A corner case is a problem or situation that occurs only outside of normal operating parameters—specifically one that manifests when multiple environmental variables or conditions are simultaneously at extreme levels, even though each parameter is within the specified range for that parameter.

Software Testing Strategies

Software testing strategies are traditionally divided into white box, black box, and gray box testing. These three approaches describe the point of view that a test engineer takes when designing Test Cases.

Black Box

Black-box testing is the testing of completed units of functional code. Testers treat the objects as black boxes using the provided interfaces. They focus on verifying that specific input will return expected output. They don't worry about the internal logic of what goes on in between. User Acceptance Testing (UAT) and Systems Testing are typical examples of black-box testing.

White Box

White-box testing, also known as glass-box testing, focuses on analyzing the internal logic of the software and the code. White-box testing is generally the domain of the developers creating and executing Unit Tests. Code coverage, code metrics, code analyses, and code reviews are also related white-box testing techniques.

Gray Box

Gray-box testing is a software testing technique that uses a combination of black-box testing and white-box testing. It involves having knowledge of internal data structures and algorithms for purposes to design the Test Cases, but testing at the user or black-box level.

You can make better informed testing choices because you know how the underlying components operate and interact. Exploring boundary conditions and error messages are typical examples.

Types of Software Testing

Many different types of software testing may be performed throughout the SDLC to assure that completed work meets or exceeds the targeted level of quality. No one testing type does it all. Rather, it is the sum collection of testing and test results that help the extended development team and stakeholders have a high level of predictability in overall project quality. Tests can be either manually scripted or automated. In either case tests should be repeatable so that you can compare progress during the course of development and refinement. You should strive for a high degree of automation and use manual testing where a high degree of human judgment and interpretation is most beneficial.

Unit Tests

A Unit Test is an automated piece of code that invokes the method or class being tested and then checks some assumptions about the logical behavior of that method or class. A Unit Test is almost always written using a unit-testing framework. It can be written easily and runs quickly. It's fully automated, trustworthy, readable, and maintainable. Unit Tests are written and run by developers as they write code. Unit Tests are typically automated as a suite to be run on code check-in (continuous integration) and used by testers as part of integration tests and regression tests.

Database Unit Tests

Just as unit testing plays a critical role in code development with languages such as C# and Visual Basic, in database development T-SQL-based Unit

Tests verify database objects during development and are also included in integration and regression test suites.

AGILE PRACTICES

Agile practices endorse test-first development—building tests before you code. Although unit testing and run-time analysis have become more mainstream, many managers still have the misconception that these procedures add unnecessary time to the schedule. In reality, schedules typically lengthen because of the time developers have to spend debugging code later in the lifecycle after QA or customers find problems. And defects discovered later are significantly more expensive. For teams that want to reduce risk and increase predictability, a well-formed, proactive QA approach by the development team is a good solution.

Smoke Tests

Smoke tests are used as an acceptance test prior to introducing new changes to the main testing process. A smoke test is usually the first test made after modifications to provide some assurance that the system under test will not catastrophically fail.

Exploratory Testing

Exploratory testing is a type of testing in which the tester does not have specifically planned Test Cases, but does the testing more to explore the software features and to discover unknown bugs. It is approached with the intention to learn and understand the software and its features. During this process, the tester also tries to think of all possible scenarios in which the software may fail and a bug can be revealed. Exploratory testing is likely the only type of testing that can help in uncovering bugs that stand more chance of being ignored by other testing strategies.

Integration Testing

Integration testing is the process to ensure that different components of the application work (interact with each other) together. Integration testing fits between unit testing and system testing. It is best performed as a continuous activity rather than waiting until the end of the development cycle and taking a big-bang approach (which never has a happy ending). You can also perform integration testing between your application and external applications with which the system communicates. This is frequently a very, very difficult task—especially if the development team has no control over the other system. This leads to issues such as how to get the other system owner to provide testing data and a test environment. This is where testing relies more on playing nice with other teams than on any specific methodology.

Functional Testing

Functional testing is testing performed to validate specific requirements (that is, not the entire system at once) and is appropriate for a continuous testing process in which each function is tested as it is completed and retested as new functions are integrated to discover regression bugs.

Load Testing

Load testing is the process to subject the system under test to a work level approaching the limits of its design specification. Load testing is usually performed in a controlled lab environment where accurate measurements can be taken under repeatable conditions. You can also perform load testing in the field to obtain a qualitative assessment of system performance in the "real world."

Automated Testing

You can use Visual Studio 2010 Ultimate or Visual Studio 2010 Premium to create automated tests of the user interface (UI) known as coded UI tests. These tests provide functional testing of the UI and validation of UI controls. Automated UI tests enable you to test that the UI is functioning correctly after code changes. They are quicker to run than manual tests.

Regression Testing

Regression testing is the process to test changes to software programs to make sure that the older code still works with the new changes (for example, bug fixes or new functionality) that have been made. Regression testing is a normal part of the application development process. The intent of regression testing is to ensure that a change, such as a bug fix, did not introduce new bugs. Regression test suites are typically automated to the extent possible including Unit Tests and integration tests but usually also include manual tests.

System Testing

System testing is the process to test the entire system to ensure that functional and nonfunctional requirements have been met. This testing is performed by the development team. (Development, test, and business analysts are usually involved in performing these tests.) It can be considered "pre-user acceptance testing" to ensure that everything works as it should. Ideally, system testing should be performed in an environment that closely reflects the physical environment that the production system runs in. Lab Management, discussed in Chapter 7, "Executing Automated Test Causes," is ideal for this.

Acceptance Testing

Acceptance testing is a functional trial performed on a completed increment of functional software before it is accepted and deemed ready for release to the market or delivery to the end user. The acceptance testing process is designed to replicate the anticipated real-life use of the product to ensure that what the consumers or end users receive is fully functional and meets their needs and expectations. In traditional predictive processes, this is usually at the end of the product development cycle, whereas with agile development, processes acceptance testing is done at the conclusion of each development iteration. As shown in Figure 2-2, acceptance testing is the pinnacle of building quality.

Acceptance Test Driven Development

"Begin with the end in mind."—Stephen R. Covey

Acceptance Test Driven Development (ATDD) is a practice in which the whole team collaboratively discusses acceptance criteria, with examples, and then distills them into a set of concrete acceptance tests before development begins. It's the best way to ensure that everyone has the same shared understanding of what is actually being built. This practice helps to uncover assumptions and confirm to everyone that there is a shared definition of "Done."

Acceptance tests are created from user stories. During an iteration the user stories selected during the iteration planning meeting will be translated into acceptance tests. The customer specifies scenarios to test when a user story has been correctly implemented. A story can have one or many acceptance tests, whatever it takes to ensure the functionality works.

Acceptance tests are black-box system tests. Each acceptance test represents some expected result from the system. Customers are responsible for verifying the correctness of the acceptance tests and reviewing test scores to decide which failed tests are of highest priority. Acceptance tests are also used as regression tests prior to a production release.

A user story is not considered complete until it has passed its acceptance tests. This means that new acceptance tests must be created each iteration or the development team will report zero progress.

Acceptance tests should be automated so that they can be run often. The acceptance test score is published to the team. It is the team's responsibility to schedule time for each iteration to fix any failed tests.

Acceptance Test Driven Development helps developers build high-quality software that fulfills the business's needs as reliably as TDD helps ensure the software's technical quality.

http://testobsessed.com/wp-content/uploads/2008/12/atddexample.pdf

http://controlchaos.squarespace.com/storage/scrum-articles/Acceptance%20Test%20Driven%20Development.pdf

http://testingguidance.codeplex.com

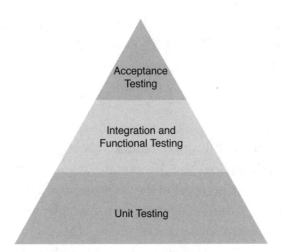

FIGURE 2-2: Building quality to completion

Test Management

You can't test everything. Accept it, understand it, and move on—but don't forget it. To prove the point, understand that testing everything means testing every possible input that an application could possibly accept. Use this small definition of everything, and you can quickly understand that even a simple application such as a calculator would take a lifetime and then some to test. Starting from this point gives you the basis for formulating your test plans and using the appropriate testing methodologies to meet your needs.

For 99.9% of the applications in the world, you cannot make them bug free. You cannot find all of the bugs; but hopefully you can find the majority of them. At a certain point in time, the law of diminishing returns applies, and beyond a certain point, the time and effort you spend to find and remove bugs becomes too expensive to be practical. This should also guide your philosophy in choosing a testing strategy.

After the Product Is Shipped or Deployed

Quality and testing continue after the product or application is placed into service. Operational downtime caused by reliability or performance problems can incur opportunity costs if customers cannot access your system or the business cannot do its work. Operations monitoring, help-desk bug logging and tracking, and user feedback must be communicated back to development and reviewed on a regular and frequent basis. Frequent inspection and adoption is a key element of agility, staying in tune with your customers and continuously improving quality.

SUMMARY

In this chapter, you went through a quick synopsis of the fundamentals of software quality and testing. The chapter taught you that software quality is a team effort and an integral part of the software development lifecycle from beginning to end. As part of that team effort, everyone must understand and agree to a comprehensive definition of "done." Defects found and corrected early are significantly less expensive than those not found until released into production. You saw the importance of "The Testing Mindset" and explored many of the types of tests commonly used in software testing. In the next chapter you start planning your testing process. Chapter 3, "Planning Your Testing," covers Test Plan components, how to create them, and how to manage them.

3

Planning Your Testing

T O BEGIN, YOU NEED A PLAN. The plan does not need to be 500 pages of documentation or a massive Gantt chart. This chapter covers how to create a Test Plan with Microsoft Test Manager (MTM) and the various options that the Test Plan provides to you. More important, this chapter covers *what* to test and how to get involved as a tester early in the development process. In addition, Microsoft provides a little-used Test Plan Word template that can help answer some questions about the testing process up front.

Another key item covered here is how to plan and test for multiple iterations. Can you reuse your Test Cases, and does it make sense to do that? Many items come into play when planning the testing for an entire release versus a single iteration. By the end of this chapter, you will know how to use the Plan tab of MTM, create new plans, and create a framework for testers to work in for a given period of time.

As mentioned in Chapter 1, "State of Testing," testers should be involved, ideally, during the requirements gathering process. In a waterfall cycle this is during the Analysis phase. In an agile cycle this is during the period of time in which the business analyst or product owner fills in the details for items on the Product Backlog but before introducing the item into an Iteration Backlog. This chapter covers what the testers' responsibilities should be and what they can do to help reduce the potential for bugs to be introduced into the software.

TEST APPROACH

When starting any testing endeavor, you need an approach to the process. Consider what is acceptable, what are the criteria for release, how you can perform each type of test, and other information that forms the framework of the approach. If you use the MSF for Agile v5.0 process template, there is a Test Approach Word template located in the sample documents on the SharePoint site. (The path to the document is Documents/Samples and Templates/Test/Document Template - Test Approach.dotx.) You can also find a sample document showing how the Test Approach looks when filled out.

Microsoft Test Manager

Microsoft provides a separate tool for testers: Microsoft Test Manager (MTM) where you can create Test Plans and add and update Test Cases and where manual and automated tests are executed from. Before getting into the details of creating Test Plans, you need to understand how to navigate within MTM. Figure 3-1 shows the navigation controls.

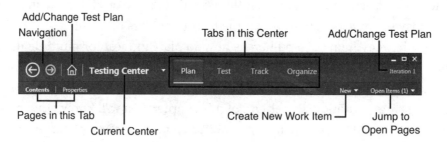

FIGURE 3-1: MTM navigation controls

MTM is organized into Centers, Tabs, and Pages, as shown in Figure 3-2.

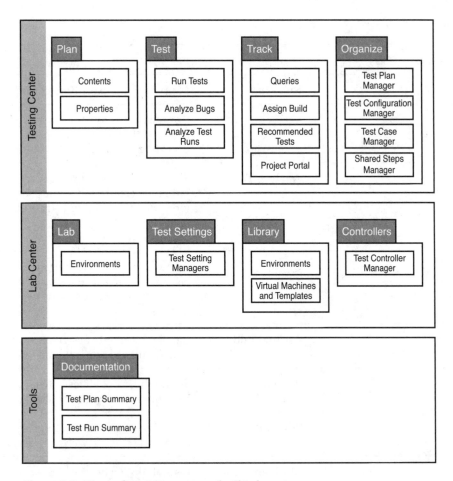

FIGURE 3-2: Microsoft Test Manager navigation layout

Table 3-1 briefly describes each section. These pages and the options they enable are described throughout the book.

TABLE 3-1: MTM Pages Described

Center	Tab	Page	Description
Testing	Plan	Contents	Contains the settings for the given Test Plan including manual and automated test settings, test configurations, and the build in use
		Properties	Contains the suites and Test Cases that need testing for the selected plan

TABLE 3-1: Continued

Center	Tab	Page	Description
	Test	Run Tests	Main page for executing test runs
		Verify Bugs	Contains bugs that have been resolved that the tester can quickly get to and verify
		Analyze Test Runs	Shows all test runs (manual and automated) but used mainly to view an automated test run and take appropriate actions based on the outcome of the test runs
	Track	Queries	Same as in Team Explorer; it enables you to execute stored work item queries or create new queries
		Assign Build	Enables a tester to assign an automated build to the Test Plan
		Recommended Tests	Shows the list of all tests that have been impacted by a code change
		Project Portal	Provides a quick link to the project portal (opens a web browser)
	Organize	Test Plan Manager	Lists all the Test Plans in the current Team Project
		Test Configuration Manager	Lists all test configurations
		Test Case Manager	Lists all Test Cases in the current Team Project
		Shared Steps Manager	Lists all the shared steps (reusable test steps) in the current Team Project
Lab	Lab	Environments	Contains all the physical and virtual environments ready for testing purposes

Center	Tab	Page	Description
	Test Settings	Test Settings Manager	Contains all manual and automated test settings
	Library	Environments	Lists all the environments prepped for use in testing, including environments that have been deployed
		Virtual Machines and Templates	Contains all the virtual machines available to be composed into a test environment
	Controllers	Test Controller Manager	Contains a list of all test controllers and all agents associated with those controllers
Tools	Documentation	Test Plan Summary	Generates a document with the selected Test Plans, associated Test Suites, Test Cases, Test Steps and related work items
		Test Run Summary	Generates a document with the results of the selected test runs

TEST SCRIBE AND THE TOOLS CENTER

The Tools Center does not exist when you first install MTM. After the release of Visual Studio 2010, Microsoft released a Test Scribe tool (available at http://visualstudiogallery.msdn.microsoft.com/en-us/e79e4a0f-f670-47c2-9b8a-3b6f664bf4ae.) (Or you can Bing "Test Scribe Visual Studio Gallery," and this link will be the first one.)

This addition is critically important to most organizations and should be installed immediately after installing MTM. The documentation it generates can be provided to users or external testers and serves as an excellent, detailed document showing the tests and test runs.

When you first start MTM, you will be asked to connect to a server (Figure 3-3), select a Team Project (Figure 3-4), and then select a Test Plan (Figure 3-5).

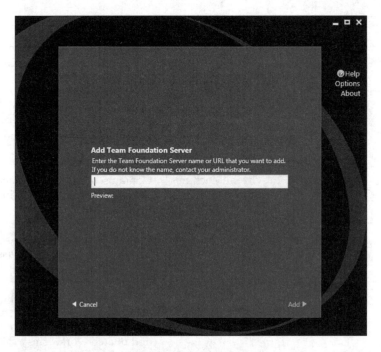

FIGURE 3-3: Connect to a Team Foundation Server

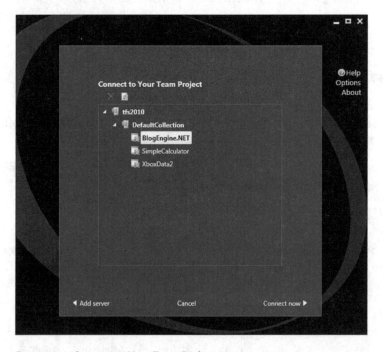

FIGURE 3-4: Connect to Your Team Project

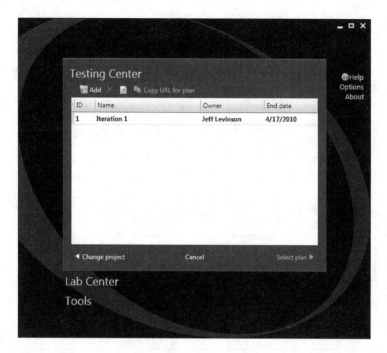

FIGURE 3-5: Select or add a Test Plan

Note the Copy URL for the plan option in Figure 3-5. MTM enables you to provide URLs to specific plans, so you can send the URL to someone who can then click it and have MTM open to the right plan. Only Active plans show up in this dialog. You can view all plans (Active and Closed) from the Testing Center, Organize Tab, Test Plan Manager page.

MTM enables you to work in one Team Project and only one Plan in that Team Project at a time, although you can change plans and projects as needed. After doing this the first time, MTM remembers your last selection, so MTM can open to the last selected Plan.

Before starting the exercises, see the section "About the Application Used in This Book" in the front matter. These exercises assume that you have followed the steps in that section.

Test Plans

Before using the testing tools, you need to understand where all the various artifacts fit together because it matters when you start to manage an actual project. Figure 3-6 shows a container view of the artifacts.

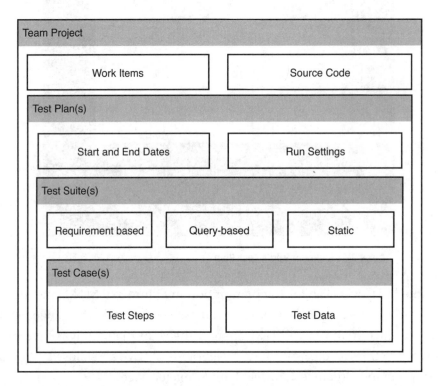

FIGURE 3-6: Relationships between Team Projects, Test Plans, Test Suites, and Test Cases

Figure 3-6 shows that a Test Plan in MTM is associated with a specific Team Project. A Test Plan is composed of one or more Test Suites, and each Test Suite is composed of one or more Test Cases. This is a straightforward structure that enables flexible reporting and easy management of the Test Plans.

▪ EXERCISE 3-1

Create a New Test Plan

This step assumes that you have not used MTM before. If you have, but you want to work through this exercise, you need to select the Home button in the upper-left corner of the screen and select Change Project:

1. Open MTM.
2. Select Add Server, or select an existing server if the correct server is listed.
3. Select the BlogEngine.NET project, and click Connect Now.
4. On the Testing Center screen, click Add to create a new Test Plan.
5. Enter the name as **Iteration 1** and click Add.
6. Highlight the Plan, and click Select Plan.

Figure 3-7 shows the Iteration 1 Test Plan.

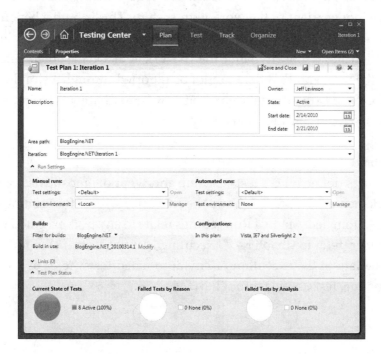

FIGURE 3-7: Test Plan

Properties

Test Plans have a name and a description, and if you use multiple Test Plans concurrently, you need to give them a descriptive name and also a more detailed description. The owner is usually the test manager but can also be a test lead if a lead is responsible for the testing that occurs within a plan. The state can either be Active or Inactive depending on whether it is currently used, and this is not customizable. Inactive Test Plans can either be previously completed Test Plans or Test Plans that have yet to be started and are still being created. The default state for new Test Plans is Active, but you might want to set the plan to Inactive if it is still being designed.

The area and iteration are the standard work item classification scheme. In general Test Plans should be related to iterations in some way (or whatever scheme the development team uses to produce software) because the testing follows the requirements or the coding, which are distinct phases in any methodology whether they are called out.

Test Plans are not work items such as a requirement, user story, or task. They are independent of the work item system. This is both a benefit and a disadvantage. The benefits are in the flexibility: the Test Plan contains more information and is more dynamic than a work item. On the other hand, items such as the Start and End date cannot be reported through a simple mechanism. You need to use the data warehouse (refer to Chapter 9, "Reporting and Metrics") to report on Test Plans.

Run Settings

Run settings define where tests execute and what diagnostic data adapters are implemented. Figure 3-7 shows the two categories of Run settings: Manual and Automated. Manual Run settings relate to any tests executed with the Test Runner (refer to Chapter 4, "Executing Manual Tests"). Automated Run settings relate to the execution of any automated tests (refer to Chapter 6, "Automating Test Cases") through MTM.

CHANGE THE TEST SETTINGS IMMEDIATELY

When the test settings are set to <Default> you have no control over them. You cannot set any diagnostic data adapters to run specifically or any other options associated with manual or automated runs. For the manual settings, simply select the drop-down list, and pick Local Test Run, or create a new test setting and change the properties as needed.

To create a new Run setting, go to the Lab Center, Test Settings tab, Test Settings Manager page, and copy an existing setting or add a new setting. These can then be assigned in the Test Plan Properties page. Figure 3-8 shows the Test Settings creation screen.

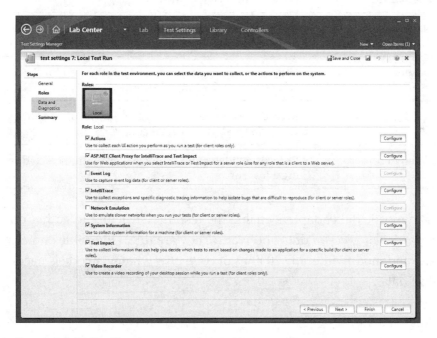

FIGURE 3-8: Test settings

Depending on whether you create an automated or manual setting, the options will be slightly different. Figure 3-8 shows a manual test setting on the Data and Diagnostics tab that contains the diagnostic data adapters. Table 3-2 lists the default diagnostic data adapters you can choose.

TABLE 3-2: Default Diagnostic Data Adapters

Collector	Description
Action Recording and Action Log	Records each step that the tester takes in the application during a manual test run.
ASP.NET Client Proxy for IntelliTrace and Test Impact	Enables you to capture IntelliTrace and Test Impact information during a test execution of an ASP.NET application. Note: This setting does not actually perform the capture; you must check the IntelliTrace and/or Test Impact collectors in addition to this collector.
Event Log	Captures selected events written to the Event Log during a test run.
IntelliTrace	Enables capturing of the debug log.
Network Emulation	Throttles the network performance based on the specified settings.
System Information	Captures system configuration information for the system on which the test is performed.
Test Impact	Records Test Impact information for calculating Test Cases affected by modified code.
Video Recorder	Records a video of all actions taken on the screen during a test run.

Diagnostic data adapters enable the test infrastructure to gather data—any particular piece of data you want. They are fully extensible and easy to create and modify (literally 20 lines of code plus whatever code is needed to collect data).

Builds

If you aren't using automated builds right now, you should be. Automated builds are one of the most effective ways to reduce the amount of time it takes to find and fix bugs. These automated builds can be Continuous Integration builds (the process of running a build immediately upon check-in to determine if the check-in broke anything) or nightly builds, and they can discover build breaks faster and with fewer lines of code to review to find the problem. They are also critical to manual testing; although not required for automated testing, they will certainly make things easier.

Builds enable you to specify which build you can execute the tests against. After you select a build to execute the Test Cases against, MTM provides you with information related to the build. Automated builds help light up the Test Impact Analysis results and provide the testing team with a list of all changes made to the code since the build they were previously using.

The build filter enables you to filter by build definition and build quality. Chapter 5, "Resolving Bugs," discusses build quality.

Configurations

On one hand configurations play an important part in test execution, and on the other hand they provide only metadata. Configurations enable you to specify various pieces of information about the tests you execute in the Test Plan. They also have a material effect on the number of tests that you need to execute and how you plan your Test Suites. For example, the default setting in MTM is Windows 7 and IE 8. If you have a Test Suite with 20 Test Cases, you need to execute 20 Test Cases. For every configuration that you add to a suite, all the tests need to be executed against the additional configurations as well. (By default, but you can change this.) So, if you have three configurations that you need to test against, you need to run 60 tests. The effect of configuration on testing and reporting are discussed in the "Assigning Test Configurations" section later in this chapter.

> Obviously, you do not have to execute any Test Cases you don't want to, and in many cases you can't execute every Test Case because of the time available to you.

The "Test Configurations" section covers Test Configuration details.

Test Plan Status

This section provides status on the current Test Plan. The first pie chart lists the total number of tests broken down by successful tests, failed tests, and tests that have not yet been executed. The Failures by Type pie chart breaks down the categories of each failure. Table 3-3 shows the available categories.

TABLE 3-3: Failure Categories

Category	Description
None	Use if the test failure is a nonissue.
Regression	Where the previous test results indicate a pass.
New issue	Has not been seen before.
Known issue	Possibly because a previous run found this bug or the development team has notified the testing team that the build is ready to test, but it knows about this particular failure.
Unknown	An error occurred, but the tester is not sure what the classification of the issue is. A test lead or manager should look further at Unknown issues.

You can also provide a category for a failure type before or after it has been fixed, but leave this empty until the defect has been fixed. Table 3-4 lists the analysis categories.

TABLE 3-4: Analysis Categories (Also Called Resolution Type)

Category	Description
None	No resolution at this time.
Needs investigation	The test team has decided to do a further investigation because it isn't sure of the cause.
Test issue	Usually set if the Test Case were at fault or the setup for the test were incorrect. This might be cause for concern because if a Test Case is wrong, the requirement it is based on might also have potential inaccuracies that need to be investigated.
Product issue	A valid failure occurred in the code.
Configuration issue	Usually a failure in the configuration files or on the machine on which the test was deployed.

FAILURE AND RESOLUTION EXTENSIBILITY

You can customize the Resolution type through the process template or the object model; however, you cannot customize the Failure type. (It looks like you can do it by editing the process template, but it does not actually work because of technical reasons.)

These graphs are updated as changes are made to the Test Plan and as test runs are completed and analyzed. (For performance reasons you might need to click the Refresh button to see the latest data.) This is a great view that quickly enables a testing team to see the progress of its testing within a given plan (as shown at the bottom of Figure 3-7).

Contents

The Contents portion of a Test Plan contains information on what will be tested; that is, it contains a list of all the Test Cases broken down into *Test Suites*. Figure 3-9 shows the Contents page of the Plan tab.

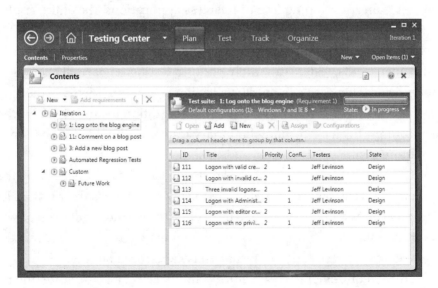

FIGURE 3-9: Test Plan contents

Refer to Figure 3-3 for the relationships between items. Test Suites can be composed in three ways: requirement-based, query-based, or customized with a static suite, and there are good uses for each of the three. The type of Test Suite is differentiated by icons next to the suite name (see Figure 3-10).

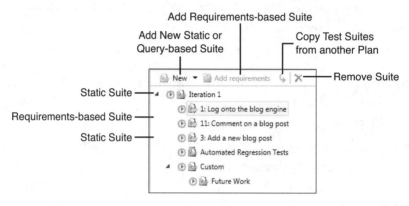

FIGURE 3-10: Test Suites

Requirements-Based Suites

For most teams developing line-of-business applications, the entire application is based around completing requirements; therefore, it makes sense that testers should test in relationship to the requirements that the developers finish. In other words, testers can rarely perform testing on partially completed requirements. They also can't perform testing on random pieces of the application because, in general, functional and integration testing relies on complete features. Even performing boundary tests must be done in the context of a requirement.

And, for the most part, customers want to know the status of their requirements. Are they close to completion? Did they pass their tests? How many bugs does a given requirement have? This is true regardless of what type of methodology you use. Grouping suites by requirement makes it extremely easy to report this information back to the customer.

To create requirements-based suites, simply select a static suite (the root node or another static suite) and click Add Requirements; then choose one or more requirements. Each requirement becomes its own suite. Any Test Cases already associated with the requirement are automatically added to the suite.

REQUIREMENTS AND WORK ITEM TYPES

Whether you use the MSF for Agile or CMMI templates, you have a requirement work item type. For the CMMI template, it is a Requirement, and for the Agile template it is a User Story. What determines a requirement from the perspective of a requirements-based suite is the category that the requirement is in. Categories are new to TFS 2010 and are a classification scheme for work item types. MTM operates on the requirement, Test Case, and bug categories. The reason it operates on categories is so that you can create a custom work item type, for example, called a Use Case that also appears in MTM if it is in the requirement category. In addition, you can create a Defect work item type that generates when you file a bug.

Query-Based Suites

These are suites created based on the results of a work item query. An example of why you might want to create a suite of this type is the need to test a specific area of your application that might be involved in different functionality. Using the requirement-based suite, you could not do this. Another reason for this type of suite can be the need to test all the bug fixes regardless of what requirement they are related to. The query-based suite simply provides you with more flexibility in selecting what you test and also enables you to run Test Cases from multiple Team Projects or requirements at the same time.

When creating this type of suite, you are limited to the results of the query, and the query specifies that you can query only work items in the Test Case category. So a query-based suite is specific to Test Cases. Because this type of suite is based on the results of a query, if the results of that query change, so will your Test Suite. Use this suite for short-term suites or suites where you don't mind them changing. An example of where this is effective is automated regression testing. You can create a query where Automation Status = Yes; when you execute the suite, all the automated tests execute.

Static Suites

A static suite is a fully custom suite; you provide the title of the suite and then add Test Cases as needed. One benefit of a static suite is that you can nest suites. This is not possible with the other two suite types. The reasons to use this type of suite can vary; however, an example of this might include final application testing where you might have time to only test requirements from various areas and iterations, and you want to break those up into subsuites so that you can roll the results up. In MTM when you select the New drop-down to add a new suite, the only two options you see are Suite and Query-Based Suite. The Suite option is the static suite.

Adding Suites and Test Cases to Your Plan

The mechanics of using the Contents window are fairly straightforward but offer a lot of options to help you control what happens when testers begin testing. The list of Test Suites is on the left side. Figure 3-6 shows a series of Test Suites starting with the Root Test Suite that is always the name of the Test Plan (Iteration 1 here). The Root Test Suite is a static suite, so you can add Test Cases directly to the root. Icons that have a red check on them are requirements-based suites. Another way to know this is to look above the list of Test Cases in the right pane; you can click the Requirement 1 link to open the requirement that these Test Cases relate to.

The Automated Regression Tests Suite in Figure 3-6 is a query-based suite, which you can tell by looking at the icon. The last suite listed, Custom, is a static suite with a Future Work subsuite that enables you to easily compose and manage your Test Suites.

You can change the default configuration for all the Test Cases here, or you can change the configuration for only individual tests. (This is not recommended because it can be difficult to keep track of which test is supposed to be run on which configuration.) You can change who the Test Cases are assigned to—either individually by selecting a Test Case and clicking the Assign button or by right-clicking the Test Suite on the left and selecting Assign Testers for All Tests (or any combination of testers to Test Cases).

In addition notice where it says State: In Progress in the upper-right corner. You can set the state to be one of three states: In Planning, In Progress, or Completed. In Progress is the default, and tests in a Test Suite that is In Progress may be executed. A Test Suite that is In Planning will not show up on the Test tab, so those tests cannot be executed. The same is also true for Completed suites.

You can also change the columns displayed for the Test Cases by right-clicking the column headers. You can filter certain columns (any column with a discrete list) to limit what displays. (For example, you can filter the Priority column in the default list of columns.)

Finally, you have the option to open a Test Case that has been added to a suite, add Test Cases that already exist in the suite, or create new Test Cases from within MTM. Any Test Cases you create or add are automatically linked with the requirement (or user story) if the suite is a requirements-based suite with a Tested By link type. The opposite is also true; if you remove a Test Case from a requirements-based suite, the Test Case is no longer in a relationship with the requirement. (The Tests/Tested By link is deleted, but the Test Case is not deleted.)

▪ EXERCISE 3-2

Create a Test Suite
This exercise assumes that you have completed Exercise 3-1.

1. Open MTM, if it's not already open.
2. Select Testing Center, Test Plan, Contents tab.
3. Select the Iteration 1 suite, which is the root suite and the only one that exists at this point.
4. Click Add Requirements from the toolbar for the suite name.
5. In the Add Existing Requirements to This Plan page, click Run (see Figure 3-11).
6. Select the requirement As the Blog Author I Want to be Able to Log onto the Blog Engine, and click Add Requirements to Plan in the lower-right corner.

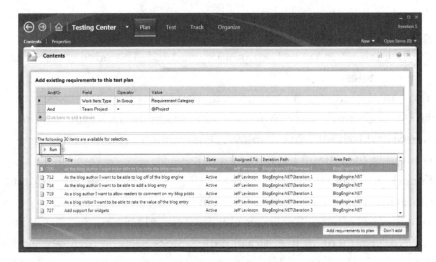

FIGURE 3-11: Add Existing Requirements to This Test Plan page

Testing Configurations

Testing configurations are configurable and can have an impact on the number of tests that need to be executed (mentioned previously). Test configurations specify any particular piece of information needed to ensure that your software is tested against all possible configuration options users could have on their machine.

> As of this release, test configurations are strictly metadata. That is, they do not have any impact on the test runs and cannot be used to specify the hardware or software a particular test is actually executed against.

The most typical example is using different browsers to ensure the rendering works correctly. Added to that may be the operating system those browsers run on. The two default configuration options are Operating System and Browser; to this you can add other things such as a Silverlight version or a particular piece of hardware, such as a webcam.

The biggest benefit to using test configurations is reporting results. All your test results can be broken down into configurations. In addition you have to write the Test Cases only one time, but this presents other issues, such as that the actions you take on one configuration may not be valid on another configuration. In some cases the differences may be so great it doesn't make sense to use the same Test Case. Consider these items when deciding on how to use test configurations.

Managing Test Configurations

You can access the Test Configuration Manager in two ways. The first is to go to Testing Center, Plan, Properties and select the drop-down arrow next to the configuration; then click Manage. The easier way is to go to Testing Center, Organize, Test Configuration Manager. This brings up the screen shown in Figure 3-12.

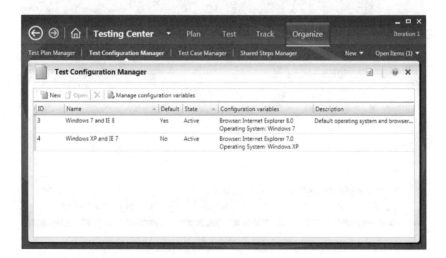

FIGURE 3-12: Test Configuration Manager

The Manage Configuration Variables option enables to you create new configuration categories. You can also add new values to an existing configuration variable.

■ EXERCISE 3-3

Adding a New Configuration Variable

To add a new configuration variable, follow these steps:

1. Click Manage Configuration Variables.

2. Click New Configuration Variable.

3. Enter **Silverlight Version** for the name.

4. Enter **Default Silverlight Versions** for the description.

5. In Allowed Values, enter the following (shown in Figure 3-13): **1**, **2**, **3**, and **4**.

6. Click Save Configuration Variables.

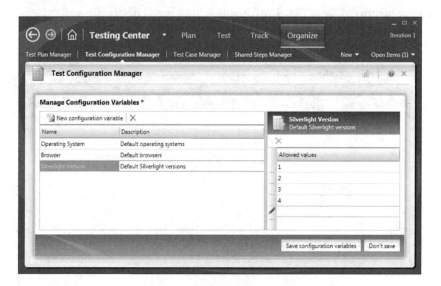

FIGURE 3-13: Silverlight Version Configuration Variable

The variables themselves cannot be used directly. You need to create an actual configuration composed of one or more configuration variables.

■ EXERCISE 3-4

Create a New Test Configuration

To create a new test configuration, follow these steps:

1. Click New from the Test Configuration Manager.
2. Enter the Name as **Vista, IE7, and Silverlight 2**.
3. (Optional) Enter an appropriate description.
4. Select the Add button, and notice that you can add configuration variables from the three existing categories. You can add only one variable from each category in a given configuration.
5. Click Operating System, and select Vista for the value.
6. Click Add, Browser, and select Internet Explorer 7.0 for the value.
7. Click Add, Silverlight Version, and select 2 for the value.
8. Click Save and Close.

You now have a new test configuration that can be assigned to plans. You can also delete test configurations if they are not being used or have not been used by previous Test Plans. If you try to delete a test configuration that is in use, you are prompted to set it to Inactive instead.

Assigning Test Configurations

To assign configurations to Test Cases, you have a few options. The first is to go to the Properties page of the plan and change the configuration. This can instantly apply the changes to all Test Cases contained within the plan and any Test Cases you add to the plan at a later date. The next option is to change the Default configurations from the Plan Contents tab (see Figure 3-9 just below the Test Suite name in the Test Suite Details pane). To make a change here, uncheck the Use Configurations from Parent Test Suite option, and check any additional test configurations you want to include. Changes you make here apply to the individual suite and any suites contained in the currently selected suite. For example, looking at Figure 3-9, if you select the Iteration 1 node and change the default configurations, the new set of configurations apply to all Test Suites in Iteration 1. If, however, you change the default configurations at Test Suite 1 (log onto the blog engine) the change applies only to this suite. Changing the configuration here is not automatically reflected on the Test tab. To illustrate this, after making one of the previous changes, select the Test tab; notice the same number of tests to be run as there are Test Cases. You see how to change this in a minute.

Another option is to assign test configurations at the suite level for existing Test Cases. To do this, right-click the suite in the left pane of the Contents tab, and choose Select Test Configurations for all Tests. This shows the screen in Figure 3-14.

One option available to you is the Reset Defaults option. If you have previously changed the default configuration at the Suite level and want to apply it to all existing Test Cases, selecting the Reset Defaults button will do this for you. (As shown in Figure 3-14, pressing this button automatically selects both configurations for all tests listed.)

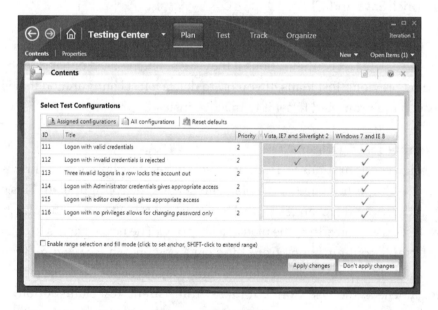

FIGURE 3-14: Assign test configurations to specific tests

After assigning one or more Test Cases to different configurations and applying the changes, you return to the Plan Contents page. The one apparent difference is the configurations column now has a value greater than 1. This column notes how many configurations are assigned to a given Test

Case; you might see the Tester for a Test Case listed as Multiple. (You revisit this when assigning testers to Test Cases is discussed.) You see the changes when you select the Test tab. You can execute two more tests than there are Test Cases; these additional tests have different configurations, as shown in Figure 3-15.

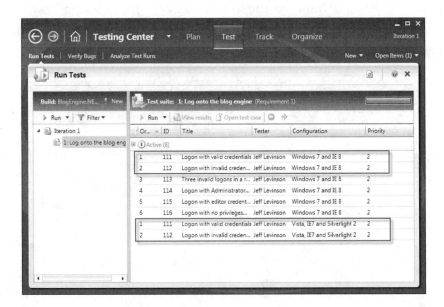

FIGURE 3-15: Testing multiple configurations

An additional option for setting test configurations is to select one or more tests and click the Configurations button. This enables you to set configurations just for the specific tests selected.

So far you have seen how to set test configurations for a plan. Options can be set at the Plan, Suite, and Test Case level, and generally they cascade down. The next step is to assign and manage testers in the context of the plan.

Assigning Testers

As with the test configurations, you can assign testers in a number of ways. The first and most obvious way (and certainly the easiest to report on) is to simply assign the Test Case work item to a tester. That person is then the "tester" of record. There are numerous scenarios in which the person who writes the Test Case does not also execute it. There are also scenarios in which the Test Case, as previously mentioned, is executed on different configurations, and different testers work those different configurations.

To assign a tester to a Test Case, you work at the suite or Test Case level. The screen for both is the same; the only difference is which testers show up. Right-click the Test Suite or the Test Case, and click Assign Testers for Selected Tests or Assign Testers for All Tests, or click the Assign button in the Suite Details pane. This brings you to the page shown in Figure 3-16.

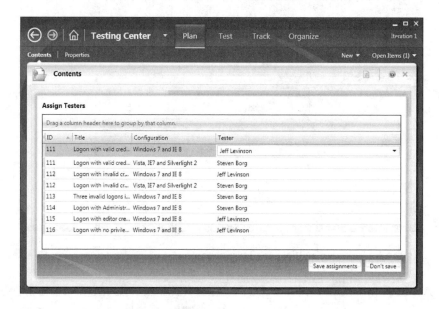

FIGURE 3-16: Assigning testers to Test Cases

You can select individual testers for each Test Case and configuration either one at a time or in bulk. To assign testers in bulk, select the Test Cases you want to assign (using the Control or Shift keys) and change the assignment for any Test Case. This change will be duplicated to all selected Test Cases. At this point some Test Cases on the Planning tab show Multiple in the Testers column. Remember that the Plan tab has a distinct list of Test Cases, but because different testers are assigned for different configurations, MTM aggregates all the testers assigned to a Test Case as Multiple. You can see the individual testers on the Test tab.

Test Case Planning Workflow

Now that you have seen the Plan tab in MTM, it's time to talk about usability. How do you use it to manage the testing workflow? What are the consequences of managing it in any particular way? How does the usage of it translate into reporting? Before jumping into the planning, take a look at a rough overall software development process. This process, shown in Figure 3-17, is not specific to any methodology.

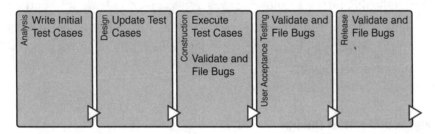

FIGURE 3-17: Basic development process with a focus on testing

What Is Presented Versus What You Should Do

It is logically impossible to present scenarios that cover every situation. Because of that much of what is presented is generalized, but some strong opinions are presented about what should be done regardless of the methodology used. Please be skeptical! What is presented here may not apply to your particular situation. There are many situations in which conventional wisdom must be discarded. In addition, theory and reality don't go together particularly well—which is why theory is discussed but is always balanced with practicality—such as with some of the advice you are about to get on creating Test Plans.

What should be obvious is that the basic steps you need to take are the same—regardless of whether you work in an agile or waterfall methodology. Someone needs to gather requirements; someone needs to write Test Cases; and someone needs to execute Test Cases. For example, using Test Driven Development is not enough to ensure the application meets the needs of the user, so even in TDD functional testing needs to be performed. However, the way in which it is performed and the emphasis placed on functional testing can vary widely. So pick and choose those practices that make sense for your organization.

Figure 3-17 presents a basic development process in which the testers come into play—and roughly when they come into play in an ideal model. The three phases of the development lifecycle where testers work are initial design and construction, testing, and maintenance.

PHASES IN AGILE

In an agile methodology, the analysis, design, construction, and testing can be tightly compressed and not visible as distinct phases. This is an important consideration to determine what works best for you. In Figure 3-17 testing is not presented as a distinct phase because it should be occurring hand-in-hand with development.

Analysis and Initial Design

During the initial design (for those plans created that deal with the analysis and design phase) the Test Plans look radically different than after the testing team can actually perform tests. Tests in these phases are created to validate the analysis and design of the application. Tests turn a subjective requirement into an objective understanding of what the customer wants.

This is a common practice. Formal specification languages—one of the best known is "Z"—enable you to precisely state requirements. (You can find more information on Z at http://formalmethods.wikia.com/wiki/Z.)

Specifications written in a formal modeling language follow strict mathematical theory that does not, in general, enable ambiguity. However, reading Z or other formal languages can be difficult. A well-constructed Test Case may not meet the rigor of a formal modeling language but can provide roughly the same benefits in an easy-to-read form in much less time. A good Test Case is one with little or (ideally) no ambiguity and provides the same result for every run.

GOOD TEST CASES

One definition for a good Test Case is that it is likely to find bugs.

Goal

The goal of Test Cases in the initial design phase is simple: Objectify and thereby validate the requirements. The following is a relatively simple, often-used example. Take a requirement that states the following: Visitors should comment on a blog post. This is a straightforward requirement—or is it? Remember that you are now looking at this requirement from the perspective of testability. You don't necessarily need to come up with all possible tests (virtually impossible in any small system and absolutely impossible in any large system) but you need to make sure that the requirement is testable. For a requirement to be testable, it cannot be ambiguous because if it is ambiguous, it is not repeatable. Before examining the details, look at Table 3-5, which is a use case that documents this requirement in more detail.

REQUIREMENT STATEMENTS VERSUS REQUIREMENT DETAILS

It is acceptable to get a requirements statement like the one just given. These are supposed to be high-level statements that provide a container for users to narrow down their requirements. The details need to be unambiguous.

TABLE 3-5: "As a Visitor" Requirement Use Case

ID	BE-1-1
Title	Visitors should comment on a blog post.
Description	Visitors should comment on blog posts. The visitors do not need to be registered to comment on posts but can comment only on blog posts that permit comments.
Actors	User (not logged on), Logged on User, System.
Preconditions	A blog post must have been published.
Post-Conditions	A blog post has a comment attached to it and displayed when the blog post is viewed.

TABLE 3-5: Continued

ID	BE-1-1
Normal Path	1. User navigates to the blog site.
	2. User selects a blog post.
	3. System displays the blog post and all associated comments.
	4. User elects to add a comment.
	5. System provides a comment entry display.
	6. User adds and saves the comment.
	7. System displays the comment at the end of the list of existing comments.
Alternative Path	[ID BE-1-1a: User is logged on]
[Branch after step 1]	
	1a. User logs onto the site. (User becomes a Logged on User.)
	[Resume at step 2.]
	5a. System prefills fields with the Logged on User's profile information.
	[Resume at step 6.]
[ID BE-1-1b: User has visited the site before.]	
	[Branch after step 5.]
	5a. System prefills all information from previously set cookie (as long as the cookie has not expired).
	[Resume at step 6.]

This use case raises a number of questions. First, what is the order of precedence when pulling cookie information or profile information? In other words, what if a user has logged onto the system before and made a comment (and thereby had the cookie set) and another user who has never made a comment before is using the system? Does the system clear the information? Does it use the cookie information? What about when a user logs onto the blog engine (from the same machine) after a nonlogged-on user has made a comment? Which information do you use? "Can a blog poster comment on his own post?" That's another good question that isn't answered by the use case.

These questions seem minor, and this is a small example, but these can lead to questions that, unanswered, can cause bugs. It also makes it difficult for developers to say they got it right. Testers have to ask these questions to create good Test Cases. Other ambiguous items show up here as well—what information is needed to create a comment? Do I just need the comment, or do I need to provide an e-mail address? What information is actually in the user profile, and just because it is there, do I use it to fill in whatever fields are available? These questions are more important because there is a data model issue here. These fields must be saved someplace, so you must know something about them; otherwise, you may end up having to rewrite the data access code to pull data from a different place.

Having seen this use case, you can roughly infer that there are three "sub" requirements:

- A visitor can add a comment to a blog post.
- Logged-on users can add a comment to a blog post, and their information should be prefilled from their profile.
- If users previously made a comment, their information should be prefilled from the cookie.

Now look at a simple Test Case to validate the requirement (see Table 3-6).

TABLE 3-6: Simple Test Case

Action	Expected Result
Navigate to the blog engine website.	BlogEngine.NET welcome page displays, and you are not logged in.
Click a blog post.	The post detail page displays with the post and all comments listed below it.
Click the Comment link.	The page displays places to enter your name, e-mail address, website, and nationality.
Enter the name **Joe**.	
Enter the e-mail address as **joe@nowhere.com**.	
Enter the comment as **Test Comment** and click Save Comment.	The comment displays above all the existing comments and below the blog post.

This simple Test Case follows the normal path. It also identifies a few details you didn't have before; the user can supply the name, e-mail address, website, and nationality. Now, it doesn't specifically say the fields are required, but it enables users to understand that this is what the developer is coding to, and if they want additional fields, they can ask for them. This Test Case does enable room for ambiguity—what blog engine website? Which post should they click? What information displays in addition to the comment? However, during the analysis phase you may not have anything concrete to latch onto or need that level of information.

The important piece here is that the user now knows exactly what to expect. This is good enough for the analysis phase. The user can say, "If this Test Case passes, the system does what I want it to do." So, at the end of the analysis and design phases, you may have a series of Test Cases marked as either In Design (the initial state of a Test Case work item type) that played a part in validating the requirements, or you may choose to change the state to Ready to indicate it is done and the users have validated the Test Case(s) against the requirement. Mostly, this will be a choice of how you want to report on these during the analysis and design phase. However, you should probably opt to leave the Test Cases in the In Design state so that you will almost always have to do minor updates after the functionality is built and ready for testing. This may include adding or removing steps and putting in concrete controls (such as Select Your Nationality From the Drop Down List as opposed to the preceding scenario in which the Test Case specified that places were merely provided for you to enter your nationality; now the control type is known). In general, a Test Case that is Ready is in a final form that can be executed.

CUSTOMIZING WORK ITEMS

Because of how flexible the work item system is, it is easy to add additional states, which is another option available to you. In general, adding additional states will not break the reports, but the reports need to be updated to see the new states.

However, this does bring up another point: Test Cases and iterations. Use the following: Iteration 1 is the analysis iteration and as such no testing will be done on this iteration, but Test Cases will be written. It is perfectly acceptable to mark Test Cases in Iteration 1 as Ready when they are completed by the standards of Iteration 1.

Then, when you begin Iteration 2, which is the start of the construction iterations, you may want to duplicate the Test Cases and reclassify them into Iteration 2. This also enables for granular tracking of Test Cases and enables you to say that a Test Case was ready in one iteration but not ready in another. Again, how you do this is up to you and how you want to report on it. The "Scenarios" section provides more detail.

Construction

The goal of Test Cases in construction is straightforward; they should be repeatable to find bugs before the user does and test the functionality of the application. The first and last items are open for discussion. Exploratory testing is not necessarily repeatable, unless you record it. Fortunately, you can record with MTM, so this isn't too much of a problem. The test may not be repeatable because of back-end data or processes, but at least a tester or developer can duplicate the steps taken to find a bug if one is found. The last item can be a bit of a problem.

In a perfect world you can achieve 100% code coverage through functional testing. Anyone who has ever done testing can tell you that this is not possible unless this is your quality bar that usually occurs only in life safety applications. So assume that this isn't going to be possible. What do you test? It goes back to the second point; you should run those tests first that are likely to be used by the user (and therefore the place to find bugs). To make it a bit clearer, in most applications, 20% of the code is used 80% of the time, and the other 80% of the code is used to handle alternative or exception paths. It's amazing how much code applications need to handle these outlying conditions. So a good rule of thumb is that the 20% of the code (100% of the normal path requirements) is tested 100%. All the other code is tested if time is available.

Will there be exceptions to this? Sure. There always are. Using this guideline can help catch the majority of the bugs before the users catch them. Testing the other 80% of the code should be done if time permits or if bugs are found that relate to the outlying conditions. That isn't to say that no testing in these areas should be done, but in general keep it to spot testing or let Unit Testing cover those conditions.

User Acceptance Testing

As an industry, there tends to be a lack of agreements (Service Level Agreements [SLAs] or other agreements) relating to the acceptance of software by the customer. This makes things difficult for the development team. Imagine completing the software for the customer, and after the "final presentation," the customer says, "Nope, this isn't what I wanted," and them asking you to redo parts of it. Who pays the cost for it? Who messed up? Does it matter? Yes. Even if the development team doesn't see it, someone has to pay for the rework, and someone cares about who made the mistake. And that's the thing: It usually isn't a mistake; it's because of changing requirements or misinterpretation. That's why it's puzzling to see this lack of an acceptance agreement.

Ideally, the conditions under which the customers will accept or reject the software are documented in a contract. The best basis for this is that an agreed upon set of Test Cases execute correctly. If this were the case, the customers would be saying that these Test Cases adequately demonstrate the features of the system that you are supposed to deliver. If these Test Cases pass, the system does what they asked you to do, and they can validate that you have delivered that functionality to them.

Now this does a couple of things: The customers have to sign off on the Test Cases. Changes to the requirements cause changes to the Test Cases that require customer signoff. Changes that go outside the scope of the agreed upon Test Cases are easily discoverable because the Test Cases are objective rather than subjective, which allows for ambiguity and therefore changes that aren't discoverable. The last benefit is that user acceptance testing is well defined. Sure, the users can do exploratory testing (that is, playing with the system to see if it works). But the real meat is the execution of the Test Cases, and this makes acceptance easy. The reason is that the Test Cases should have all been executed, at a minimum, twice: once by the developers and once by the testers. The users should almost never find problems with UAT Test Cases. So these Test Cases you create now are of benefit when delivering the software as well.

A GOOD UAT OPTION

One potential benefit of MTM being separate from Visual Studio is that for users performing UAT, this can be installed, and the users can run their exploratory testing through the Test Runner. In this way, if the user does find a bug, the development team has a complete record of the steps the user took to arrive at the bug. (This does require the end user to have a license for the software.)

Are SLAs going to be used? After all this, it is sad to say that the answer is probably no, because there will almost always be some last-minute items the customers want that can cause problems somewhere. Keep a process but be aware of the customer needs. Finding a way to fit both the process and the customer needs together can give you the power to use what has been discussed here. Even if you can't get there right now, start thinking about it now so that when the opportunity comes you can take advantage of it.

Common Scenarios

This section covers some common scenarios and how you can handle them from a planning and tracking perspective.

Scheduling and Tracking Test Case Creation and Execution

Before everyone on the team rushes to write features and write Test Cases, you need a plan for how to manage and track this work. Out-of-the-box, you can notice that the Test Case work item type (regardless of whether you use the MSF for Agile or MSF for CMMI template) lacks the Remaining Work and Completed Work fields. There is a reason for this. What would that time track? Is it tracking the creation of the Test Case or the execution of the Test Case? Or both? It would be hard to say.

Another item to consider is projects in which the project manager uses Microsoft Project to track work. It uses a Work Breakdown Structure (WBS) that uses parent/child relationships between work items to create that WBS. The Test Case work item is related to the requirements with a Tests/Tested By relationship, so Test Cases will not show up in the WBS, and the project manager cannot schedule them the way they would schedule a task.

The best way to handle this is with the structure shown in Figure 3-18.

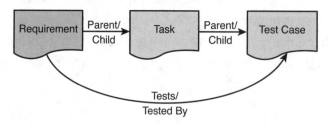

FIGURE 3-18: Work item relationships

This structure solves a number of problems. First, a project manager can assign the task of creating a Test Case to the test team, which means that the activity can be captured in a Microsoft Project WBS. Second, the project manager has the option to schedule the Test Case for creation and for execution separately. When doing it this way, the Assigned To field would be the person creating it in the first case and executing it in the second case. You do not need to use the Assign To Tester functionality unless testing on multiple configurations. This enables the project manager to track the time discretely for each activity; however, you may not want to assign a task to execute a Test Case. This is quite difficult for a tester to realistically keep track of. The task would be associated with the Test Case and not the test run, which makes reporting even more difficult.

The Parent/Child relationship between the Task and Test Case is not necessary. It provides some additional structure and enables the Test Cases to show up in a tree query (as opposed to a directed links query) but does not feed any reports.

Feature Driven Development

In FDD, software development is done on multiple branches. That is, you may have a branching structure like the one shown in Figure 3-19.

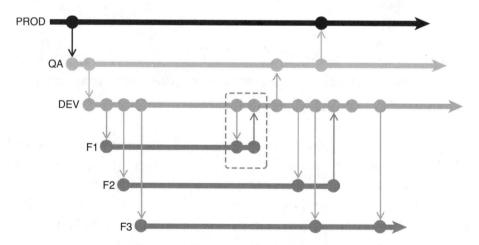

FIGURE 3-19: A typical FDD source code structure

In this type of branching structure, it is generally considered a best practice to perform comprehensive testing on all code in each feature branch before merging it to the main development environment. As part of this process, Test Cases need to be "migrated." For example, if you create a series of Test Cases (Test A, Test B, Test C) for code on feature branch F1 and that code is merged to Dev and then back down to feature branch F2, those Test Cases may need to be executed against the code in branch F2. How do you keep track of it?

The recommended solution is to create one Test Plan per feature branch. Because you can copy suites between Test Plans, this becomes relatively simple. Figure 3-20 shows the Copy Suites screen.

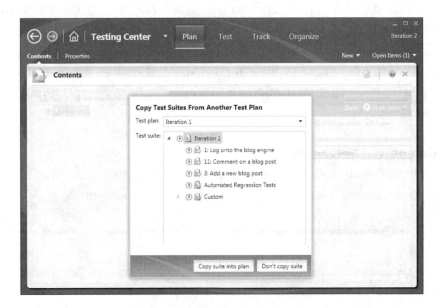

FIGURE 3-20: Copy Test Suites from Another Test Plan dialog

To get to this dialog, right-click Test Suite in the Plan, Contents page, and select Copy Suite from another Test Plan. You can either copy the entire suite (which includes the root node) or you can copy individual suites. It is critical to note that this does *not create a copy of the Test Case*. It simply references the existing Test Cases, which in this situation is exactly what you want—change the Test Case in one place and it changes it in all places. In this way multiple Test Plans can be associated with different code from different branches (because each Test Plan can be associated with its own build) but the results can all be reported on together.

Moving from One Iteration to Another

When you move from iteration to iteration, you need to deal with a number of issues. Some of these include uncompleted Test Cases, and in others the Test Cases were completed but never executed. Do you simply "copy" them from one suite to another, which creates a reference, or do you duplicate the Test Cases? This depends on how you want to report on them.

If you have a Test Case with the area set as Iteration 1 but then you copy the suite that it is part of to another Test Plan, which is testing Iteration 2, you have a problem. Because a suite copy is actually a "reference," the Test Case continues to show up in Iteration 1—not Iteration 2. This can significantly skew your reporting depending on how you report on it. On the other hand, creating actual copies of the Test Cases adds to the "number" of Test Cases, even though this number doesn't change.

What are your options? In the first case, the suite copy is an expedient way to handle the problem. But the recommendation for this is to go one step farther. After you perform a suite copy, update all the Test Cases that were copied to be the same iteration that the new plan is in. To make this clearer, consider the following: You have a plan (Analysis) that is set for Iteration 1. All Test Cases in the plan are also set for Iteration 1. The analysis phase is complete, and you move to the next phase in which these Test Cases will be updated. If you plan to do work on these Test Cases, use the suite copy to add them to a new Test Plan called Construction. After they are copied over, update all the Test Cases so that the iteration is set to Iteration 2 (to match the iteration in which they will be worked on). Then continue to work on them as you normally would.

The second option in many ways is more appealing. Creating copies of the Test Cases allows you to preserve the Test Case as it was executed against the code in a given iteration. An example is that Iteration 3 ended in a release to the customer. The team begins work on Iteration 4, which will modify some of the features in Iteration 3. (This is an every-day occurrence in agile development but less so in waterfall.) However, between the current release and the next release, those Test Cases may need to be re-executed against production code. If you are actively changing those Test Cases, you need to go back into the Test Case work item type history to get back to the Test Case executed against the current release. In this way it acts almost as a branching mechanism for your Test Cases and enables you to preserve the Test Cases executed against a release. This may be handy for auditing purposes.

The advice for this issue is "It depends on what you're trying to do." There are no "best practices" because everything is dependent on your situation. Just be aware of what can happen in the various scenarios, and think it through before developing your plan.

Handling Different Test Configurations

As previously mentioned you can use configurations as metadata for reporting purposes and to cut down on the number of Test Cases that you need to maintain. But does it always make sense to do this? The answer is no. No tools can easily solve this problem, so it takes some planning. First, you need to determine if the different configurations require different tests. If they do, your answer is simple: Do not use the MTM test configurations to differentiate configurations. In this scenario, it requires you to create separate Test Cases and differentiate by Area. In addition, you would be better off creating separate Test Plans. Why? As noted earlier, Test Plans have one manual test setting and one automated test setting. It can be assumed that for different configurations you may be testing on different systems or with different settings, so it is easier to manage with separate Test Plans. If you do this, you do not need to use Areas to break up your configurations; MTM can work for you.

This is one item that should absolutely not be overlooked. The test settings can be cumbersome to manage if you have to change them on a per-run basis. It is easy enough to group Test Plans in different areas and then arrange the Test Cases under them. If you have to group Test Cases together that require different test settings, you are adding more work for the testers, so plan this before you get to the point where it is a problem.

SUMMARY

In this chapter, you learned about Test Plan components and how to create them. You learned the relationships between all the different test containers and about the goals of different stages of testing: analysis, construction, and user acceptance testing. This chapter also showed you how to create different testing configurations and their effects on Test Cases. You learned how to start managing a Test Plan by assigning testing configurations and testers to different Test Cases and configuration combinations. Most important, you explored a number of different scenarios that require you to think about the structure of your testing environment and common problems to these scenarios. In the next chapter, you learn how to execute tests using Microsoft Test Manager.

4

Executing Manual Tests

IN CHAPTER 1, "STATE OF TESTING," one of the goals mentioned for the Visual Studio 2010 family of products was the no-more-no-repro scenario. The first step in this process is to run tests in a repeatable fashion and to file "actionable" bugs. What is an actionable bug? It is a bug that the developers can act on, which means that the bug can be fixed with the available information in a reasonable period of time. Today, much of the problem is that developers are not exactly the happiest people in the world when someone comes to them and says, "We found a bug in screen x, please fix it," and then walk away. That's not actionable; that's a recipe for wasting hours of developer time.

For testers to file actionable bugs, they need good Test Cases. Or do they? What happens when testers runs exploratory tests or ad-hoc tests and the tests fail? They aren't working from a good test script, so it's hard to document how the failure occurred. With Test Runner (TR) the problems caused by trying to reproduce the results of an exploratory test are a thing of the past. In this chapter, you see how TR works.

This chapter also exposes the power of having the testing tools, requirements, and code base linked together because it enables testers to gather detailed information to provide back to developers to virtually ensure that they can re-create the problem. This information includes stack trace information and the ability to actually walk through the code that was executing during the test using a technology Microsoft calls IntelliTrace.

By the end of this chapter, you will know how to work with the Test Case work item type, execute a manual test, and file bugs through TR. All aspects of executing manual tests from straight execution to restarting a test and creating and running parameterized tests are covered. In addition you start to learn how to use the built-in data collectors to gather important information.

Using the Test Case Work Item Type

The Test Case work item type contains the normal fields that you expect in a TFS work item type. One difference is that the priority setting has an actual function other than notification to the tester of what needs to be worked on first. When coupled with automation, the Priority field filters out automated tests that you don't want to run. Keep this in mind as you set and change the Test Case priority. The Test Case also adds a new control: Steps. Figure 4-1 shows the Test Case work item type.

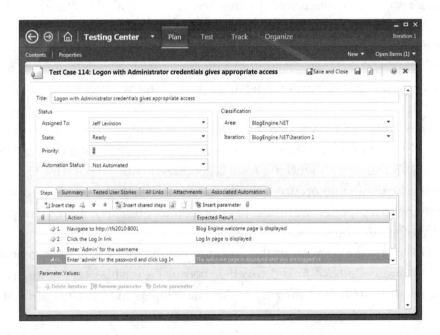

FIGURE 4-1: Test Case work item type

The Steps tab contains an Action column that shows the steps testers must take. The Expected Result column explains what testers should see after they complete the step. The first column shows any attached items for that step. As you can see in Figure 4-1, not every step requires an expected result. This plays into how the test execution behaves and how test automation works. Below the steps are the parameters that show information related to parameterized Test Cases. Figure 4-2 shows the specific controls and information related to test steps.

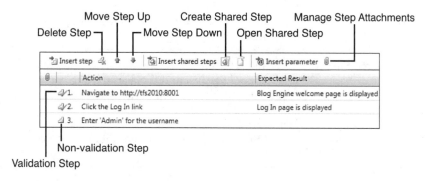

FIGURE 4-2: Steps control details

EDITING TEST STEPS

Test steps can be edited only in MTM. Opening the Test Case work item in Team Explorer or Team Web Access displays a read-only view of the test steps.

In the second column of the Steps tab is an icon indicating if the step includes a validation or expected result, which are the same things. An expected result requires that you validate that a step is successful, which is why the terms are used interchangeably. The check mark indicates an expected result; the step without a check mark indicates there isn't an expected result.

Above the Steps tab are a series of buttons that enable you to perform different actions on the selected step. Table 4-1 explains these options.

TABLE 4-1: Steps Control Options

Option	Description
Insert Step	Inserts a step before the currently selected step.
Delete Step	Deletes the currently selected step.
Move Step Up	Moves the currently selected step up one step. Move Step Down Moves the currently selected step down one step.
Insert Shared Step	Inserts a Shared Step before the currently selected step.
Create Shared Step	Takes the currently selected steps and creates a Shared Step set and replaces the current selection with the Shared Step. This works only with contiguous steps.
Open Shared Step	Opens the Shared Step work item type for viewing or editing.
Insert Parameter	Displays a dialog for adding a parameter, but in practice you do this manually.
Manage Step Attachments	Enables you to associate attachments with each step in the test.

The associated Automation tab contains the information necessary to automate the Test Case. I explore this in more detail in Chapter 6, "Automating Test Cases."

EXERCISE 4-1

Creating a Manual Test Case

This exercise assumes that you have performed the exercises in Chapter 3, "Planning Your Testing." To create a manual Test Case, follow these steps:

1. Select the Plan tab, Contents page.
2. Select the As the Blog Author I Want to Be Able to Log onto the Blog Engine Test Suite from the list of suites.

3. Click New from the toolbar in the Test Suite Details pane.

4. Type the title **Logon with Administrator credentials gives appropriate access** and click Save.

5. Click the Action column in the first row of the test steps.

6. Type **Navigate to http://[*servername*]:8001** and press Tab.

7. Type **Blog Engine welcome page is displayed** in the Expected Results column, and press Enter.

8. Type **Click the Log In link**, and press Tab.

9. Type **Log In page is displayed** in the Expected Results column, and press Enter.

10. Type **Enter 'Admin' for the username** and press Enter. (There are no expected results for this step.)

11. Type **Enter 'admin' for the password and click Log In**, and press the Tab key.

12. Enter **The welcome page is displayed and you are logged in–verify this by noting that the Admin control is displayed**, and press Enter.

13. Set the State to Ready, and click Save.

Refer to Figure 4-1 to see the results of this exercise.

Shared Steps

The first item that needs some explanation is the Shared Step, which has many interesting and time-saving effects on a Test Case. A Shared Step enables you to create a reusable set of steps, but you need to follow some rules. Using the example steps shown in Figure 4-1, you might presume that many tests require a user to log on as an administrator to carry out tests related to administration functions. The first Test Case is a basic "does the logon work correctly" Test Case, but these steps can be applied to many Test Cases. To create a Shared Step, complete Exercise 4-2.

EXERCISE 4-2

Create Shared Steps

To create Shared Steps, follow these steps:

1. Select the test steps you want to reuse (in this case all test steps).

2. Select Create Shared Steps.

3. Enter the name as **Log on as Administrator** in the Create Shared Steps dialog, and click OK.

Figure 4-3 shows the resulting test steps.

FIGURE 4-3: Results of creating a Shared Step

The first question to ask is, "What happened to my steps?" Good question. To see the list of Shared Steps you created, select the Organize tab, Shared Steps Manager page (see Figure 4-4).

FIGURE 4-4: Shared Steps Manager

Here, you can open the Shared Step, which is just another work item type. Shared Steps cannot contain other Shared Steps, so there is a limit to how Test Cases can be composed. You can have as many Shared Steps in a given Test Case as you want, but not in a Shared Steps work item type. As part of the Shared Steps Manager you can copy Shared Steps, open them for editing, and create new Shared Steps. You can also create an action recording for Shared Steps independent of any tests that may implement the Shared Steps. You see the action recording in the section on Test Results.

You can also edit Shared Steps by clicking the Open Shared Steps button in the Test Case work item type with the Shared Steps selected. The next section discusses how a Shared Step affects the run.

IMPORTING EXISTING TEST CASES

Microsoft released a tool (Test Case Migrator) to import Test Cases from either Excel or from an existing .mht file used by the testing framework in Visual Studio 2008, which can be downloaded from http://tcmimport.codeplex.com. The download contains extensive documentation and walkthroughs on how to use the tool.

Data Driven Test Cases (Test Parameters)

You can augment any set of test steps by using parameters that enable you to specify how many iterations a given Test Case will go through and provide different data for each iteration. To add a parameter to a Test Case, simply add a space, an @ symbol, and the name of the parameter. For example, @Value creates a parameter named Value. However, P@ssw0rd will not create a new parameter named ssw0rd because a space does not proceed the @ symbol.

The best way to show this is through an example. In the previous example you created a specific Test Case for logging on as an administrator. This is helpful when running many different types of tests but causes more work than you need when you want to validate different logons. To put it another way, you can create three Test Cases to validate the Administrator, Editor, and Guest permissions, or you can create one Test Case with three sets of parameters. Exercise 4-3 shows how to do this.

■ EXERCISE 4-3

Create a Parameterized Test Case

To create a parameterized Test Case, follow these steps:

1. Create a new Test Case called Logon with Valid Credentials.

2. Enter the following actions to receive the expected results.

Action	Expected Result
Navigate to http://[server name]:8001.	Blog engine welcome page displays.
Click the Log In link.	Log In page displays.
Enter the username as @username.	
Enter the password as @password and click Log In.	The welcome page displays, and the administrator widget contains the following entries: @result.

3. In the Parameter Values section, you now see username, password, and result (Figure 4-5). Click in this section and add the following values:

username	password	result
admin	admin	Users
jeff	P@ssw0rd	Add Entry but does not contain Users
steve	P@ssw0rd	Change Password only

4. Change the state to Ready, and click Save and Close.

Figure 4-5 shows the outcome of Exercise 4-3.

Here, the Test Case validates that valid logins are successful and grants the right level of access. Instead of writing three separate Test Cases, you can simply write one with multiple iterations. Note the Parameter Value section at the bottom of the Steps tab. Select Delete Iteration to delete a set of parameters because each new parameter is a new iteration.

The parameter columns displayed in the Parameter Values list are automatically created as you add parameters to the Steps control. Step 3 and 4 each have parameters that display in the Parameter Values list.

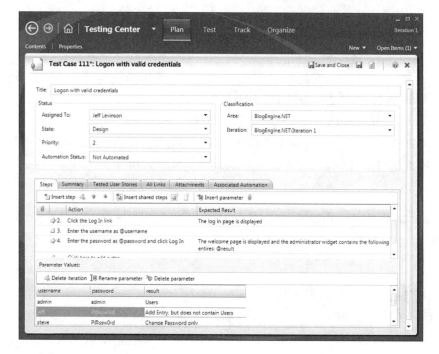

FIGURE 4-5: Parameterized Test Case

Running Your First Tests

For this example, execute the tests selected in Figure 4-6.

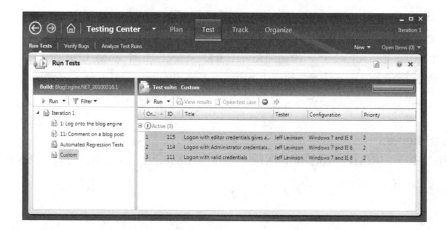

FIGURE 4-6: Test Tab, Run Tests Page

As shown in Figure 4-6, three tests are selected to be executed for this first run.

USING STATIC (CUSTOM) SUITES

The suite the Test Cases are contained in is a static suite for this test run. The static suite has one major benefit that a requirements or query-based suite does not have; you can order the Test Cases for the run.

The test settings for this specify Test Impact Analysis, System Information, IntelliTrace, and the Video Recorder.

INTELLITRACE SETTINGS

By default, IntelliTrace information is not collected for ASP.NET applications. You must click the Configure button in the Test Settings creation screen and specifically select this option. (See Chapter 5 for more information about IntelliTrace Settings.)

A build has been assigned to this Test Plan, and each Test Case is Active. You can find the build number above the Test Suites in Figure 4-6. Each Test Case is marked as Active, Passed, or Failed. Because none of the Test Cases have been executed, they are listed as Active. To execute the test run, simply click Run, or select the drop-down and select Run with Options, which enables you to change the build in use, test settings, or the test environment on a per-run basis.

Test Runner

Clicking the Run button hides Microsoft Test Manager and brings up the Test Runner, as shown in Figure 4-7.

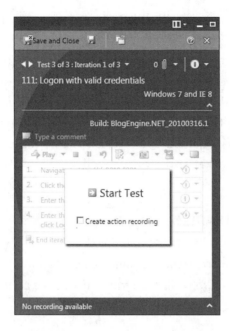

FIGURE 4-7: Test Runner before the start of a test run

Before running the test, here's a quick tour of Test Runner, which is detailed in Figure 4-8 for your reference.

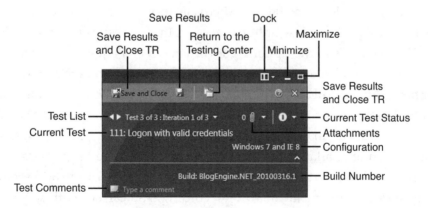

FIGURE 4-8: Test Runner Layout (header)

In the upper-left corner is the number of tests to be executed as part of this run (three in this case) with the first test listed (111: Log on with valid credentials). To the right you can see a "0" with a paperclip. This denotes that no attachments are associated with this test execution run. The icon to the right of that indicates the status of this Test Case in this run. In Figure 4-8 this is the Active icon and indicates that no status exists yet (that is, it hasn't been run yet); a green check mark indicates a successful run; and a red X indicates a failed run. Below this is the test configuration that this run should be executed with; clicking the down arrow below that displays the build that this Test Case is executing against. You can also add comments related to the Test Case result during and after the run as well.

BUILDS AND BINARIES

Although a build has been associated with a Test Plan, you aren't actually executing those binaries when running manual tests. This is especially true of Web Applications. You still need to make sure the builds are deployed to the appropriate location for the testers to execute the right binaries.

In the upper-right corner of the Test Runner is an icon that looks like a little Windows Explorer icon. This enables you to dock TR. Dock Left is the default or Undock It makes it float.

You can exit TR and go back to Microsoft Test Manager in three ways. You can use the Save and Close button that saves the test results to TFS and closes TR. Or click the X in the upper-right corner, which is the same as Save and Close. Any completed tests have their results reported to TFS; any that have not been run are still in the Active state. Or click the Return to the Testing Center button to the right of the Save disk. This returns you to MTM but leaves the run in an "in progress" state. This enables you to pause and resume testing at a later time. Only one test run can be in progress at any given time. If you start another test run, the run in progress will be discarded.

To start the test, create an action recording. You can select this option as part of the test settings, but in some cases, you may not want to record an action log, so this displays as part of the normal test start process. For this example an action recording is created. To do that, select this check box and click Start Test. Figure 4-9 shows the Test Runner during a test execution.

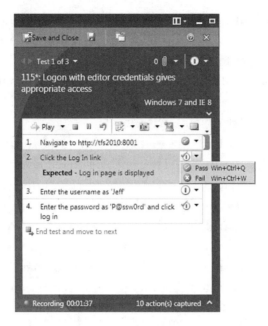

FIGURE 4-9: Test Runner during a basic test execution

Each step in the Test Case is listed with the expected result listed directly below it. Each test step expands to show the expected result. This enables you to see the full text of the step and the results without taking up more room than necessary. To the right of each test step is the Active/Pass/Fail indicator. The third line of the Test Case, Enter the Username as 'Jeff', has a different icon because no validation is associated with this step. You can still mark it as Passed or Failed, but you don't have to do anything for this step if you don't want. However, if you don't mark it, you have to manually move to the next step by clicking it.

Marking a step as Pass/Fail or not marking it at all has three consequences. First, when you turn the manual Test Case into an automated Test Case, every step marked pass becomes a separate method that enables you to apply discrete validations. (Refer to Chapter 6.) Second is when you manually play back the Test Case in TR (covered in the "Replaying Test Steps" section). For steps where no validation exists, the tester does not need to examine anything, so the playback plays back the step but doesn't stop at that point. The idea of stopping at only a validation point enables the tester to visually inspect the screen to make sure everything is correct. Finally is a trade-off that you have to make when creating a CodedUI (automated) test. By marking every step as passed, if the user interface ever changes, it becomes much easier to replace a section of the CodedUI test (the cheaper option). If you mark only validation steps as passed, when the user interface changes you might need to put in more work to maintain the CodedUI test than you might need to do otherwise.

Across the top of the test steps (detailed in Figure 4-10) are various options you can take during the test run. They enable you to Play back a section of the Test Case, Stop the test execution, Pause the test execution, and Redo the Test Case. (This resets everything as though the test never started.) Following this you can file a bug (or an Exploratory Bug covered in the "Exploratory Testing with MTM" section) or update an existing bug, capture a screenshot, attach it to the step, connect to or snapshot a virtual environment (covered in Chapter 7, "Executing Automated Test Cases") or add a comment to the current step.

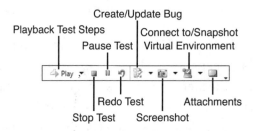

FIGURE 4-10: Test Runner Layout (toolbar)

The bottom of Test Runner shows how long the existing Test Case has been running; clicking the up arrow to the right shows you the action log for the existing recording. This list of actions also serves another purpose. An example is a scenario in which an unexpected dialog displays (more than likely this applies only to browser-based applications, but it could be caused by any number of items) such as the Internet Explorer First Run Customization dialog, and you click through it. If you try to play the test back, it fails because the dialog displays only once. You can select individual steps to delete or a range of steps, as shown in Figure 4-11, to complete the Internet Explorer First Run Customization dialog. To delete the steps, expand the action log steps, select the steps to delete, right-click the steps, and select Delete, or press the Delete key.

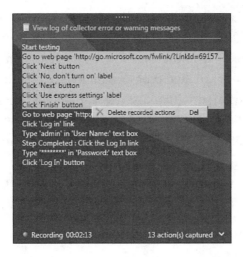

FIGURE 4-11: Action log list

Executing a Test

To begin executing a test, simply select Start Test and check the Create Action Recording check box. This begins recording the test; the time the test is running starts to increment. For each step that you are on (assuming this is not a Shared Step) do the following:

1. Execute whatever actions the step tells you to take.
2. Optionally, if there are expected results, validate that they are correct.
3. Optionally, add a comment or take a screenshot that is attached to the test execution step. (The distinction between associating something with a test step and what the effect is of associating something with an executing test step will be covered shortly.)
4. Optionally, Pass (Win+Ctrl+Q) or Fail (Win+Ctrl+W) the step. (You can also just click the active icon, once for Pass, twice for Fail.)
5. Move to the next step (manually if it is not a validation step).

Any comments you make or screen captures you take are automatically associated with the given test run and step. At this point it is worthwhile to take a minute and explain test step association in a Test Case versus test step association with an executing Test Case. From a development perspective, think of the Test Case as a class and each execution of the Test Case as an object of that class. You can spool up an unlimited amount of test executions for a given Test Case. Therefore, when you attach an item to a test step from within the Test Case work item type, that item is available to you during any test run. Items associated with a test execution step become part of the test results for that Test Case.

If you pass or fail a step, Test Runner automatically moves you to the next step. If you choose not to pass or fail a step, you must manually move to the next step in the Test Case. There are no negative effects for not passing or failing a step with no validation.

Figure 4-12 shows the second of the three tests executing that contains the set of Shared Steps.

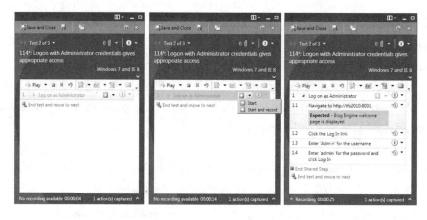

FIGURE 4-12: Shared Step execution

In the first panel, the Shared Step is listed as a collapsed, single step with a green option drop-down next to it. The second panel shows the available options: Start and Start and Record. A third option is also available here if you have already run a Test Case with this particular Shared Step: Play. Start will start the test but will not record an action log. Start and Record starts the test and records an action log for the Shared Step. The last panel shows the Shared Step being executed. There are two items to note here: Each step in a Shared Step is part of the Shared Step, and you can see this by looking at the step numbers, 1, 1.1, 1.2, 1.3, and 1.4. You must end the Shared Step separately from the test (bottom of the third panel).

Executing a Parameterized Test

A parameterized test executes once for each row of data. It displays in Test Runner, as shown in Figure 4-13.

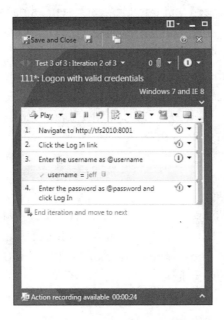

FIGURE 4-13: A parameterized Test Case

A few differences in this Test Case execution are immediately obvious. First is the test designation at the top of Test Runner, Test 3 of 3: Iteration 2 of 3. This indicates that the current Test Case has three rows of data associated with it, so to complete the run the test must be executed three times with different data. The second item is the currently selected test step with username = jeff and a check mark and a data symbol next to it; jeff is the value from the parameters grid filled in for you on each iteration. The check mark and data symbol display after you have successfully bound a value to a field. A third difference is that at the end of the test, you end the iteration and not the test. After all iterations have been completed you can end the test.

One other nice feature of parameterized tests is that the parameter values are copied to the clipboard for you. This means that, for example, when you select Step 3, you can click in the username textbox and do a Ctrl+v and the value "jeff" will be pasted into the username textbox.

BEST PRACTICES FOR RUNNING PARAMETERIZED TESTS

To make the testing experience as fast as possible, execute the first iteration in a parameterized test (marking each step as passed) and then play
back subsequent iterations. One of the great benefits of data binding is that
for each subsequent test run the correct parameters will be inserted for you.
Then simply note the end result and mark the overall test as passed or failed
(using the status icon in the upper-right corner of TR). For tests that require
validation along the way, you can selectively play back test steps by Shift-
clicking test steps to select them.

Finding and Filing a Bug

So far you have looked at running a basic set of manual tests and a parameterized test. The next feature of Test Runner is filing bugs, which is where the
magic happens. This shows the power of MTM to find and trace bugs and
track them to their resolution.

In Figure 4-14, you can see the selected step for which a Test Case failed.

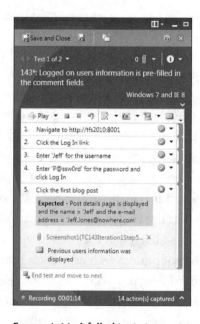

FIGURE 4-14: A failed test step

At the point of failure, note a few pieces of new information. A screenshot of the failed step is automatically attached to the failed test step. You take a screenshot by clicking the camera icon on the toolbar and either selecting the full screen (which includes TR), a window, or a rectangle (the default) that enables you to select the area you want to capture. This screenshot is automatically attached to the test step. Next, a comment has been added to the test step to indicate what was displayed, which was the information from a previously executed Test Case. After taking the appropriate screenshots and notes, make sure you fail the step before you click the Create Bug button on the toolbar. (You also have the option to update an existing bug.) If you don't do this step first, when developers look at the bug, they cannot see a step marked as failed, and you want them to know where things went wrong. This brings up a new Bug work item type (or whatever work item type you denoted in the Bug category) with all the information for the entire test attached. You can look at the generated bug in the Results section.

Pausing and Resuming Test Runs

Complex test runs may take several hours. If you need to stop testing to address other issues, MTM enables you to pause test runs. The test run is not completed but is still "in progress" and you can resume at any time. This makes it easier to handle testing tasks without losing your place.

To pause a test run, click the Return to MTM button at the top of the Test Runner window (shown to the right of the Save icon in Figure 4-14) instead of Save and Close. After doing this, you see a screen similar to Figure 4-15 on the Test tab, Run Tests page.

Figure 4-15 shows the test run in progress. Note that above the Run Tests page is the small Test Runner icon with an arrow that is the Return to Test Runner button. Essentially Test Runner is hidden and still runs in the background. The state of your application (the one tested) is not saved, so you should pause between tests and not in the middle of a test.

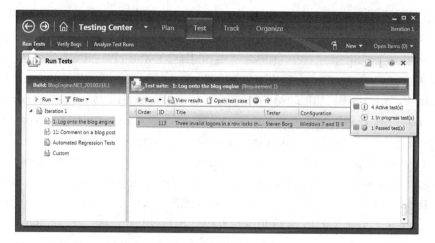

FIGURE 4-15: Test run in progress

VIRTUALIZED TESTING

This situation is remedied to a certain extent through the use of virtualized testing environments. Chapter 8, "Lab Management," covers this topic in great detail.

To continue a run in progress, simply click the Return to Test Runner button. If you close MTM or take any number of other actions (such as closing all the pages in MTM without actually exiting MTM), MTM automatically completes the test run for you and records the results. Test runs do not survive MTM sessions. Also, you cannot have multiple test runs in progress simultaneously. If you have a run in progress, you must stop or complete the run before starting a new run. MTM automatically ends the run for you if you start a new test run without explicitly taking an action.

Replaying Test Steps

A strip of orange or blue color is along the right side of the Test Runner; this is the playback strip. Any place you see this strip, you can select test steps and click the Play button in Test Runner. A blue playback strip represents a previously recorded strip; an orange strip represents a strip currently being recorded. Notice the grouping of test steps in relationship to the strip. Figure 4-13 shows that the grouping of the playback strip has a one-to-one relationship with every step because every step has a validation. Playback groupings are created based on validations with an obvious benefit: When you are simply running a test back, you do not want (in general) the playback to stop at steps on which there is nothing to validate. For example, if you work in a form with many fields to fill in and each field is its own step, there is nothing to verify; however, after you cause an action to be executed based on that data, you need to verify the results. So the strip helps avoid time-consuming steps and takes the testers to where they need to be to verify the results of one or more actions.

In Figure 4-12, the Log On as Jeff (Editor) Shared Step has been executed before. You know it works. There are no problems, so why go through each step for every test run? The answer is that you shouldn't do this, therefore the playback. Figures 4-13 and 4-14 show the playback strip. To play back a portion of the script, highlight steps you want to play back (or select a step within the strip) and click Play. If you record a new Test Case and the Test Case contains a Shared Step for which you already have a recording, a small icon appears to the right of the Shared Step and enables you to Start, Start and Record, or Play. When you are not recording a Test Case, simply press the Play button on the toolbar above the test steps.

Figure 4-16 shows the playback in progress.

Test Runner plays back each action and notifies you of where it is in the list of steps. As shown in Figure 4-16, don't play with the keyboard or mouse during playback. The playback goes as quickly as the application can respond. This is another feature of the testing tools in Visual Studio; they understand the application. There are no "wait" commands for the browser or application to respond. Test Runner knows, for example, when a page finishes loading or a response is completed, so your tests will not go off track because Test Runner tried to process a command before the application was ready. This feature is called Fast Forward for Manual Testing.

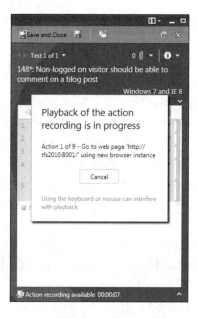

FIGURE 4-16: Playback in progress

Examining Test Results

After you complete a test run, it's time to look at your results and understand what was collected and what it is used for. Upon completing a test run, the Run Tests page changes to display the results of the latest run, as shown in Figure 4-17.

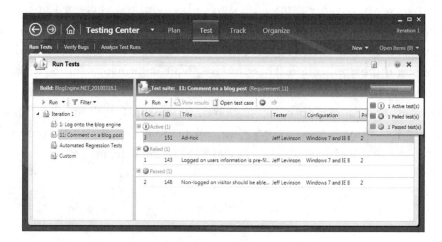

FIGURE 4-17: Run Tests page after a completed test run

From Figure 4-17, you can see that one of the tests passed on the last run and one test failed. One test has never been run before and is in the active state. Tests can also be in the blocked state, which is discussed later. To block a test, select the Test Case, and click the Block icon on the toolbar.

In the upper-right corner, you can see a bar graph showing the status of the test suite; holding your cursor over it creates a summary.

THE ACTIVE STATE

Tests can be in the active state because they haven't been executed before or because you manually set them back to the active state because a Test Case needed to be verified after a bug fix. They may also be active because the Test Case was copied from another suite and had to be reset or was set to be rerun to verify existing functionality had not been broken.

Test Run Results

Instead of seeing just the last set of results in the Run Tests page, you can select the Analyze Test Runs page that shows the results of all completed or in-progress runs, as shown in Figure 4-18.

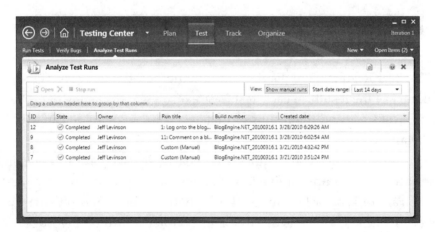

FIGURE 4-18: Analyze Test Runs page

The Show Manual Runs toggle is off by default, so if you work only with manual runs, make sure you select this; otherwise, nothing shows up in the list. This page is designed more to analyze automated test runs that might need some analysis after the fact. For a manual test run, it is assumed that if any work on the test results is needed you would do that immediately after the fact. Select any run, and click Open to view the overall test run results, as shown in Figure 4-19.

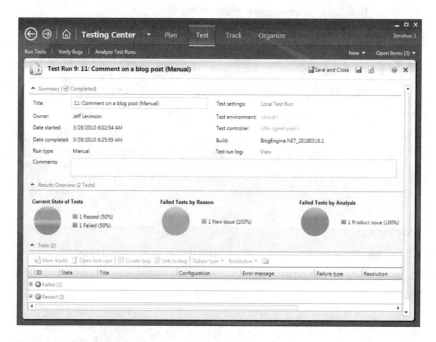

FIGURE 4-19: Test run results

The Test Results page displays information on the test run including a summary of the results of each Test Case executed and a listing of each individual Test Case and the results of that Test Case so that you can drill into the details of the test.

This view enables you to quickly and easily update various items in all Test Cases. For example, if five tests fail, instead of drilling into each test to set the Failure Type or Resolution (typically the resolution is set after the fix has been verified, which is discussed in Chapter 5, "Resolving Bugs") you can simply set it for every test from this screen. If you decide that a test was successful but you still want to file a bug against the test run, you can do that here. Any items that you want to attach to the overall results can be attached and viewed on this page. This page is actually the dashboard for an individual test run.

Detailed Test Results

Double-clicking a Test Case in the list displays the detailed Test Results page, as shown in Figure 4-20.

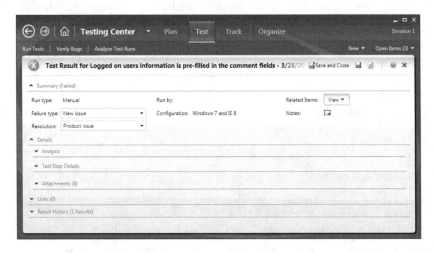

FIGURE 4-20: Detailed Test Results

This is the collapsed view of the test results. The summary section provides a high-level view of the test result. In this case you are told that the test failed, it was a manual run, and the configuration for this run was on Windows 7 and IE 8. Any notes that you added to the run results can display by hovering over the Note icon or double-clicking it to open up the Notes page.

Analysis

Figure 4-21 shows the Analysis section.

FIGURE 4-21: Analysis section

The Analysis section enables you to add comments to the Test Case if any additional details are discovered during analysis. (The Comments section is for general purpose notes about the run.)

Test Step Details

This section displays each step taken during the test and any comments or attachments associated with each step. In addition, whether the step passed, failed, or was not marked is shown here. The Test Step Details section is partially shown in Figure 4-22.

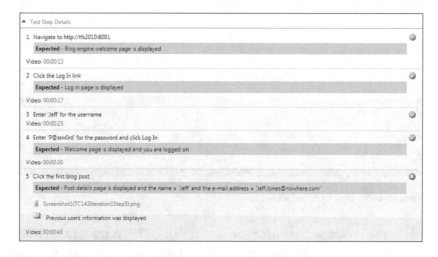

FIGURE 4-22: Test Step Details section

You can begin to see how things come together. (You will complete this understanding when you examine the bug that was created from this failure.) Here the screenshot from the failed step is available, as well as the notes the tester put in for the test failure. The video link is the fun one. One of the options is to use video recording to record the test set up for this particular test run. Test Runner indexes the video with each step taken and marked as passed or failed. This is one reason why it is better to mark each step; if you have to zip through a long video, this makes it much easier. Clicking this link opens a video recording of the test at mark 00:30. A screenshot of the video playback is shown in Figure 4-23.

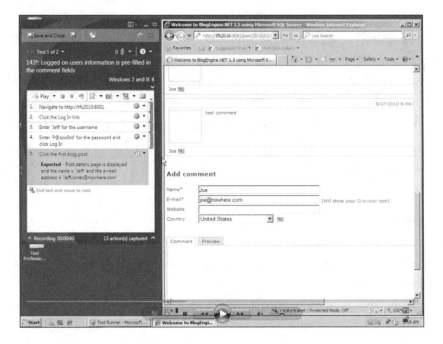

FIGURE 4-23: Video playback screen capture

The actions of the tester are recorded along with the application, so you can see what the testers were doing when they were not stepping through the application. This also enables developers and testers to verify that the tests were executed correctly. In addition the developers can see the exact steps and expected results the way the testers saw them. From a time-saving perspective, this is priceless and can give testers and developers huge efficiencies when trying to repro and fix bugs.

ANOTHER USE FOR THE VIDEOS

When time gets short, budgets get cut, and deadlines loom; usually two things get cut: code reviews and documentation. Even testing gets cut. One purpose that these videos can be used for is documentation. Think about it. The Test Case executed tests a feature because these are system tests in many cases. And you test the major features in their entirety. So if you don't have time to do end-user documentation, you can simply provide them videos from the testers. By capturing the test steps as well, you have built-in documentation for how to use every major feature of your application. No additional time, money, or work is needed to produce them. (They output in Windows Media Video format.) Use them wisely.

You must configure the Data Diagnostic Adapter for video recording to save the video even if the Test Case passes. Do this from the test settings Data and Diagnostics tab.

Attachments

The Attachments section stores all attachments generated for the test, either manually or as a result of a data collector running. Figure 4-24 shows a typical set of attachments.

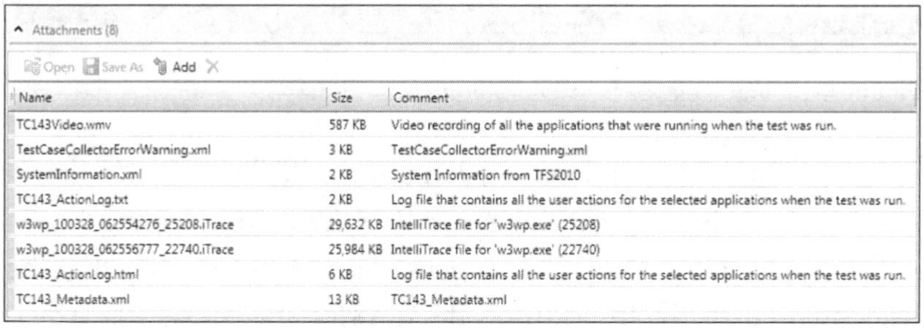

FIGURE 4-24: Test result attachments

Table 4-2 describes each of the file types.

TABLE 4-2: Test Result File Attachments

File Type	Description
System Information.xml	Contains all the information collected about the system on which the test is running (if the system collector is enabled)
Action Log.txt	A list of all steps taken against the application and recorded by Test Runner in a raw text format (if an action log is recorded)
Action Log.html	A formatted view of the contents of the Action Log.txt file

File Type	Description
Video.wmv	The video file of the test (if the video collector is enabled)
IntelliTrace log (.iTrace)	The IntelliTrace file with detailed debugging information (if the IntelliTrace collector is enabled)

In Figure 4-24, certain files appear to be duplicates. The reason for the duplicate files is because a test step failed during the test run. For example, the IntelliTrace file size is slightly different from one to the next. At the point that a step fails, a snapshot of everything is taken and stored for use by any bug that you may file. In the IntelliTrace log, the two logs combined are not taking up 55MB on the server. The smaller of the two files is "pointing" to a subset of the full IntelliTrace log, and that subset is 25,984KB but is not a separate file.

Figure 4-25 shows the contents of the Action Log.txt file in a formatted state.

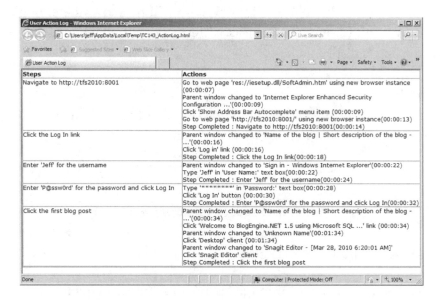

FIGURE 4-25: ActionLog.html

The Action Log.txt contains the raw text of the log whereas the Action-Log.html file contains the table format shown in Figure 4-25; however, they have the same contents. The action log plays a large role in both automated testing and manual exploratory testing, which is covered in the next section.

Links

This section contains links to work items generated from the test results. You can also create additional linked work items from this screen. Figure 4-26 shows the Links section from this test run.

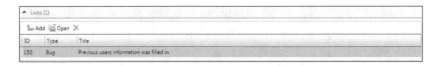

FIGURE 4-26: Links section

Bug #150 is the bug created as a result of the test failure on the last step. You can see what the generated bug looks like in the next section. A list of all work items linked by a Tested By link type will be shown here. Bugs are Tested By a Test Case while Test Cases "Test" a Requirement, which is why only the Bug is displayed here.

Result History

This section shows the test result for every run of this particular Test Case. The history of this Test Case is shown in Figure 4-27.

Result	Created date	Failure type	Resolution	Notes	Run by
Blocked	3/28/2010 8:49:58 A...	None	None		Jeff Levinson
Failed	3/28/2010 6:02:54...	New issue	Product issue		

FIGURE 4-27: Test Case Result History

This Test Case has gone through "two" runs. Two is in quotes because it was actually only run once. However, when you set a Test Case to Blocked, a new test run is automatically created, and "Blocked" is the result of that test run. You can view the results of any test run from here.

BLOCKED TEST CASES

A blocked Test Case is one that cannot be executed for some reason. Maybe there is a reason the code can't be fixed or some dependency such as an external system that isn't ready to be part of a test yet. Whatever the reason, a blocked Test Case is one that a tester should not attempt to run until it is un-blocked. A Test Case can be blocked by any tester, and the block can also be removed by any tester. There is no particular ownership of a blocked Test Case. This is a process that each team must work out.

Another feature of the Result History is that you can create a new bug directly from this section. Assume that you failed a test step during the test run but you forgot to file a bug. Going to this screen, selecting the test result, and clicking Create bug creates the bug with all the information that the developer needs, just as though you had created it from MTR. (With the exception that the log files will include the entire test run rather than just stopping at the point the failure occurred.)

Exploratory Testing with MTM

So far you have seen scripted testing; that is, a test in which the testers know exactly what steps they will take. Certainly this is critical in any testing process, but there has been an uptake in ad-hoc testing, the only form of testing performed. Although this is not ideal, budget and resource cuts and schedule cuts seem to frequently necessitate this step.

MTM has an exceptionally cool feature built into it so that you do not actually need to have a Test Case with test steps in it to run the test with Test Runner. Exercise 4-4 demonstrates how to perform ad-hoc testing with MTM. It does require at least an empty Test Case; you need one test step so that you can automate it.

■ EXERCISE 4-4

Exploratory Testing

This exercise walks you through executing a Test Case with no test steps and filing a bug against a Test Case of this type.

1. Create a new Test Case with the title **Ad-hoc** and save it.

2. Add the new Test Case to a Test Suite in MTM.

3. Go to the Test tab, select the Ad-hoc Test Case, and run it.

4. When MTR comes up, select Create action recording, and click Start Test.

5. Perform a series of actions. (The amount of time does not matter.)

6. At some point in the test, assume a failure occurs; click the drop-down next to the Create Bug icon in MTR, and select Create Exploratory Bug. (This displays the Time Range dialog, as shown in Figure 4-28.)

7. Move the slider about half way to the left, and click Use Range to Create Bug.

8. Click Resume and End Test.

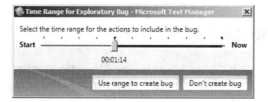

FIGURE 4-28: Range Selector for creating an exploratory bug

The Range Selector enables you to specify the time period you want the bug to cover. With the entire range selected (which is the default and which you should probably leave it at unless it is an extraordinarily long test) everything from the beginning of the test to the current point in time is included in the bug. In some cases a bug might have been caused by recent actions rather than a string of actions, so you don't need to clutter up the developers' list of things to check with meaningless steps that occurred early in the test. There are no hard-and-fast rules as to what to select; it's up to the testers' judgment about what caused the failure.

Exercise 4-4 shows some good practices and bad practices of using exploratory testing; understanding these is critical to performing good testing. You do not need a test step to perform exploratory testing, but notice that you could not grab a snapshot of the screen. You need at least one test step to do that. Also, you can associate only comments with the entire Test Case and not a particular step if there are no steps. In addition, the default action for ending an exploratory test is to pass the test. In general, you need to leave it that way; the reasons for this are discussed in the next section.

When the test concludes, go to the Test tab, Verify Bugs page. This page lists the bug you just filed (refer to Chapter 5). One of the options available at the top of the page is the option to Create Test Case from Bug. Select the bug you created, and create a Test Case from the bug. Figure 4-29 shows the created Test Case.

FIGURE 4-29: A Test Case created from an exploratory bug

Figure 4-29 shows the list of steps created from the action log attached to the bug. Granted, the output doesn't look that great, but from developers' perspective they know every step the tester took while performing exploratory testing. And more important, they can re-create the steps. From a testers' perspective, when they find a bug, they have a number of advantages: They can track this failed "test" and add the exploratory steps to the list of valid Test Cases to rerun when the bug has been fixed. They also have a better understanding of how they got to where they found the bug—no more guessing about what steps they took.

When creating a Test Case from a bug, there will be some cleanup work. In Figure 4-29, for example, you can delete many of the lines, and some of the steps in the action column can be moved to the expected results column. One thing you can't do though is update an existing Test Case (that is, the exploratory Test Case) with these steps unless you want to do it manually.

For this reason, you need to determine how to maintain exploratory Test Cases from normal tests. In general the exploratory Test Cases are throwaways, one-use-only tests. Make sure to close them afterward, or have an administrator destroy them. On the other hand, you can also have just one exploratory Test Case and use it as the basis for all exploratory testing. Either situation works but using individual exploratory Test Cases enables you to assign testers to perform exploratory testing.

As a recommendation, keep one exploratory test for each feature. When a bug is found, you should create a Test Case that reproduces the bug. The following are the recommended steps in this process:

1. Run the exploratory test. If you find a bug, file one and then generate a Test Case from that bug.
2. Execute the Test Case to verify that it finds the bug. (In other words, your exploratory test might hit upon something data-driven or something else that makes it not easily reproducible.)
3. After you have done that, you can create a "real" bug. The original bug can then be set to Closed.

Chapter 5 discusses the lifecycle of a Bug work item type. This may skew your metrics a little, but some simple work item customizations can handle this problem (refer to Chapter 5).

SUMMARY

This chapter gave you your first taste of working with Microsoft Test Manager and Test Runner. You can now create Test Cases, execute manual tests, and file bugs from those tests. More important, you know how Test Plans can be tracked and how Test Cases, test results, and Test Plans relate to each other through actual use.

The data collectors provide powerful tools for gathering data to help developers fix bugs. You can use the action logs and video logs to find and document the cause of bugs in your application.

The power of using a testing tool is integrated with your development tool. Developers have access to everything that testers have access to. With this power comes a decreased amount of time to find and solve problems. In addition, with this integration the communication barriers between developers and testers are eliminated.

In the next chapter you learn how the information generated by the work of the testers is used by developers to resolve the discovered bugs. At the end of the next chapter, you learn how to manage the process full circle—after the developer fixes the bug, how does the tester verify that the bug is fixed? Chapter 5 covers this information in detail.

5

Resolving Bugs

C HAPTER 4, "EXECUTING MANUAL TESTS," covers how to execute Test Cases and file bugs. This chapter walks you through the contents of bugs and how developers use this information to find and resolve bugs. After a bug is resolved, the tester verifies that the bug was actually fixed. At the end of this chapter, you will have an understanding of the lifecycle of a bug.

This chapter includes one of Visual Studio's most interesting and time-saving new features: Test Impact Analysis (TIA). You look at what it does and how, and how you can take advantage of it to give your team more confidence because it has identified and tested those areas most likely to have a regression bug.

A Bug's Life

Before examining a bug, you need to understand the Bug work item type so that you know how to handle it. In many cases, there are no easy answers, and each team (or organization) must decide how to handle bugs. Depending on whether you use the MSF for Agile or MSF for CMMI process template, a bug's life slightly differs. After looking at the lifecycle of the bug, you may decide to make some changes. Make some recommended changes based on certain scenarios in the next section. Also, depending on how the bug is filed, it may be treated differently and require different lifecycles depending on the submission process. Figure 5-1 shows the bug states and transitions for both MSF for Agile and CMMI.

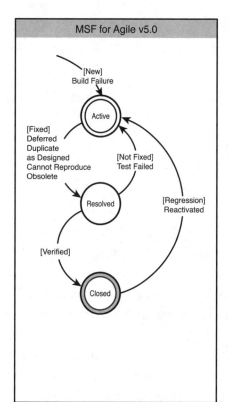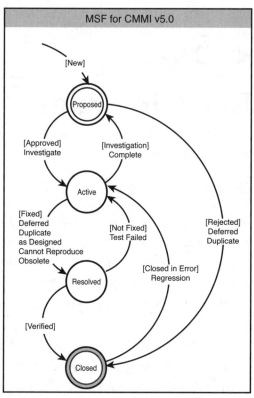

FIGURE 5-1: Life of a bug

The first and most obvious item is that all bugs in Agile start off as Active. Bugs in CMMI start off as Proposed. This is an important distinction and has ramifications for how a team handles the bug in scheduling and for reporting.

Figure 5-2 shows the MSF for Agile bug, and Figure 5-3 shows the MSF for CMMI bug.

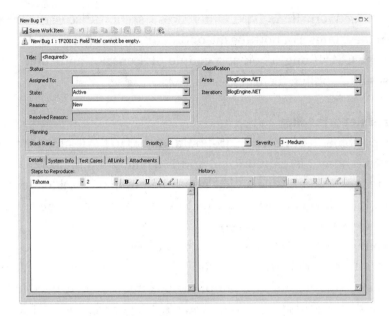

FIGURE 5-2: MSF for Agile Bug work item type

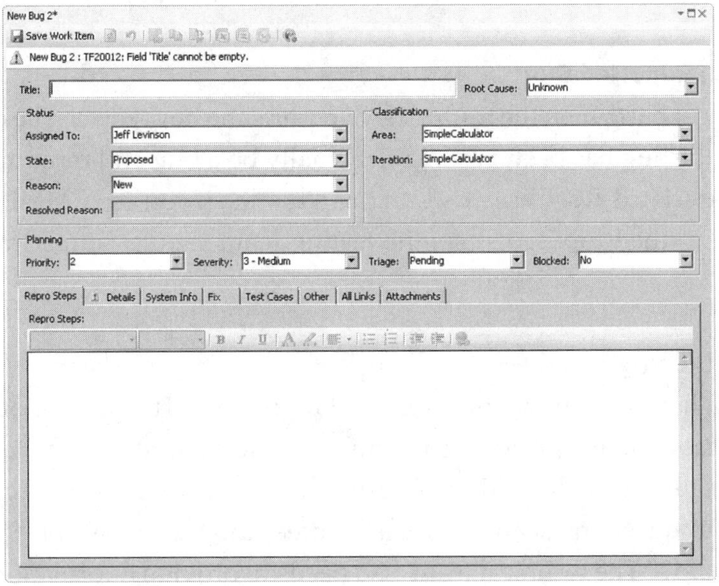

FIGURE 5-3: MSF for CMMI Bug work item type

The "Bug Work Item Type Differences" section discusses differences between these bugs. For now the major differences are that more data is gathered in the CMMI bug. Look at a couple of scenarios and some potential processes for handling them.

Customer Reported Bug

When a customer reports a bug, it should first go to the testing team for validation to ensure it is reproducible and is actually a bug (as opposed to a change request). In an Agile project it may be put in the backlog for the next iteration. In a CMMI project it may go to a change board before going to the testers; it depends on your processes.

When the test team gets the bug, as part of the verification process, a Test Case should be created. In addition the Test Case should then be linked to the requirement. This provides the out-of-the-box traceability needed to light up the various reports discussed in Chapter 9, "Reporting and Metrics." If the "bug" is not actually a bug, it should be transitioned to either a Change Request (CMMI) or a User Story (Agile) and handled appropriately.

Test Team Reported Bug

For the most part when the testing team reports the bug, you can be quite certain that the bug has been verified to actually be a bug and reproduced and that an associated Test Case exists. In this situation if you use CMMI, the team should skip the Proposed state; the testing team should simply move it to Active.

Triaging the Bug

After you have a verified bug, you need to triage it. The process of triaging is simply assigning a priority to the bug. You do need to have certain pieces of information to help with this process. The business needs to provide answers to questions such as "Does it affect the business?" or "Is there a workaround?" The technical team also needs to provide information such as what is the impact of fixing it? How long will it take to fix it? (That is, an estimate is needed.)

Reactivations

An important point is in dealing with reactivations of both bugs and requirements. Bugs can either be new bugs or "fixed" bugs that were not actually fixed. The following process applies in each situation: For the testers to begin testing a feature, the feature must be complete (or should be, in most cases). This is indicated by the developer setting the requirement to Resolved. (This is true in both process templates.) When testers find a new bug, they should not only create the bug but also set the requirement back to Active. This causes the story to appear in the Reactivations report (discussed in Chapter 9).

For an existing bug that has been resolved, the tester should set the bug back to Active if the bug is not actually fixed. It is up to the team to determine whether the tester should also set the requirement that the bug is associated with back to Active. The act of setting the bug back to Active can cause the bug to show up on the Reactivations report. A bug appearing in the Reactivations report is likely more critical than a requirement appearing in the report because it indicates the bug has occurred multiple times. But it is critical that this be done correctly so that the process can be improved.

Bug Differences and Modifications

To this point you have seen the out-of-the-box work items and a basic process flow for handling bugs. In many cases teams want to revise the Bug work item type definition in the process template to capture additional information. This decision depends on what type of information you want to capture and if it is worthwhile to capture it. Table 5-1 lists the major fields in the MSF for CMMI Bug work item type but which are not in the MSF for Agile Bug work item type.

TABLE 5-1: Fields in MSF for CMMI Bug WIT That Are Not in MSF for Agile Bug WIT

Field	Need
Blocked	Indicates that work cannot proceed on this work item because of some issue (waiting on someone else, unable to get needed materials, and so on).
Found in Environment	Which physical environment was it found in? (Development, testing, testing with one operating system versus another, production, and so on; this is a free form field.)

TABLE 5-1: Fields in MSF for CMMI Bug WIT That Are Not in MSF for Agile Bug WIT

Field	Need
How Found	What was going on when this bug was found? This is a free form field.
Original Estimate	How long is it going to take to fix this bug?
Proposed Fix	What is the developer proposing to fix this bug?
Root Cause	How did this bug get in the code? The default values are Unknown, Coding Error, Communication Error, Design Error, and Specification Error.
Symptom	How was this bug manifesting itself? (The screen didn't complete a redraw, the data was incorrect, and so on.) This is a free form field.
Triage	Where is the team in the triage process? The default values are Pending, Info Received, More Info, and Triaged.

The questions are, "What do you do about these differences?" and "Are they important?" Answering the second question first, the answer is an unqualified "yes." The first question is a little bit more involved, so it helps to look at each field and what the benefits might be.

This discussion is highly subjective, and there are reasons to do things and not do things. One of the major issues between an Agile process and a more formal process is the involvement of users. With the daily interaction between developers and users, much of the need for recording information goes away because there is such a short time between being given the information and acting on it to fix the problem. The same goes for developers and testers working together. Because of this if your team has the luxury of being in this type of environment, you can easily exclude some of these fields; however, not all of them, and other changes may make sense as well. What follows are some items to think about as you determine your strategy.

Out of the gate you should consider changing the Bug work item type (if you use the MSF for Agile template) to start as Proposed or another state such as Unverified. The reason for this should be obvious: Just because a bug is filed does not mean that a) anyone is actively working on it, b) that it is a verified bug, or c) that it is a bug. Because everything starts as active, this can tend to skew the metrics by reporting a higher than accurate number of bugs.

BUG WORKFLOW

The discussion of workflow is based on the built-in MSF process templates and not by any other influences. For that reason you should also determine if the process flow makes sense for your team. For instance, when a bug has been verified (assume this is a more formal CMMI type of process), moving a bug from Proposed to Active doesn't make a lot of sense if you want to manage work in progress. After a bug has been investigated (and it is back in the Proposed, Investigation Complete state), when it is approved for work does not mean anyone is actually working on it. In Agile, the bug would be accepted into an iteration. In CMMI there needs to be a way to say it is a valid bug (maybe by adding a Verified state) and that the team has agreed to fix the bug (maybe by adding an Accepted state). Then when the developers work on the bug, they set it to Active. This enables far more granular tracking of what is occurring with the bug to the point in which you can run a report saying, "x number of bugs have been reported, y number are not actually bugs, and z number have been verified; and of those that have been verified, the team is going to fix n number of them." You get all this information just from adding two states that you cannot otherwise get.

The Blocked field is an all or nothing field; you add it to all the work items or none of them because applying it to just one work item type does not make sense. In addition, it depends on your feedback mechanism. One reason this is missing from the Agile template is because if you work in an environment in which you do daily stand-ups or your team is close together, you can simply inform someone that there is an issue—barring that you can create an issue work item to notify the appropriate people. For a more waterfall process or a larger team that is geographically distributed, the Blocked field has the potential to quickly and easily notify project managers and team members that an issue exists, and you can create an issue work item to further detail why something is blocked. Adding this field is at your discretion and depends on whether you have a problem which you need to solve.

The Found in Environment field is not necessary in its default form. A free form field provides no benefit for quantification purposes (and doesn't provide benefit for fixing the bug). The main reason for this is that with the System Info data gathered (see this in the "The Generated Bug" section), all the information you need is collected for you. Where this provides some benefit is when you can quantify where in the process the bug was found (Development, Testing, denoting internal team testing, User Acceptance Testing, or Production). This helps gauge the successfulness of the testing process. To do this, update the work item with an Allowed Values rule and put in these values (refer to Chapter 9).

The How Found field is also free form and provides little or no benefit. The reason is that there are only three answers: through production use, as a tester was testing, or as a developer was testing. This information is essentially provided by the Found in Environment field. For more detailed "how found" information, the team would look to the Test Case. This field is redundant and does not provide any benefit.

The Original Estimate field provides a huge benefit, which is why you need to update the Agile Bug work item type. It lets a team receive a bug and then include it in planning the next release or phase of work. Even in Agile, bugs go on the backlog for a future iteration, but there is no way to estimate these bugs. For this reason, update the Agile Bug work item type to include the Story Points field, which is equivalent to the Original Estimate field.

UPDATING THE BUG IN AGILE

If you choose to update the bug to add a Story Points field in Agile, you should also update the Product Planning query and the Iteration X queries. This enables the bug to show up in the Product Planning workbook and the Iteration Planning workbook. In the default implementation, this is not the case, but a bug is simply another backlog item to be addressed.

The Proposed Fix field is valuable if there is a period of time between the bug being found and the developer starting on the fix, or if there needs to be a design review process for a complex bug. There are no hard-and-fast rules for this one. It is valuable, but it may not be valuable to you in your current situation.

The Root Cause field is valuable no matter what methodology you use. Without pinpointing how a bug was introduced, you can never make changes to prevent it from occurring again. The root cause default values are fairly broad and encompass almost everything you will encounter. However, if you can add additional values that can help narrow the root cause, that will be beneficial in devising a plan to fix it. This field should be retrofitted to the Agile Bug work item type. In addition, make the list of Allowed Values a Global List so that it can easily be updated for every Team Project.

CUSTOMIZING THE PROCESS TEMPLATES

The process of customizing work items is beyond the scope of this book because although it is generally a simple process, there are so many options it is almost another book in itself. For more information on customizing process templates, see this MSDN topic: http://msdn.microsoft.com/en-us/library/ms243849(VS.100).aspx. Again, the MSDN documentation team has done an excellent job with the 2010 release, and this topic links you to all the information you need to know to perform a customization.

This page also includes a download link to the Team Foundation Server Power Tools, which includes the Process Template Editor to make the editing process easy.

The Symptom field is actually a description of what happens when the bug occurs. This information is critical for the initial bug report (customer telling the development team what happened). This information is not captured at all in the Agile Bug. Whether you want to call this a Symptoms field (it can't be reported upon because it is a Plain Text field), there should be a way to capture the users' perception of the bug. The reason why this is not in the Agile Bug work item is again because of the proximity of users to the development team; they can just call someone over and show them. This, however, does not take into account the maintenance period after the application is released; the development team is not going to be there forever, and there will be some communication done through the use of work items in the future.

Triaging bugs is always necessary; you need to know the priority of the bug. The big difference here is that the product owner sets the priority with the team during a planning meeting. For the CMMI Bug work item, it doesn't make sense to have this field. The reason is that the Priority field is required. Theoretically, you can look at the Triage field first, and if it does not say "Triaged," you know the priority is invalid but that doesn't make much sense. So there are two options you can take: Make the priority field not required for the CMMI Bug and remove the Triage field, or add some ridiculous priority and set it as the default. (Use a value like 99 that indicates it hasn't been triaged and is easy to filter out of results.) Any of these options enhance these fields above what is available in the default structure.

The Generated Bug

Now that you have seen the Bug work item, its workflow, and from Chapter 4 how easy it is for testers to file rich bug reports, look at the generated bug. A *bug* is the primary means of communication between testers and developers for problem solving. The Bug work item is important to the developer because the goal is to allow the developer to track down the source of the bug as quickly as possible *and to fix it*. In many environments today, that goal is often hindered because of a lack of good information and sometimes just a lack of context. How Visual Studio handles bugs is a key benefit to everyone. Figure 5-4 shows the Bug work item filed from the failure, as shown in Figure 4-11 of Chapter 4. This benefit is only available because of the tight integration between the testing and development tools. It enables the testers to file incredibly accurate and *actionable bug reports* with no extra effort and no wasted time.

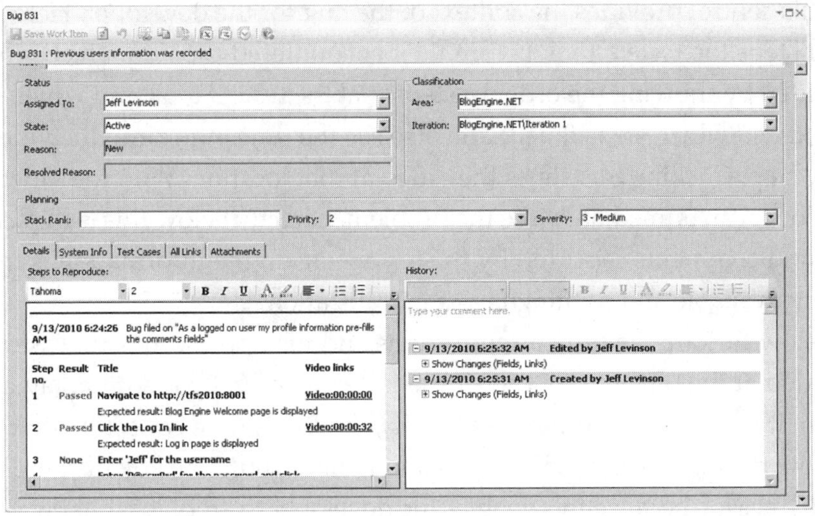

Figure 5-4: Bug work item type

The information contained above the tabs is fairly standard across the different work item types. The critical pieces of information to the developer are contained on the Details, System Info, and Test Cases tab. The Details tab contains two controls: Repro Steps and History. Figure 5-5 shows the repro steps for the bug.

Figure 5-5: The Repro Steps control

This control provides the context of the bug for the developer. Here is the set of steps the testers took before they encountered the bug. The context is provided by showing the order of steps that the testers took and which steps passed and which steps failed. You also see the time index into the video for every step. Clicking this starts the video at that location. With the video, the developer can immediately see the problem. Directly below this is the screenshot and comments captured by the tester—again the information is immediately available and nothing is lost in translation.

Below this are the test configurations and the applications that were not recorded at the time of the test. (If the tester specifically identified an application, it will be called out here.) Finally, the list of data collectors that were running during the test is displayed and their output. The key file here is the IntelliTrace log because this enables the developer to "replay" what was happening—in code. The IntelliTrace log and capabilities of IntelliTrace are covered in the "How a Developer Uses IntelliTrace" section. Not only can the developers replay the session, but also the IntelliTrace log can take the developers to the exact point in the code where step 5 began, so they don't need to trace through the entire application!

The System Information tab contains two (and eventually three) important pieces of information. The first is the build that the bug was found in. This makes it easy for the developers to know which build the testers were working with and for them to quickly grab it and go. Eventually, when the bug is fixed, built, and re-tested, the Integrated In field will contain the information that the build was fixed in.

The system information provided is shown in Figure 5-6.

This is the information for the system that the test was running on. In many situations (especially when dealing with specific hardware that your software may interact with), what was happening with the system makes a big difference. Sometimes, it's the operating system version that makes the difference, and sometimes it is the language or the amount of available memory. This information is captured in the SystemInformation.xml file and is formatted and displayed here.

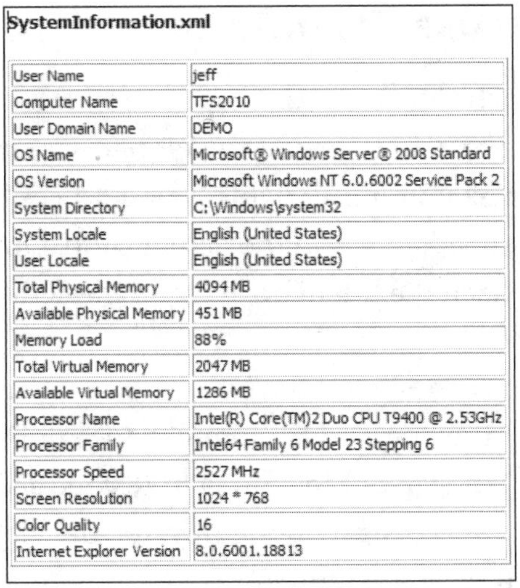

SystemInformation.xml	
User Name	jeff
Computer Name	TFS2010
User Domain Name	DEMO
OS Name	Microsoft® Windows Server® 2008 Standard
OS Version	Microsoft Windows NT 6.0.6002 Service Pack 2
System Directory	C:\Windows\system32
System Locale	English (United States)
User Locale	English (United States)
Total Physical Memory	4094 MB
Available Physical Memory	451 MB
Memory Load	88%
Total Virtual Memory	2047 MB
Available Virtual Memory	1286 MB
Processor Name	Intel(R) Core(TM)2 Duo CPU T9400 @ 2.53GHz
Processor Family	Intel64 Family 6 Model 23 Stepping 6
Processor Speed	2527 MHz
Screen Resolution	1024 * 768
Color Quality	16
Internet Explorer Version	8.0.6001.18813

FIGURE 5-6: System Information

TEST ATTACHMENTS *WARNING*

Test attachments are stored with Test Results, not with the Bug WIT. For this reason, be extremely careful when deleting a test result. Check to make sure no bugs are in the active state. If you accidentally delete a set of test results, the links in the Bug work item type no longer connect to anything, and you cannot undo the deletion of the test results (without a full restore of the SQL Server database).

The last important tab, Test Cases, provides a link to the Test Case that caused the bug, so the developer can view the entire Test Case and its history—and the requirement to which the Test Case was related.

TOUCHING THE SURFACE ABOUT INTELLITRACE

IntelliTrace provides so many options and has so many different possibilities that a full book could be written on just how to debug problems with it. The view provided here gives you a somewhat detailed introduction to IntelliTrace but leaves out many features and skips over much of what occurs.

How a Developer Uses IntelliTrace

By way of an introduction, IntelliTrace captures historical data related to the code executed by the test. In this way, developers can move back and forth through the test run examining variable data and conditions at a point in time, and they don't need access to the actual code. On the other hand, the developer can also attach the IntelliTrace log to the code and replay the testing session after the fact.

When developers are assigned the bug, one of the first things they do is look at the context of the bug and try to reproduce it. For this, they can just walk through the list of steps in the Steps to Reproduce section of the filed bug. When they have successfully done this, the developer will most likely jump into the IntelliTrace log (Figure 5-7).

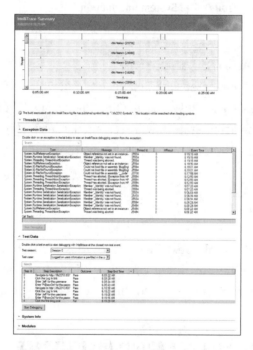

FIGURE 5-7: IntelliTrace Summary Log

Figure 5-7 shows those sections that are most important for the discussion. The top section lists the threads that were running before, during, and after the test failure occurred. The Exception Data shows all exceptions thrown during the test. The Test Data shows all information related to the actual tests that were run, including the Test Case and the test steps taken during the Test Case and whether they passed or failed.

Before you step into finding and fixing the bug, it is worth noting that you can find two types of bugs during a test: an exception bug (the application does something it cannot actually do, such as creating a file in a location where the application does not have permission to create that file) and a logic bug. Exception bugs will be listed in the Exception data, and debugging these problems is extremely simple; the developers just double-click the exception and are taken to the line of code that it occurred on. Logic bugs are a different problem because developers can't point to a single spot in the code and say this is where everything went wrong; they need to track it down.

A NOTE ABOUT THIS PARTICULAR INTELLITRACE FILE

You can see the rather large amount of exceptions thrown by this particular application. Some basic assumptions are made (incorrectly as it turns out) and some prevalidations are not done (such as checking to see if a file exists before trying to load data). The exceptions are handled, but it is much cheaper to prevalidate rather than handle an exception, so this would be detrimental to application performance. This is the type of information that IntelliTrace helps you discover quickly and easily.

For this situation, the developers can start debugging by double-clicking the failed test step, which takes them to the point in time at which the test failed. Now the developers have a number of options. This bug is fairly straightforward (it is the result of incorrect data populating a text box), so the developers can just search for that text box in the IntelliTrace file, as shown in Figure 5-8.

Here, you can see the number of occurrences called during the test run (2 of 2 at the top of the code pane) and the developers are taken to the spot where the txtName text box is populated. It is easy to see that the application is checking the cookie file before the authenticated users' information, even if they are logged on. So it's a case of simply reversing these values.

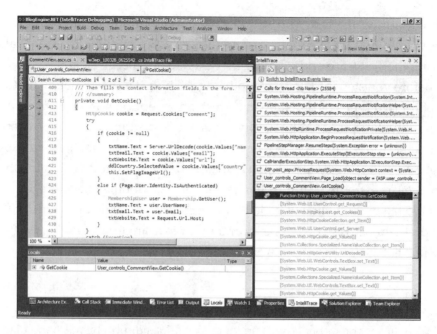

FIGURE 5-8: Finding the bug

For additional help, the pane on the right shows the entire stack trace up to this point. Although the image is hard to see, you can see that there is a lot there—there always is when debugging an ASP.NET application because of the calls made by IIS—but that's for the developers to worry about, not the testers!

Fixing the Bug

This bug can easily be fixed by moving a little bit of code around. After moving this code, the developer can check the code in.

A part of fixing this bug, when the code is checked in it, is associated with Bug #155, which is the bug generated as a result of the test failure. This creates a changeset association between the code and the work item that is critical to making the rest of this scenario work. The Pending Changes window and Associated Work Items tabs are shown in Figure 5-9.

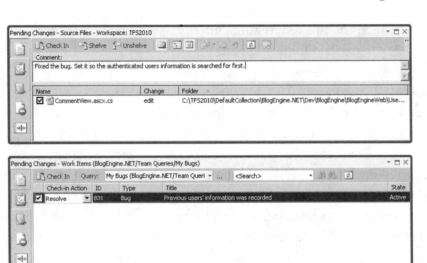

FIGURE 5-9: Pending Changes and Associated Work Items tab

Next, the changes need to be included in an automated build. To do this, the developer would rerun the build definition in use by the testers (in this case, the BlogEngine.NET build). The build report is shown in Figure 5-10.

FIGURE 5-10: Build output, which contains the bug fix

Three items on this report are of interest: Associated Changesets, Associated Work Items, and Impacted Tests.

Associated Changesets

If you have used TFS but have never used automated builds, you are missing out on a big feature. In many organizations, a manifest must be created showing which files and which versions of files are included in a release. This is painstaking (and painful) and time consuming to do correctly. Automated builds solve that problem with no work. All you need are automated builds! Changesets are associated with builds through the following mechanism: As part of a successful build (this is not true if the build fails), Team Build creates a label. (This label is per build definition.) When performing a new build, TFS looks at all the changesets added after the previous build (which is identified via the label) and incorporates them as associated changesets.

Figure 5-10 shows that only one changeset is associated with the build, and the comment for the changeset displays.

Associated Work Items

Associated Work Items is a list of all work items affected by the code changes in the build from the last successful build of this particular build definition. This is tracked by changesets associated with work items. If you have not used work items before, or automated builds, this is an extremely valuable tool and one of the key reasons for using TFS. Often, testers or users (or both) ask what changed from the last build of software they tested or used. This information isn't usually available unless the project manager or build master is keeping detailed notes on what is going on.

In Figure 5-10, you can see that only one work item, Bug 155, is associated with this build. This information (which you can see in Figure 5-12) is also available to the testers when they decide to accept a new build. The only way this information is available to them is through the use of automated builds.

NOT ALL WORK ITEMS ARE ASSOCIATED WITH BUILDS

A word of caution: Not all the work items associated with a build are listed. Consider the following: A requirement has a task. A developer writes code and checks the code in and associates it with the task. The build runs, and the report show that only the task is associated with the build. Why? There is no changeset related to the requirement work item.

So what can you do about this? When you do a code check-in, make sure to associate it with both the task and the requirement. This can also be done as a post check-in step but is easier to do at the time of the check in. You need to be aware of this out-of-the-box limitation.

Impacted Tests

This section comes to you courtesy of a new feature in Visual Studio 2010 called Test Impact Analysis (TIA), which was covered briefly in Chapter 1, "State of Testing." This is where you can see it in action. In Chapter 4, a number of tests were executed; among them were the tests that involved adding blog entries and making comments. Every one of those tests passed, which means that you don't have to run them again, right? Of course not! What TIA is telling us is that these two tests had been previously run and were successful, but that this code change may cause the results of those tests to change. Note that it did not list the Test Case that actually caused the bug because that test had not been successful before. Also it did not list the logon tests that were run because they did not touch the changed code.

Test Impact Analysis works for Unit Tests as well. This is helpful when the number of Unit Tests grows to a large number or when there are some Unit Tests that take a while to run and you don't want to wait. This can also help testers because they can execute the Unit Tests created by developers as part of executing automated tests.

Setting the Build Quality

In the upper-right corner of Figure 5-10, you can see the Build Quality selection. This option was available in TFS 2005 and 2008 but was not used frequently because there were many options that had to be set from a different screen. In addition, there were no integrated functional testing tools to take advantage of this value. With 2010, this might change; if it does you should use this setting to inform and communicate to testers whether a build is suitable for a variety of things. In addition, testers can update this field to further communicate with the release team. You must decide what you are going to use the build quality for. For example, the first quality available to you is Initial Test Passed. Well, what initial test? The Unit Tests that ran as part of the build or when the testers got the build and ran their regression tests? It can mean different things to different people, so you must define these before using them so that everyone has a common understanding.

Table 5-2 describes the default options available to you.

TABLE 5-2: Build Quality Usage and Description

Quality	Description/Usage
Initial Test Passed	Indicates that the build has been tested in some capacity and that the tests passed.
Lab Test Passed	Indicates that the build executed tests in a lab environment and that those tests passed. This generally refers to automated UI tests but can also refer to Unit Tests that ran as part of the lab build.
Ready for Deployment	This quality should be set only by the test team after all tests have passed and the build is "signed off" that it is ready to go to UAT or production.
Ready for Initial Test	Indicates that the build was successful and is ready for testers. Successful may mean that the Unit Tests passed (if there are Unit Tests) or simply that the build did not break.
Rejected	For whatever reason (usually test failure or build failure) this build is unsuitable for use. This can be set by the developers or the testers, but in general a failed build will not be used, so this will be set by the testers after a series of tests has failed.
Released	Indicates that the particular build has been used to release to production or beta testing.
UAT Passed	Indicates that the users approved the build after running their series of tests.
Under Investigation	Indicates that the build is used by the developer or tester to discover a problem.

To customize these build qualities, go to the Build Explorer page in Team Explorer, and select Manage Build Quality. After the build is complete, the testing team should redeploy the code to wherever it is the testers are testing from.

DEPLOYING TEST CODE

Test code can be deployed automatically as part of the build. This is much easier to manage with a virtual testing infrastructure because you can have many more different versions of the build available to testers. So whose responsibility is it? The testers are responsible for deploying and testing the code, but it's nice when the developers help with an automated deploy script or an MSI package or a set of instructions.

Assigning a New Build

After the build with the fix has been deployed, the testers can be notified in a number of ways: by e-mail alerts, build alerts (via the build notification tool), or by word of mouth. In any case, the first step for the testers is the determination of whether they will use the build. For this explanation, they can use the build. Testers can use the build filter to make sure they do not select from a build that is not ready for testing. One point to be aware of is that the build quality filter is an exact match—you cannot set an "at least this quality" filter. This is why, as noted, the team should agree on how they will use the build quality setting.

USING A BUILD NOT ASSIGNED TO THE PLAN

To use a build that has not been assigned to the plan, use the Run with Options selection on the Test tab, Run Tests page. However, this requires that you configure a separate test environment from the one the plan is using. In addition you don't get the benefit of the Test Impact Analysis notifications or the Verify Bugs functionality (discussed next).

In MTM, you can assign a new build in two ways: from the Plan tab, Properties page or from the Track tab, Assign Build page (Figure 5-11). (They are the same screen, so it's just a matter of preference.) When you assign a new build, MTM lists the latest build for the given build definition.

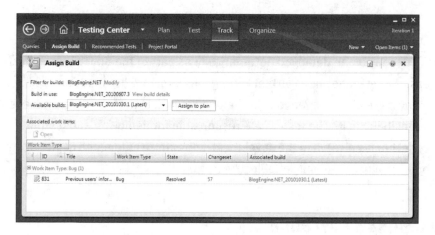

FIGURE 5-11: Assign Build page

In the example scenario covered in the last few chapters, you know that there are impacted tests, so selecting the latest build displays a test impact dialog. The impacted tests are shown in Figure 5-12.

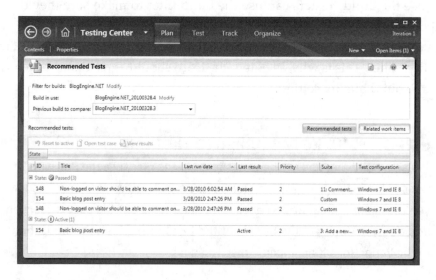

FIGURE 5-12: Test Impact Analysis, Recommended Tests

The impacted tests between two different builds are shown; the builds do not need to be consecutive, so you can see all the tests that have been impacted over a period of time. Each impacted test is shown once for each Test Suite that the test is a part of. (This is why the same test shows up twice in Figure 5-12.) When you select one or more tests, you have the option to reactivate the Test Cases. You cannot run these tests directly from this dialog. To return to this list, select Track tab, Recommended Tests page. On this page is the option to show the related work items. Selecting this shows the screen in Figure 5-13.

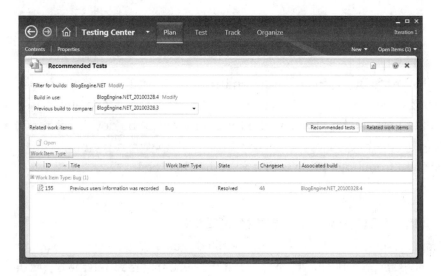

FIGURE 5-13: Related work items

In this case, the related work item is a single bug fixed by the previous build. However, all related work items of any type are shown here.

Verifying That the Bug Is Fixed

View all the bugs filed for the Team Project that this plan is associated with on the Test tab, Verify Bugs page. These bugs are grouped by state and, as you may imagine, the resolved bugs are of most interest to a tester (Figure 5-14). Bugs in the resolved state (as noted in Figure 5-15) indicate that the bug has been fixed and is ready to be verified by the testing team.

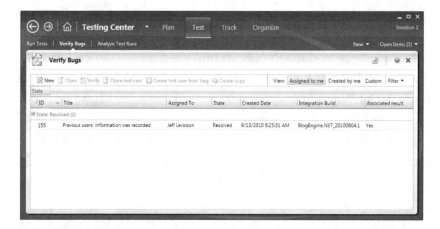

FIGURE 5-14: Verify Bugs screen

The Verify Bugs screen has a number of options. The default view shows the bugs assigned to you. As you can see in Figure 5-14, one bug is assigned to Jeff. Open the bug to view the fix or any notes the developer may have added to the bug, or open the Test Case that spawned the bug. The Create Test Case from bug option is discussed in Chapter 4.

BUILD RETENTION POLICY MATTERS

You must retain builds that a bug was filed against. You must decide upfront who is responsible for this because if the build that reported the bug is deleted, when testers click Verify, they receive an error message stating that the original test results are not available. In this situation, the tester needs to re-execute the Test Case and then mark the bug as Closed manually after the test passes.

Use the Verify button to make sure that the bugs are resolved. With this method, you can verify only one bug at a time. Select the bug that you want to verify, and click the Verify button. This launches Test Runner loaded with the Test Case associated with the bug you want to verify.

Generally when verifying a bug, you need to create an action recording because the first time you ran the test a bug occurred, so there is a strong likelihood that the original action recording is not suitable for use in generating an automated Test Case. As soon as you create an action recording, the play-back is not available to you, so determine when this makes the most sense. However, when using the playback feature, the benefit is immediately appar-ent. Now you simply play back the existing recording until you get to the point in which the bug occurred and simply execute that part of the test man-ually. This makes bug verification simple and virtually painless. When you complete the test run of the bug and click Save and Close, a bug resolution dialog displays (as shown in Figure 5-15).

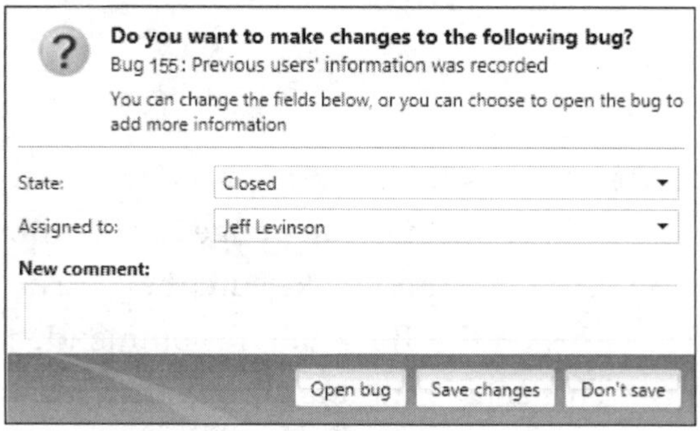

FIGURE 5-15: Bug resolution dialog

The bug resolution dialog enables you to quickly update the bug that has been resolved. In this case, it is setting the bug to Closed. You can also add a comment, which will be applied to the bug.

Dealing with Impacted Tests

In Figure 5-12, you saw the tests that were impacted by the code change, but how should you actually handle them? In a small suite of tests, such as what is shown here to demonstrate functionality in this book, you don't need to worry about it too much. If there is only a small list of Test Cases, the assump-tion is that you can rerun them all to verify regression bugs have not been introduced. On the other hand, consider a system that has hundreds or thou-sands of Test Cases and a limited period of time and limited testers to run regression testing. This situation is specifically what Test Impact Analysis was built for. This scenario requires that testers pick from all the tests avail-able to them with the hope that they pick high-value Test Cases that can find defects. To do this, they have only the information provided by the developers and their experience in running these Test Cases before to determine which Test Cases are best to execute.

TEST IMPACT ANALYSIS WON'T FIND EVERYTHING

TIA does not know about changes made to external components or to things such as data. For this reason it is still the responsibility of the testers to make sure that the right tests are executed. Use TIA as a guide but not as the only guide.

For a small number of tests, the easiest option is to reset all the impacted tests to Active. Use the Test Plan Summary page to determine how many are Active in the overall set of tests and make sure they are all executed. To do this, select the Test Cases on the Track tab, Recommended Tests page, and select Reset to active. This enables testers to see which tests are active on the Test, Run Tests page. The testers can then execute those tests again.

For a large number of tests, things become a little more complicated, and you can use several techniques. First, use the Priority field of the Test Case—that's what it's there for. By default all the Test Cases are set at Priority 2. If you might be in this situation, consider changing the default setting from 2 to 4 so that as you reprioritize them, it makes more sense. In combination with the priority setting, you can create a query-based suite where the Priority = 1 for example; then testers will know that this suite must be completely tested. Maybe the suite based on Priority 2 should be mostly tested, and suites based on Priority 3 and 4 are on an as-time-permits basis. By creating tiers in this manner, it becomes easier to report on their status and to ensure the testers are testing the right features at the right times.

SUMMARY

In this chapter, you examined the workflow structure of bugs in the Agile and CMMI templates and explored all the critical fields in these work items. You also explored a bug created through the testing process and the information

contained in the filed bug, and you know the value of the information collected for you automatically by Microsoft Test Manager and Test Runner.
Knowing what information is gathered and how developers can use that
information is critical to improving the communication between developers
and testers. When the developers have completed their bug fixes, testers can
be notified through a number of different mechanisms. After the testers have
the resolved bug back in their hands, they not only can verify that the bugs
were fixed, but also rerun high-value tests to increase their confidence that no
regression bugs were created by the bug fixes.

You have been dealing with manual Test Cases and a completely manual
process for testing and verifying code, but starting in Chapter 6, "Automating Test Cases," you learn how to automate many aspects of the testing
process, execute those tests, and verify the results.

6

Automating Test Cases

Up to this point, you have seen how to perform manual testing and file bugs and how to verify those bugs. However, manual testing is not efficient for use in regression testing. Regression testing takes time and, in few cases is performed comprehensively because of a lack of automation. Visual Studio 2010 enables you to create automated Test Cases from your manual tests (or as completely stand-alone automations), which enables you to use many tests without having someone babysit the Test Cases or take away from other testing opportunities.

WHO SHOULD READ THIS CHAPTER

Read this chapter if you need to create automated tests. You might be a technical tester or developer who wants to create your own automated functional tests. Although it does not have to be a coding-intensive process, it might be depending on what you want to accomplish. Therefore, this chapter presents a large number of coding examples. Chapter 7, "Executing Automated Test Cases," covers executing already-created automated tests and is more appropriate if you do pure testing, as opposed to coding work.

Automation in Visual Studio is accomplished through three technologies: Microsoft Active Accessibility (MSAA), User Interface Automation (UIA), and Internet Explorer Document Object Model (IE DOM). MSAA is an older technology still used in web automation, whereas UIA is a newer implementation for providing automation. For this reason MSAA is used to automate C++ applications and Web Applications (with the IE DOM) whereas UIA is used to automate WPF applications. This chapter overviews both technologies. You also examine the code that Visual Studio generates in both cases. The chapter concludes with showing how to associate automated tests (both Coded UI and Unit Tests) with Test Cases.

DEVELOPERS CAN WRITE AND EXECUTE TESTS ALSO

Coded UI Tests are not relegated to the next step after a manual test. Developers can write Coded UI Tests that validate a user interface where a Unit Test would either not be possible or practical. Don't let that this is part of a "testers" toolkit dissuade developers from taking full advantage of every quality tool available to ensure that the code is free of bugs. The section "Adding Additional Recorded Steps" describes the process of recording automated tests from within Visual Studio.

To Automate or Not to Automate

This simple question deserves some serious thought. The answers can run the gamut from "Automate everything" to "It isn't worth it to automate anything." Or another favorite is "We have Unit Tests; why do we need to automate functional tests?" The reality is that the first response is appropriate (but rarely achievable); the second is almost never appropriate; and the third question is actually a good question. If you have large amounts of Unit Tests that give you high code (and maybe even functional) coverage, why bother with automated functional tests? The answer is that although many people like to think that Unit Tests are the be all and end all of testing, they aren't— regardless of how far down the path you go. Unit testing done properly, by definition, does not test integration. It doesn't test a whole series of events, and that's what functional testing does. (Also, unit testing user interfaces is fairly difficult, so many teams don't do it.) So although Unit Tests may give you 100% code coverage, they can never give you 100% functional coverage.

Having accepted this reality, you then need to determine what to automate. The answer is always "everything," but that rarely works out. The reason for this is that you can't afford it. Automating tests, even with a framework as slick as what Visual Studio 2010 offers, takes time. And that costs money. And it usually isn't worth it to automate everything because your ROI diminishes as you automate more tests.

Tests, by one definition, are only good if they are likely to find bugs. This was discussed earlier when the case for what makes a good test was laid out. This same holds true for automating tests; automated tests are only useful if they have a high likelihood of finding bugs. So what types of tests are likely to meet this criteria and what questions should you ask yourself?

- Is the work to automate the test to provide benefits in the future?

  If it takes 10 man hours to automate a test and the test is only 2 minutes long and you're only going to run the test maybe 10 times in the foreseeable future, this is not a beneficial use of your time.

  Tests that can quickly and easily be automated are good candidates, whereas complex tests that take a long time to automate are not usually a good choice.

- How often is the feature you're testing likely to change in the future?

  If there is a high degree of likelihood that the feature will undergo many changes, it is not a good candidate because too much maintenance work would need to be done.

- Is the feature tested used frequently?

  This is where trade-offs come into play. A frequently used feature is likely to be changed frequently because users will create new ideas that they want to see implemented. However, a frequently used feature is also an area in which users can find bugs because they use every aspect of it, so it must be tested to a higher degree than other parts of the system.

In general, frequently used features are not good candidates because of the maintenance costs. In addition, testers also write and update new test scripts all the time to take into account the changes. However, if the feature is frequently used and stable (that is, the customers like it the way it is) it might make a good candidate for automated tests.

- Is the test likely to find regression bugs?

  Finding regression bugs is one of the key reasons for creating automated tests. Regression bugs can, of course, be found anywhere, but they are typically found in areas of the application that are central and shared by many features. This includes common business logic and user interface portions of the application. If it is the business logic that is shared, a comprehensive set of Unit Tests as opposed to Coded UI Tests are probably the best way to go. A cost is associated with Unit Tests as well, but these tests are prime candidates for automation.

  If the test you devise is not likely to find regression bugs, avoiding it can lower your maintenance costs because an automated test provides value only if it is likely to find regression bugs. Well, peace of mind is another reason to automate tests, but this reason may not be as compelling.

- How many different versions of the software do you need to maintain?

  If you are maintaining many different versions side by side, you probably have the same test in each version (or a derivation of the same test, which is much worse). The maintenance can be phenomenally expensive when all other things are considered. If you maintain only one or two versions of the software in production, automation is okay. If you maintain more, consider sticking with manual testing.

You might not have all these answers the first few iterations because you don't know this information. Talk with the developers and have them give you some ideas. Keep these points in mind as you go through this chapter.

The Automated Testing Framework

Before diving into Coded UI testing, it is helpful to understand the automated testing framework in Visual Studio and to become familiar with the various screens. All types of automated testing in Visual Studio rely on this framework, so if you understand how it works once, you understand how it works for everything. Unit Tests, Coded UI Tests, Web Performance tests, Generic tests, and Database Unit Tests all use this infrastructure. The basic structure of these tests is the code that supports them. When you create, for example, a new Unit Test, the generated code enables you to use certain attributes, which are shown in the order executed in Figure 6-1.

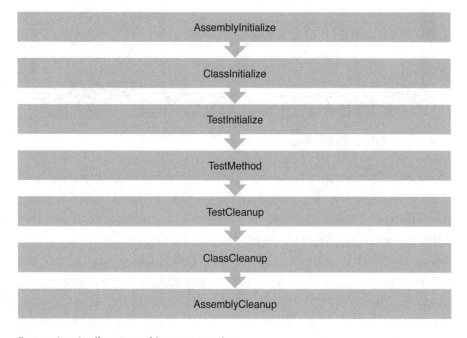

FIGURE 6-1: Attributes used in test execution

These attributes are identical for all tests, but some variations exist in the different test types. Some classes that contain tests (such as a Unit Test) are decorated with the TestClass attribute, and others such as the Coded UI test class are decorated with the CodedUITest attribute. There are other differences such as that the Web Performance test supports plug-ins and other features such as extensible validation and extraction rules. And Database Unit

Tests support executing SQL statements that are the test. But at their core, they all support these basic attributes and are executed in the same manner.

Two screens support executing automated tests: the Test List Editor and the Test View window (see Figure 6-2). From the Test menu select Test List Editor and Test View.

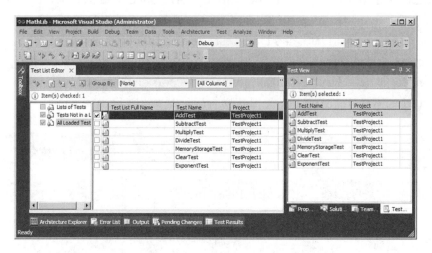

FIGURE 6-2: Test List Editor and Test View

Both windows enable you to execute automated tests of any type, but the Test View window is a light-weight window that is meant to be docked. The major difference between the two windows is that you can create test lists to use for whatever purpose you want. The most common use of test lists is to break up tests so that only certain tests are executed as part of a build or for developers to quickly and easily run blocks of tests rather than all tests.

Each test has properties such as Owner, Test Name, Test Categories, Description, and Data Connection information. This means that tests such as Coded UI Tests can be data-driven using an external data source or the para-meterized data (as opposed to manual tests that can use parameterized data stored in the Test Case). In many cases setting, these properties add additional attributes to the test method to store the data. VS2010 introduces two additional options of importance to these tests to those managing automated tests. The first is that you can right-click a test and select Associate with Test Case; this walks you through associating the automated test with a specific

Test Case Work Item. The other is the ability to right-click a test and select Create Test Case from Test. This provides the ability to automatically create an automated Test Case. And this enables developers to now associate developer level tests with requirements so that they can understand the Test Case coverage of a requirement from the developer tests. This also means that one existing property should not be used anymore: Associated Work Items. This value is not reported to the data warehouse and therefore cannot be used for reporting. If you currently use this property, consider associating your test with an actual Test Case work item type.

UNIT TEST REQUIREMENTS COVERAGE

Normally, you don't see Unit Tests and requirements coverage in the same sentence because Unit Tests are blocks of code that aren't associated with a requirement, in any reportable way. Using the Test Case work item type and associating it with a Unit Test means a couple things: First, you can now report on requirements coverage by Unit Tests, even if you don't use the features of MTM, and second, this enables testers to execute the Unit Tests to help verify code quality.

Creating an Automated Test from a Manual Test

The most common scenario is to create an automated test, for the purpose of regression testing, from a previously passed manual test. Continuing the example from the last few chapters, you start by automating the Test Case that a bug was found against and fixed. The Test Case is As a Logged on User My Profile Information Prefills the Comments Field. Exercise 6-1 walks you through the automation process.

■ EXERCISE 6-1

Automating a Manual Test Case

To automate a manual Test Case, follow these steps:

1. Open Visual Studio.

2. Select Test, New Test from the main menu.

3. In the Add New Test dialog, select Coded UI Test, give the test a name (in this case **LoggedOnUserPreFilledTest.cs**), and click OK.

4. When the New Test Project dialog displays, enter a name (in this case **BEAutomatedTests**), and click Create.

5. In the Generate Code for Coded UI Test dialog, select Use an Existing Action Recording, and click OK.

6. Search for the Test Case you want to automate in the Work Items Picker dialog, and click OK.

You can do a few things to make the process of selecting the appropriate Test Case easier. The first is that a tester can set the Automation Status to Planned so that the developer doing the work can easily find it. The second is to notice the icons next to the result of the query that you run to find the Test Case. Any item with a red circle and a line through it indicates that no test automation strip exists, and as such you cannot use that Test Case to generate an automated test.

Examining a Generated Web Application Coded UI Test

This particular Test Case is about as simple as it gets, so spend some time stepping through it to become familiar with every aspect. The `Logge-dOnUserPreFilledTest` code is shown in Listing 6-1. This code has been slightly condensed, and unnecessary comments have been removed from what is actually generated.

LISTING 6-1: LoggedOnUserPreFilledTest Class

```
using System;
using System.Collections.Generic;
using System.Text.RegularExpressions;
using System.Windows.Input;
```

LISTING 6-1: Continued

```csharp
using System.Windows.Forms;
using System.Drawing;
using Microsoft.VisualStudio.TestTools.UITesting;
using Microsoft.VisualStudio.TestTools.UnitTesting;
using Microsoft.VisualStudio.TestTools.UITest.Extension;
using Keyboard = Microsoft.VisualStudio.TestTools.UITesting.Keyboard;
namespace BEAutomatedTests
{
  [CodedUITest]
  public class LoggedOnUserPreFilledTest
  {
    public LoggedOnUserPreFilledTest()
    {
    }
    [TestMethod]
    public void Coded UITestMethod1()
    {
      this.UIMap.Navigatetohttptfs20108001();
      this.UIMap.ClicktheLogInlink();
      this.UIMap.EnterPssw0rdforthepasswordandclickLogIn();
      this.UIMap.ClicktheWelcometoBlogEnginepost();
    }
    public TestContext TestContext
    {
      get
      {
        return testContextInstance;
      }
      set
      {
        testContextInstance = value;
      }
    }

    private TestContext testContextInstance;
    public UIMap UIMap
    {
      get
      {
        if ((this.map == null))
        {
          this.map = new UIMap();
        }
        return this.map;
      }
    }
    private UIMap map;
  }
}
```

To begin with, the class must be tagged with the `CodedUITestAttribute` to identify this to Visual Studio as a Coded UI Test. Each Coded UI Test that you generate is placed into its own class. The method that actually runs the test is marked by the `TestMethodAttribute` and is given the name of `CodedUITestMethod1`. It is a good practice to immediately rename this to a more descriptive name such as LoggedOnUserInformationIsPreFilled1 or something similar. This makes it easier to identify in subsequent dialogs.

The `TestContext` object provides access to information about the currently executing test. This is the same test context instance provided for Unit Tests as well. The information provided by test context enables you to access data in a data-driven test (discussed later), where the test is executed from, where the logs are written to, the results of the test, and other information.

Understanding a Coded UI Test

The UI Map class is where the real work takes place, and an assortment of supporting classes are generated. The code you saw in the previous listing wraps the code in the UI Map class. This code file actually contains several classes that you can look at. Before diving into a rather convoluted set of generated code, it helps to look at a class diagram to understand the relationships and the classes involved. Figure 6-3 shows the class diagram for the generated code.

Now look at each of the steps in the Test Case and their associated methods. You need to understand how these calls work—not so much for using Coded UI Tests out-of-the-box but for using them in Lab Management, which is covered in the next chapter. Listing 6-2 contains the methods and classes used to support the Navigate to http://tfs2010:8001 test step. These listings include code from multiple classes to show all the relevant code together. For example, Listing 6-2 contains the `Navigatetohttptfs20108001` method in the `UIMap` class and the `Navigatetohttptfs20108001Params` class.

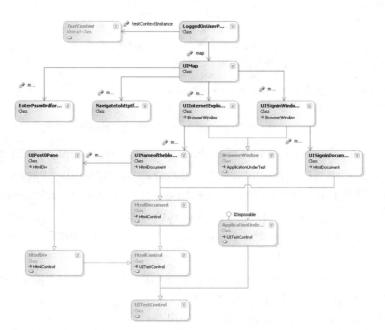

FIGURE 6-3: Coded UI Test generated code

LISTING 6-2: Navigate to http://tfs2010:8001 Test Step

```
[GeneratedCode("Coded UITest Builder", "10.0.30319.1")]
Public partial class UIMap
{
  public void Navigatetohttptfs20108001()
  {
    this.UIInternetExplorerEnhaWindow.LaunchUrl(
    new System.Uri(this.
     Navigatetohttptfs20108001Params.UIInternetExplorerEnhaWindowUrl));
  }
  public virtual Navigatetohttptfs20108001Params
    Navigatetohttptfs20108001Params
  {
    get
    {
      if ((this.mNavigatetohttptfs20108001Params == null))
      {
        this.mNavigatetohttptfs20108001Params = new
          Navigatetohttptfs20108001Params();
      }
      return this.mNavigatetohttptfs20108001Params;
    }
  }
}
```

LISTING 6-2: Continued

```
[GeneratedCode("Coded UITest Builder", "10.0.30319.1")]
public class Navigatetohttptfs20108001Params
{
  public string UIInternetExplorerEnhaWindowUrl =
  "http://tfs2010:8001/";
}
```

First, the actual values used for the test are not stored inline with the test. For each test step that requires parameters, a corresponding `Params` class is created. This provides a great benefit because the values returned by the params classes can be set elsewhere. A common use is for data binding, which is discussed later. Using the `params` classes you can simply override the default values provided.

Second, each method in the UIMap.designer.cs file has the `Generated-CodeAttribute`. Any class with this attribute will be regenerated upon any change made with the Coded UI Test Builder.

MAINTAINING CODED UI TESTS

This is your first lesson in maintaining automated tests. For tests that you don't need to customize, this is something you don't have to worry about. For tests with a high amount of customization, regeneration can cause some problems. This is why you should always keep any custom code in the UIMap class located in the UIMap.cs file and not the designer file. Then all you need to deal with is removing the ambiguous calls from the UIMap.designer.cs when you regenerate code.

LISTING 6-3: EnterPsswordforthepasswordandclickLogIn Test Step

```
[GeneratedCode("Coded UITest Builder", "10.0.30319.1")]
Public partial class UIMap
{
  public void EnterPssw0rdforthepasswordandclickLogIn()
  {
    HtmlEdit uIUserNameEdit =

this.UISigninWindowsInterneWindow.UISigninDocument.UIUserNameEdit;
    HtmlEdit uIPasswordEdit =
```

LISTING 6-3: Continued

```
    this.UISigninWindowsInterneWindow.UISigninDocument.UIPasswordEdit;
        HtmlInputButton uILogInButton =

    this.UISigninWindowsInterneWindow.UISigninDocument.UILogInButton;
        // Type 'Jeff' in 'User Name:' text box
        uIUserNameEdit.Text =

    this.EnterPssw0rdforthepasswordandclickLogInParams.UIUserNameEditText
    ;
        // Type '********' in 'Password:' text box
        uIPasswordEdit.Password =

    this.EnterPssw0rdforthepasswordandclickLogInParams.UIPasswordEditPass
    word;
        // Click 'Log In' button
        Mouse.Click(uILogInButton, new Point(35, 13));
    }
}
[GeneratedCode("Coded UITest Builder", "10.0.30319.1")]
public class EnterPssw0rdforthepasswordandclickLogInParams
{
    public string UIUserNameEditText = "Jeff";

    public string UIPasswordEditPassword =
"Cf6+rNQubXkqzKc/jQXexQKmdE+3YIke";
}
```

In the methods presented in Listing 6-3, a couple of items are not seen in the previous method: The first is that the code references controls on the user interface. The first three lines in this method grab references to the username, password, and login button controls. After that they provide parameters to the username and password controls, and finally the Login button is clicked. There have been many comments made about the point that you see created when the mouse-click is simulated and whether this means the controls are found based on their location on screen. The answer is that they aren't. How controls are found is covered in the next section. The point referenced here is, for all intents and purposes, not used. This is actually the point, from the upper-left corner of the parent control where the mouse-click was recorded for playback, but it isn't used to find the control except as a last resort.

Finally, the password is encrypted, so it is okay to have this information stored in the test. (Also, because this was run, hopefully, against a test server with test accounts, this should not be a big deal.)

ENCRYPTED PASSWORDS

Although it is okay to have throwaway usernames and passwords stored in the Test Case, do not use actual accounts that have access to a network or sensitive information as a prudent security measure.

Searching for Controls

Continuing with the preceding example, now dive into how the control hierarchy is structured. Figure 6-3 accurately represents the class structure but leaves out some detail covered here. When a test is recorded, the structure of the test is as follows: The test contains a series of test steps that reference a UI element (the browser in this case) that has instances of controls. The question is, how does the test find the control on the user interface?

Now look at a single line in the `EnterPssw0rdforthepasswordandclick-LogIn` method presented in Listing 6-3.

```
HtmlEdit uIUserNameEdit =
    this.UISigninWindowsInterneWindow.UISigninDocument.UIUserNameEdit;
```

The first step is to get a reference to the web page that the code is going to operate on. Drilling down into the `UISigninWindowsInterneWindow` property, you see that the property creates a new instance of the class with the same name (see Listing 6-4).

LISTING 6-4: UISigninWindowsInterneWindow Class

```
[GeneratedCode("Coded UITest Builder", "10.0.30319.1")]
public class UISigninWindowsInterneWindow : BrowserWindow
{
  public UISigninWindowsInterneWindow()
  {
    #region Search Criteria
    this.SearchProperties[UITestControl.PropertyNames.Name] =
      "Sign in";
```

LISTING 6-4: Continued

```
      this.SearchProperties[UITestControl.PropertyNames.ClassName] =
        "IEFrame";
      this.WindowTitles.Add("Sign in");
      #endregion
    }

    public void LaunchUrl(System.Uri url)
    {
      this.CopyFrom(BrowserWindow.Launch(url));
    }

    #region Properties
    public UISigninDocument UISigninDocument
    {
      get
      {
        if ((this.mUISigninDocument == null))
        {
          this.mUISigninDocument = new UISigninDocument(this);
        }
        return this.mUISigninDocument;
      }
    }
    #endregion

    #region Fields
    private UISigninDocument mUISigninDocument;
    #endregion
  }
```

First, this class inherits from the BrowserWindow class, so you know it represents, in this case, Internet Explorer. The constructor is what is interesting, though. All the values for the search properties gathered during the test are fed into the search properties here. So the test recorded that the name of the page was "Sign In", it was in an IEFrame class, and the window title was also "Sign In". With this information the testing framework can get a reference to the right browser window. The next step is to get a reference to the UISignin-Document. This is the HTML document loaded in the browser (that is, the contents of the browser window). Listing 6-5 shows the UISigninDocument class (reformatted for readability). Before looking at Listing 6-5, the last point to note about this class is the LaunchUrl method, which uses the CopyFrom method to grab the browser window from the base BrowserWindow class. The

Launch method is static and enables this step to reuse the browser window from the previous step.

LISTING 6-5: UISigninDocument Class

```
[GeneratedCode("Coded UITest Builder", "10.0.30319.1")]
public class UISigninDocument : HtmlDocument
{
  public UISigninDocument(UITestControl searchLimitContainer) :
        base(searchLimitContainer)
  {
    #region Search Criteria
    SearchProperties[HtmlDocument.PropertyNames.Id] = null;
    SearchProperties[HtmlDocument.PropertyNames.RedirectingPage]
      = "False";
    SearchProperties[HtmlDocument.PropertyNames.FrameDocument]
      = "False";
    FilterProperties[HtmlDocument.PropertyNames.Title] = "Sign in";
    FilterProperties[HtmlDocument.PropertyNames.AbsolutePath] =
      "/login.aspx";
    FilterProperties[HtmlDocument.PropertyNames.PageUrl] =
      "http://tfs2010:8001/login.aspx";
    WindowTitles.Add("Sign in");
    #endregion
  }

  #region Properties
  public HtmlEdit UIUserNameEdit
  {
    get
    {
      if ((this.mUIUserNameEdit == null))
      {
        this.mUIUserNameEdit = new HtmlEdit(this);
        #region Search Criteria
        mUIUserNameEdit.SearchProperties[HtmlEdit.PropertyNames.Id] =
          "ctl00_cphBody_Login1_UserName";
        mUIUserNameEdit.SearchProperties[HtmlEdit.PropertyNames.Name]
=
          "ctl00$cphBody$Login1$UserName";
        mUIUserNameEdit.FilterProperties
          [HtmlEdit.PropertyNames.LabeledBy] = "User Name:";
        mUIUserNameEdit.FilterProperties[HtmlEdit.PropertyNames.Type]
=
          "SINGLELINE";
        mUIUser
NameEdit.FilterProperties[HtmlEdit.PropertyNames.Title]
          = null;
        mUIUser
```

LISTING 6-5: Continued

```
NameEdit.FilterProperties[HtmlEdit.PropertyNames.Class]
        = null;
    mUIUserNameEdit.FilterProperties
      [HtmlEdit.PropertyNames.ControlDefinition] =
      "id=ctl00_cphBody_Login1_UserName name=ct";
    mUIUserNameEdit.FilterProperties
      [HtmlEdit.PropertyNames.TagInstance] = "5";
    this.mUIUserNameEdit.WindowTitles.Add("Sign in");
    #endregion
  }
  return this.mUIUserNameEdit;
  }
}

public HtmlEdit UIPasswordEdit
{
  get
  {
    if ((this.mUIPasswordEdit == null))
    {
      this.mUIPasswordEdit = new HtmlEdit(this);
      #region Search Criteria
      mUIPasswordEdit.SearchProperties
        [HtmlEdit.PropertyNames.Id] =
        "ctl00_cphBody_Login1_Password";
      mUIPasswordEdit.SearchProperties
        [HtmlEdit.PropertyNames.Name] =
        "ctl00$cphBody$Login1$Password";
      mUIPasswordEdit.FilterProperties
        [HtmlEdit.PropertyNames.LabeledBy] = "Password:";
      mUIPasswordEdit.FilterProperties
        [HtmlEdit.PropertyNames.Type] = "PASSWORD";
      mUIPasswordEdit.FilterProperties
        [HtmlEdit.PropertyNames.Title] = null;
      mUIPasswordEdit.FilterProperties
        [HtmlEdit.PropertyNames.Class] = null;
      mUIPasswordEdit.FilterProperties
        [HtmlEdit.PropertyNames.ControlDefinition] =
        "id=ctl00_cphBody_Login1_Password value=\"";
      mUIPasswordEdit.FilterProperties
        [HtmlEdit.PropertyNames.TagInstance] = "6";
      mUIPasswordEdit.WindowTitles.Add("Sign in");
      #endregion
    }
    return this.mUIPasswordEdit;
  }
}
```

LISTING 6-5: Continued

```
public HtmlInputButton UILogInButton
{
  get
  {
    if ((this.mUILogInButton == null))
    {
      mUILogInButton = new HtmlInputButton(this);
      #region Search Criteria
      mUILogInButton.SearchProperties
        [HtmlButton.PropertyNames.Id] =
        "ctl00_cphBody_Login1_LoginButton";
      mUILogInButton.SearchProperties
        [HtmlButton.PropertyNames.Name] =
        "ctl00$cphBody$Login1$LoginButton";
      mUILogInButton.FilterProperties
        [HtmlButton.PropertyNames.DisplayText] = "Log In";
      mUILogInButton.FilterProperties
        [HtmlButton.PropertyNames.Type] = "submit";
      mUILogInButton.FilterProperties
        [HtmlButton.PropertyNames.Title] = null;
      mUILogInButton.FilterProperties
        [HtmlButton.PropertyNames.Class] = null;
      mUILogInButton.FilterProperties
        [HtmlButton.PropertyNames.ControlDefinition] =
        "id=ctl00_cphBody_Login1_LoginButton oncl";
      mUILogInButton.FilterProperties
        [HtmlButton.PropertyNames.TagInstance] = "8";
      mUILogInButton.WindowTitles.Add("Sign in");
      #endregion
    }
    return this.mUILogInButton;
  }
}
#endregion

#region Fields
private HtmlEdit mUIUserNameEdit;
private HtmlEdit mUIPasswordEdit;
private HtmlInputButton mUILogInButton;
#endregion
}
```

A key takeaway from this class is that key properties that the test could record are used in the search. This has some major implications depending on your application. The biggest issue is the constructor of the class, which has a distinct signature:

```
public UISigninDocument(UITestControl searchLimitContainer)
```

This is crucial to understand later for modifying search properties. Any search criteria it uses to find a specific value or control on a section of the application is contained by the parent control, which also has distinct properties. Consider this situation (as is the case with the BlogEngine.NET Web Application).

Every time you add a blog post, that post is listed on the home page using a repeating mechanism so that the first post on the page is contained in a div tag called postpane0; the next one is postpane1; and so on. Well, what if you execute and record the test when there are two or three other posts so that the post you want to validate is contained in postpane2? As part of the validation step, look for the innertext of some field within postpane2. But what if when you play back the test, there was another post added, and the post you wanted to validate is now in postpane3? Now you are in trouble because the code may be searching for the right properties in the wrong location.

There are only two solutions to this problem. The first is to ask the developers to write the code in such a way that you can consistently perform the tests. In other words, ask them to use a record ID or something else that is not auto-generated and independent of the data. The second option is to manually expand the search scope. The way to do this isn't so obvious but is quite easy. For each of the control property methods, there is a constructor for the control that takes the value `this`. This ensures that the control is searched for only in the parent that it was originally found in. To expand the search scope, replace `this` with `this.TopParent`. That expands the scope to the top of the page. This may be too far, but you can narrow down the scope from there. To narrow the scope down, you have a number of options. Use the `GetChildren` method to return a list of all controls contained by the top level control and iterate through them (`this.TopParent.GetChildren()`). Another option is to use the `SearchProperties` to provide specific values that you want to search for and then call the `Find()` method.

Another key point is the `PageUrl` property. The full URL for this page is also stored as part of the class. This can cause complications when the test is used as part of Lab Management because the server name will probably be different. Chapter 8, "Lab Management," discusses this scenario and ways around it.

MAINTAINING CODED UI TESTS

This is your second lesson in maintaining Coded UI Tests. You can make many changes to controls without having to rewrite your automated tests. The reason for this is that if you change the label, the test still looks for the control by control name. If you change the name, it still searches for the control by ID, and so on. A cascading series of changes need to be made to mess up your tests. One such change may be renaming a control and then adding a new control with the original name. As long as something like that doesn't happen, in most cases you won't need to change automated tests because of simple control changes.

The last portion of generated code that you need to examine to round out your understanding of a Coded UI Test is where everything is actually stored. Up to this point, you looked at the methods responsible for running the tests and some of the information those actions represent, but not all of them. The UIMap.uitest file contains the rest. This is an XML configuration file that stores the steps, actions, and additional information needed to execute the tests.

This file is rather large, so the entire file is not be presented here; however, to illustrate several points, Listing 6-6 shows an excerpt of the file.

LISTING 6-6: Partial Listing of the UI Test File

```
<TestStepMarkerAction MarkerInformation="ClicktheLogInlink">
     <ParameterName />
     <StepId>1</StepId>
     <Direction>Both</Direction>
     <Outcome />
     <Disabled>false</Disabled>
     <WorkItemId>815</WorkItemId>
```

LISTING 6-6: Continued

```xml
            <MarkerRegionType>Default</MarkerRegionType>
        </TestStepMarkerAction>
        <SetValueAction UIObjectName=
"UIMap.UISigninWindowsInterneWindow.UISigninDocument.UIUserNameEdit">
            <ParameterName />
            <Value Encoded="false">Jeff</Value>
            <Type>String</Type>
        </SetValueAction>
        <SetValueAction UIObjectName=
"UIMap.UISigninWindowsInterneWindow.UISigninDocument.UIPasswordEdit">
            <ParameterName />
            <Value Encoded="true">Cf6+rNQubXkqzKc/jQXexQKmdE+3YIke</Value>
            <Type>String</Type>
        </SetValueAction>
        <MouseAction UIObjectName=
"UIMap.UISigninWindowsInterneWindow.UISigninDocument.UILogInButton">
            <ParameterName />
            <ModifierKeys>None</ModifierKeys>
            <IsGlobalHotkey>false</IsGlobalHotkey>
            <Location X="35" Y="13" />
            <WheelDirection>0</WheelDirection>
            <ActionType>Click</ActionType>
            <MouseButton>Left</MouseButton>
        </MouseAction>
        <TestStepMarkerAction MarkerInformation=
"EnterPssw0rdforthepasswordandclickLogIn">
            <ParameterName />
            <StepId>3</StepId>
            <Direction>Both</Direction>
            <Outcome />
            <Disabled>false</Disabled>
            <WorkItemId>815</WorkItemId>
            <MarkerRegionType>Default</MarkerRegionType>
        </TestStepMarkerAction>
```

Listing 6-6 contains the steps for logging onto the blog engine and includes all the information needed to generate the code that performs the automation. Further in the file (not shown) is a section that contains all the search conditions for each element that appears in this uitest file. When you use the Coded UI Builder, it actually creates this "map" file and generates the code based on the contents of this file. This is included here to complete your understanding of the underlying pieces of the test, but editing this file directly is not supported. However, to ease this situation and enable you to add search properties, configurations, and other items directly to this file, Microsoft will be releasing a UI Test Editor Visual Studio Extension. (This has been released as Team Foundation Server Feature Pack 2 available to MSDN subscribers. More information on this Feature Pack can be found here: http://msdn.microsoft.com/en-us/vstudio/ff655021.aspx.) Figure 6-4 shows an early version of this tool, which means it will most likely change before the release.

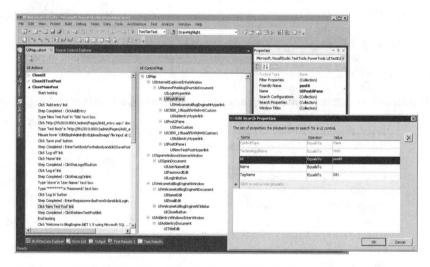

FIGURE 6-4: UI Test Editor Visual Studio Extensibility Add-In

The features planned for this release (again, no guarantees) are as follows:

- Undo/Redo support
- Cut/Copy/Paste of actions
- Keyboard Accessibility
- Find Next & Search up in UI Control Map
- Find Missing controls
- Add Actions
- Merge two controls
- Clean up unused methods
- Move controls/methods to another UI Map
- Promote controls/methods to a shared/global UI Map

As you can see from Figure 6-4, this enables you to edit the file, not in XML but in a nicely structured editor. It also generates code updates when you finish with it. This tool simplifies the process of making modifications that will not be deleted upon the regeneration of the code.

At this point, you should now have a relatively good understanding of how the test actually works, and you have a limited amount of knowledge on how to make changes to the test. One area that you should research that is not covered in this book is the options available to you on different controls. The control definitions can be found in the Microsoft.VisualStudio.TestTools.UITesting.HtmlControls namespace. (WinForms and WPF controls can be found in the WinControls and WpfControls namespaces, respectively.) For each control class, there is an associated `PropertyNames` class.

Before leaving this section, here are a few tips that, as a tester, you must impart to the developers:

- Use meaningful names when naming UI controls.
- Assign as many properties as practical; don't just use a single property unless it will never change (such as the control name or ID).
- Change the test method to a meaningful name; CodedUITestMethod1 is not a good choice.
- Never make any changes to the UIMap.designer.cs file; always use the UIMap.cs file (or the UI Test Editor).

Adding Validations

In its generated state, the Coded UI Test will always pass (unless the application doesn't run, or in the case of a Web Application the web server isn't configured correctly) because there are no validations. In the manual test, the validations are visually checked, so you can't turn those into programmatic checks. Here, you add a couple of validations to the test to ensure it works correctly.

MULTIPLE VALIDATIONS

For this example, you can see how to add a simple validation on a single step. However, in many cases, you will not simply validate the last step in the test; you will add validations every place the manual test contained those validations. This ties into when you mark steps as passed or failed during the manual test run. To avoid a large number of methods that do not require validation afterward, just mark steps where there actually is something to validate as passed.

To begin with, execute the Coded UI test. Select Test, Windows, Test List Editor, or double-click the .vsmdi file in the Solution Items folder to open it. Click the Refresh button so that the latest version of your test is compiled and displayed in the Test List Editor. Select the test, and click Run Tests. Allow the test to run. (And don't play with your mouse and keyboard while the test is running; although, in general the test will still work fine.)

USING THE TEST LIST EDITOR

Because of how the test names are generated, it is strongly recommend that you add the Class Name column to the Test List Editor. This shows you the class names that coincidentally are the test names!

After the test has completed, and with the Coded UI Test open, place your cursor after the step that you want to validate in the method marked with the TestMethod attribute and add a new line. In this example that would be after the this.UIMap.ClicktheWelcometoBlogEnginepost(); line. From the main menu select Test, Generate Code for Coded UI Test, Use Coded UI Test Builder (Figure 6-5).

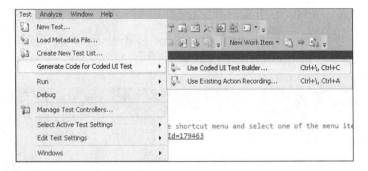

FIGURE 6-5: Add Validations with the Coded UI Test Builder

EXECUTING THE TEST FIRST

Now you can see why you should execute the test first. Executing it leaves the application open to the point at which you want to add validations. If you want to add multiple validations to a test, simply comment out all the steps after the point where you want to add the validation, and the test will complete at the appropriate page or form so that you can simply select which controls and values you want to validate. Another option is to set a breakpoint, run to the breakpoint, and then stop the application.

The Coded UI Test builder (see Figure 6-6) enables you to record actions and add them into your existing Coded UI Test, view the steps that are/were being recorded, select controls to validate, and generate code for the whichever actions you have taken. In this example you can see how to validate field controls.

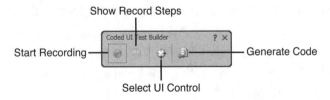

FIGURE 6-6: Coded UI Test Builder

To validate a control, click and hold the crosshairs, and drag them over the control you want to validate. In this case, the control is the Name text box that contains the value Jeff, as shown in Figure 6-7.

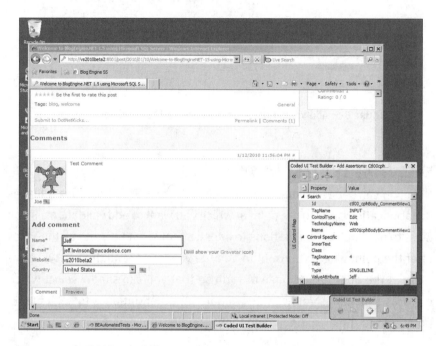

FIGURE 6-7: Validating a Field Control

This action brings up the Add Assertions dialog shown in the lower-right corner of Figure 6-7. Because the goal of this test is to ensure that Jeff is in the Name text box and "jeff.jones@nowhere.com" is in the E-Mail text box, you can select any control setting that has the value Jeff in it; however, it is not a good idea to use the CopyPastedText field or DefaultText field. In this case the Text property will be used. Highlight the property, and click the Add Assertion button at the top of the Add Assertion dialog. Set your comparator (AreEqual in this case) and click OK. A check will be displayed next to the property indicating that the assertion has been added; however, no code has been generated at this point.

Before doing anything else, it is worthwhile to take a good look at the Add Assertions dialog, which is shown in its entirety in Figure 6-8.

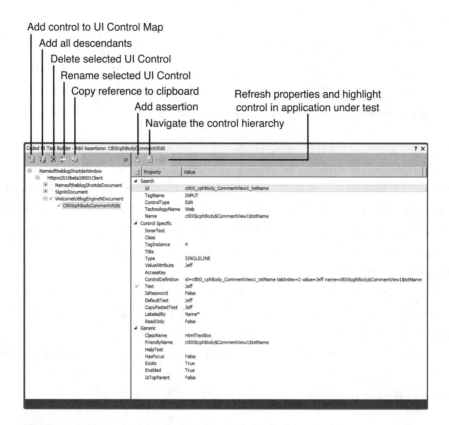

FIGURE 6-8: Add Assertions dialog

The pane on the right contains three sections: Search, Control Specific, and Generic. This window is designed to interrogate the application you are testing to determine its information. It also contains a wealth of useful information that will be covered in detail. The search section determines how the code will find your control. As you can see, it has a variety of ways to do so. In this instance it can search for either the ID or Name values that both contain information helpful to locating the control. As noted previously, if you change the name of the control but not the ID, there is still a good chance the test can find it. It does not rely on coordinate positioning to discover the control. This makes Coded UI Tests less fragile than they might otherwise be.

The Control Specific section contains those properties that can logically be validated against. (It doesn't make much sense to validate anything in the search section because it doesn't contain any information about what the control contains.) The Generic section contains high-level information about the control and is usually not specific enough to use in validation.

DIFFERENT TECHNOLOGIES

ASP.NET applications rely on MSAA, and there will be different properties in this dialog than there would be for a test that uses UI Automation. It also greatly depends on how the automation framework was implemented.

One helpful control is the last one located on the toolbar of the right pane: the Control hierarchy control. When you have a specific control selected (and depending on which control it is), you can use the arrows to move to the parent control (up arrow), child control (down arrow), or a peer control to the left or right. This lets you drill down to the lowest possible level or move up from the selected control easily.

The pane on the left is the UI Map pane and displays a "map" of the user interface. From Figure 6-8, it is evident that the NameoftheblogShortdeWindow is the application. Clicking Show All Properties at the bottom of the Properties pane displays even more information. Table 6-1 shows the properties and values.

TABLE 6-1: IEFrame Properties

Property	Value
Search	
ClassName	IEFrame
ControlType	Window
TechnologyName	MSAA
Name	Welcome to BlogEngine.NET
Control Specific	
Uri	http://vs2010beta2:8001/Welcome-to-BlogEngineNET-15-using-Microsoft-Sql-Server.aspx
Version	8.0.6001.18865

Property	Value
Generic	
FriendlyName	Welcome to BlogEngine.NET 1.5 using Microsoft SQL....
HelpText	
HasFocus	False
Exists	True
Enabled	True
IsTopParent	True

This window, as you can see in Table 6-1, displays the technology you are dealing with (MSAA in this case) and the version of the browser. The control can't be interrogated for detailed information if it can't be found. For example, the PostPane and LoginHyperlink don't exist on the current page, so more detailed information can't be provided. If you need detailed information on a control, open up the application to that point, and then launch the Coded UI Test Builder tool.

The next UI element down, Httpvs2010beta28001Client, is the client window through which you access the application (see Figure 6-9).

FIGURE 6-9: Close up of the UI Elements pane from Figure 6-8

Going down further, the NameoftheblogShortdeDocument is a control of type Document that represents the HTML page that displays. Below that is the PostPane, LoginHyperlink, SigninDocument (this represents the ASP.NET Login control), username, password, login button controls, and finally the WelcometoBlogEngineNDocument, which is the current page displayed and the page that hosts the post details information. The InnerText is where all the text is stored; below that is the Name control. Both of these last two elements were added to the Coded UI Test Builder when the last validation was added.

One of the benefits of this tool is you can add other UI elements that you want to interact with as part of the test, even if they were not directly involved in the test, by adding the UI element to the UI map. After you generate code, you can make programmatic changes to it or interrogate it as necessary.

When the validations are added, click the Generate Code button on the Coded UI Test Builder, and in the Generate Code dialog (see Figure 6-10) provide a method name, and click Add and Generate. (Every time you click Add and Generate, all the work up to that point is generated into a single method.)

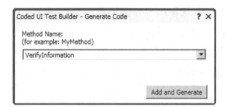

FIGURE 6-10: Generate Code dialog

Adding Additional Recorded Steps

This particular test used for this example is basically a stand-alone test as far as the Coded UI Test is concerned. Because of this, Internet Explorer should close after the test has been completed. This was not done as part of the manual test, so an additional bit of code needs to be added. Because this is code, you can simply wire up a simple step that closes the browser. But if you have a series of complex actions to take, you can record additional steps from the Coded UI Test Builder.

RECORDING FROM SCRATCH

The process for recording a Coded UI Test from scratch is the same as recording an additional test. The difference is that you would select Test, New Test from the main menu, and select Coded UI Test. Then you simply select the Record actions, edit UI map, or add assertions from the Generate Code for Coded UI Test dialog.

To record additional steps, click the red Record button on the Coded UI Test Builder, select the window you want to record (in this case, IE), and click the X in the upper-right corner of the window. Press the Pause button on the Coded UI Test Builder and then select Add and Generate code. For this option, the Coded UI Test Builder generated the code shown in Listing 6-7.

LISTING 6-7: Coded Generated from Closing the IE Browser Window

```
public void CloseIE()
{
    #region Variable Declarations
    WinTitleBar uITestPostWindowsInterTitleBar =
this.UITestPostWindowsInterWindow.UITestPostWindowsInterTitleBar;
    WinButton uICloseButton =
this.UITestPostWindowsInterWindow.UITestPostWindowsInterTitleBar.
UICloseButton;
    #endregion

    // Click 'Test Post - Windows Internet Explorer' title bar
    Mouse.Click(uITestPostwindowsIntertitleBar, new Point(854, 6));

    // Click 'Close' button
    Mouse.Click(uICloseButton, new Point(3, 10));
}
```

The recording grabbed a reference to the title bar and the Close button and then simulated two mouse clicks: one to select the window and one to click the Close button. The points are relative to the control selected and not relative to the entire window or the screen. The Coded UI Tests still work if the screen resolution changes because of this.

This code still works if the WinTitleBar declaration were deleted (and the associated mouse-click) because the only important thing is the mouse-click that closes the window. There is another way to close the window as well:

programmatically. To do this programmatically, you need only add this line of code: this.UITestPostWindowsInterWindow.Close(). That's it. Both the MSAA and UIA frameworks give you access to a variety of properties to let you manipulate the applications in code.

FRAMEWORKS AND APPLICATIONS

The properties available depend on how the application implements them. For example, all applications that use a particular version of IE support the same properties. However, the same code cannot simply be switched to Firefox because it supports a different set of properties. You need to create a basic Coded UI Test to determine the available properties.

Parameterized Coded UI Tests

This example is a Test Case to validate that basic HTML tags work as they are supposed to when adding a new blog entry. Figure 6-11 shows the Test Case.

FIGURE 6-11: Entry should accept HTML tags Test Case

When generating a new Coded UI Test in an existing project, the UI map is re-used and the test steps generated from shared steps. This at least makes it easier if you need to regenerate the shared steps because they changed and makes it so you don't need to regenerate the entire Test Case.

Listing 6-8 shows the code generated for the CodedUITestMethod1.

LISTING 6-8: BlogEntryHTLMBasicTest CodedUITestMethod1 (Line Numbers Added for Readability)

```
1  [DataSource("Microsoft.VisualStudio.TestTools.DataSource.TestCase",
2  "http://tfs2010:8080/tfs/defaultcollection;BlogEngine.NET",
3  "818", DataAccessMethod.Sequential), TestMethod]
4  public void CodedUITestMethod1()
5  {
      // To generate code for this test, select
      // "Generate Code for Coded UI Test"
      // from the shortcut menu and select one of the menu items.
      // For more information on generated code, see
      // http://go.microsoft.com/fwlink/?LinkId=179463
6  this.UIMap.LogonasJeffEditor();
7  this.UIMap.ClicktheAddEntrylink();
8  this.UIMap.ClicktheHTMLbuttonabovethebodysection();
9  this.UIMap.EnterhtmlandclicktheUpdatebuttonParams.
      UIHtmlSourceEditText = TestContext.DataRow["html"].ToString();
10 this.UIMap.EnterhtmlandclicktheUpdatebutton();
11 this.UIMap.ClicktheSavePostbutton();
12 }
```

The first item to note is the DataSource attribute (lines 1–3). These lines tell you that the test is accessing a TestCase data source (as opposed to a SQL Server or other type of data repository) and that the Test Case is located in the default collection and the BlogEngine.NET project. In addition, the data comes from work item number 818 (the Test Case shown in Figure 6-8) and the data will be accessed sequentially. (You can use only sequential data access on a Coded UI Test.)

The biggest difference between the actual test code and the previous test that was not parameterized is line 9, which accesses the TestContext. DataRow property that retrieves the parameter arguments from the Test Case work item. The tool does this to make your life easier by enabling you to view and change parameters and bindings here rather than having to search in the methods for where this value is assigned.

One initial problem with this is that the htmlresult parameter in the Test Case is not sufficient for the automated Test Case. A good practice if you plan to automate an iterative Test Case is to add a third parameter, something such as automatedresult, so that everything is in the same Test Case, and you can use it for both manual and automated testing. (You see this in the next section.)

TEST CASE DATA SOURCE

One small note on the data source: You cannot set this data source using the properties grid—there are just no options for it. So, if you decide to parameterize a generated test at a later point in time and use data in the Test Case, you need to regenerate it; otherwise, you have to add information manually.

Handling Issues Due to Inconsistency

Sometimes coding inconsistencies can cause problems for teams trying to automate Test Cases. Take the test shown in Figure 6-11. The goal is to validate that the text that is the result of the post is This is a test. If you were to select this line of text (which is in a DIV tag) you would find that the InnerText property reads This is a test. Sure, this is helpful to verify that the right text is displayed but hardly enough to verify that the format is right. In this case you can drill down into the children of the DIV tag to get to the "control" that you want. The goal isn't to find a control but a property. For this particular application, you have to drill down two levels until you come to a control of type Pane with an InnerText of "test" and a Generic ClassName of HtmlTag.STRONG (or HtmlTag.EM for italics). This particular application presents a problem because it does not use consistent methods of formatting its code, which is something you need to think about in the design of the application. The way an underlined piece of text is encoded is to use the ControlDefinition of "style="TEXT-DECORATION: bold"".

So, how do you get around this particular problem? Unfortunately it isn't easy, and for every application there are issues like this. What you need to take away from this is how to best determine what to do and how to best address these issues.

First, the easiest and most expedient thing is to talk to the developers to see if they can change how they handle the anomaly. And it is an anomaly. Anything that is different is more difficult to maintain. One of the jobs of the tester (but certainly not the primary job) is to point out inconsistencies that may make it more difficult to maintain in the future. If developers can change how they do things to be consistent, that is the best approach. Mark the test as a bug, and note that it is a technical bug rather than a functional bug because it may not be that high on the priority list; then move on.

Another option is to split your Test Case. Copy the Test Case so that you have two versions: one to handle the bold and italic text and one to handle the underlined text case. This is expedient and easy to do. This also makes the Test Cases more maintainable but has the drawback of requiring testers or the developer who is automating the Test Cases to have deep technical knowledge about the application. This knowledge is sometimes difficult to acquire and can be time consuming to figure out.

A final option is to simply handle the issue by saying that for run number three, you will use an "if" statement to selectively validate the third run differently from the first two runs. Although this is fairly simple, it becomes incredibly complex to maintain—especially if you have to change the order of the data or you add new data that fits one pattern or the other, or even a third pattern. This is not a good option but might fit your needs.

Resolving the Data Inconsistency

For this particular resolution, the Test Case was altered to look like that in Figure 6-12. (The Underline test was moved to a different Test Case and additional parameters were added.)

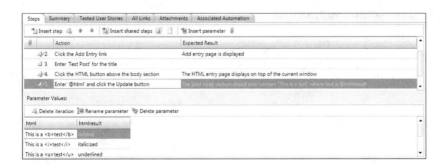

FIGURE 6-12: Updated parameterized Test Case

Unfortunately, although this is easy to fix in the Test Case, a lot more work is required for the actual test. Note that you do not need to re-record the test unless you are binding additional information to the UI because the additional columns are used in Assert statements. This is not for the faint of heart and requires a fair bit of looking around until you get comfortable with it. Listing 6-9 shows the updated CodedUITestMethod1 to work with the Test Case shown in Figure 6-12.

LISTING 6-9: Updated CodedUITestMethod1

```
[DataSource("Microsoft.VisualStudio.TestTools.DataSource.TestCase",
"http://tfs2010:8080/tfs/defaultcollection;BlogEngine.NET", "818",
DataAccessMethod.Sequential), TestMethod]
public void CodedUITestMethod1()
{
  // To generate code for this test, select "Generate Code for Coded UI
  // Test" from the shortcut menu and select one of the menu items.
  this.UIMap.LogonasJeffEditor();
  this.UIMap.ClicktheAddEntrylink();
  this.UIMap.EnterTestPostforthetitle();
  this.UIMap.ClicktheHTMLbuttonabovethebodysection();
  this.UIMap.EnterhtmlandclicktheUpdatebuttonParams.
    HtmlSourceEditText = TestContext.DataRow["html"].ToString();
  this.UIMap.EnterhtmlandclicktheUpdatebutton();
  this.UIMap.ClicktheSavePostbutton();
    this.UIMap.ValidateHTMLInfoExpectedValues.UIItemCustomInnerText =
      TestContext.DataRow["word"].ToString();
    this.UIMap.ValidateHTMLInfoExpectedValues.UIItemCustomClassName =
      TestContext.DataRow["htmlformat"].ToString();
    this.UIMap.ValidateHTMLInfo();
    this.UIMap.CloseIE ();
}
```

Before examining the contents of this listing, let's go through Exercise 6-2 to generate the supporting code.

■ EXERCISE 6-2

Generate ValidateHTMLInfo Code

To generate the supporting code, follow these steps:

1. Execute the test to get the application to the appropriate screen; don't worry about the test failing as it will because IE is not yet closed between test runs.

2. Next, place your cursor after the `this.UIMap.ClicktheSavePostbutton();` and press Enter.

3. Select Test, Generate Code for Coded UI Test. Use Coded UI Test Builder from the main menu.

4. Select the crosshairs and drag it over the This Is a Test line until it is surrounded by the blue box; then let go of the mouse button.

5. Click the Move to Child Control button twice (last control on the Coded UI Test Builder toolbar, down arrow).

6. Select Control Specific, InnerText property, and click Add Assertion; then click OK.

7. Select the Generic, ClassName property, and click Add Assertion; then click OK.

8. Click Generate Code, and name the method ValidateHTMLInfo; click OK and close the Coded UI Test Builder.

After completing this, add a method to close Internet Explorer. You reused the `CloseIE()` method generated earlier because it had the same title, but you can override the search criteria if needed so only one `CloseIE()` method should be needed.

Finally, the two calls to the ValidateHTMLInfoExpectedValues were hand added. (The method with the parameters is generated by the Coded UI Test Builder; you just need to supply the values.) When you perform validation in a parameterized test, the values are set in a class that is the name of your validation class + ExpectedValues. This is a class generated by the testing framework for a parameterized test. The set statements here exactly mimic the columns in the Test Case.

As you can see, the most difficult part of this process is determining what you actually need to validate against, which requires generating the Coded UI Test and running to examine which values are important. The good news is that after you do this, adding the additional parameters and validations are simple.

Handling Dynamic Values

In this application, BlogEngine.NET (and most blogging tools), the URLs are constructed based on the date that the pages are created. In looking at the posts created in the previous set of tests, the URLs all follow the following pattern: http://[server]:[port]/post/[year]/[month]/[day]/[post name].aspx. You need to pull these values out to use as search criteria for the right link to click. To make this clearer, after a post is added, the link for the post shown on the welcome page is (for example) http://tfs2010:8001/post/2010/04/27/Test-Post.aspx. The problem is that if the test that generated this URL were rerun on 4/28/2010, the test would fail because of the following search criteria:

```
this.FilterProperties[HtmlDocument.PropertyNames.AbsolutePath] =
    "/post/2010/04/27/Test-Post.aspx";
this.FilterProperties[HtmlDocument.PropertyNames.PageUrl] =
    "http://tfs2010:8001/post/2010/04/27/Test-Post.aspx";
```

Because of this the link would not be found. To be insulated, tests need to feed the results of generated values to subsequent actions. This applies to applications such as order entry systems and other systems that perform navigation based on a unique ID. So how do you handle it?

To demonstrate this, let's look at one more Test Case, which logs a user on, adds a new post, and then has another user log on afterward, and click that added post to view the details of it. Based on the previous information, playing this back on another day will also cause the test to fail. Listing 6-10 shows the generated code for this test.

LISTING 6-10: Initial Add New Post and Read Test

```
[TestMethod]
public void CodedUITestMethod1()
{
  this.UIMap.LogonasJeffEditor();
  this.UIMap.ClickAddEntry();
  this.UIMap.EnterTestBodyforthebodyandclickSavePost();
  this.UIMap.ClicktheLogoffbutton();
  this.UIMap.ClicktheLogOnlink();
  this.UIMap.Enterthepasswordaspssw0rdandclickLogin();
  this.UIMap.ClicktheNewTestPostlink();
}
```

The third method is the one that creates the URL that needs to be consumed by the last method. However, this URL is never returned in code, so you need to figure out how to fix it so you can actually click the link in the last method. In this case you need to do something a little different: Alter the UI Map by adding another control to it without adding any validations. This is a relatively simple example because you can construct the URL because you know the date the test is running, but you need to find the right control on the web page to click the link.

EVERY CIRCUMSTANCE IS DIFFERENT

This is just one example to show you the thinking behind how this is done. If you were to try this with an actual order entry system, for example, you might examine the order confirmation page and find the control that outputs the value and grab it from that. Or you might want to read the value directly from the database. Many approaches can be taken, and this is just one of them. It would be impossible to demonstrate every example in every technology that the Coded UI testing framework supported.

In this case, another option is also open to you: Controls can search for the name using the contains function, so you would have to pass in only the name of the post, and the date is ignored. Of course, this also has a drawback because if you run the test on multiple days without cleaning up your test environment, the test would probably pick the wrong control.

So, to do that, comment out all the lines after the first three lines and execute the test. (You want the browser to be open at the point that the new post has been created.) Open the Coded UI Test Builder, and select the link for the new post using the crosshairs. Next, expand the Coded UI Test Builder window using the double arrow in the upper-left corner to show the control section. Click the Add Control to UI Map button in the upper-left corner. A dark red check mark displays next to the control, and its parent controls and a message display at the bottom of the window indicating the controls have been added to the UI Map. Next, select the Generate Code button (Alt+G is the shortcut key); you will see a message stating a new method is required and only code related to the UI control map will be generated. Click Generate and close the Coded UI Test Builder.

To all outward appearances no changes were made, but some underlying changes in the UIMap class were made; it just takes a little work to find. The best way to find changes to code is to search for a known property of the control (that is, the value that was in the UI). In this case, Listing 6-11 shows the class that was added.

LISTING 6-11: Generated Control Class (Partial)

```
public UINewTestPostDocument(UITestControl searchLimitContaine
        base(searchLimitContainer)
{
  #region Search Criteria
  this.SearchProperties[HtmlDocument.PropertyNames.Id] = null;
  this.SearchProperties[HtmlDocument.PropertyNames.RedirectingPage] =
    "False";
  this.SearchProperties[HtmlDocument.PropertyNames.FrameDocument] =
    "False";
  this.FilterProperties[HtmlDocument.PropertyNames.Title] =
    "New Test Post";
  this.FilterProperties[HtmlDocument.PropertyNames.AbsolutePath] =
    "/post/2010/04/27/New-Test-Post.aspx";
  this.FilterProperties[HtmlDocument.PropertyNames.PageUrl] =
    "http://tfs2010:8001/post/2010/04/27/New-Test-Post.aspx";
  this.WindowTitles.Add("New Test Post");
  #endregion
}
. . .
public UIPost0Pane2 UIPost0Pane
{
  get
```

LISTING 6-11: Continued

```
    {
        if ((this.mUIPost0Pane == null))
        {
            this.mUIPost0Pane = new UIPost0Pane2(this);
        }
        return this.mUIPost0Pane;
    }
}
```

The search criteria are the first critical element because that helps you find the pane, and the second critical item is the Post Pane that contains the actual hyperlink that you want to click. Drilling down into the UIPost0Pane2 class gives you access to the actual hyperlink. Now, the search criteria for this control look similar to the actual information you need to find the hyperlink. In this case, generating the additional control was not necessary because you needed that information to find it. However, in many cases, you won't, for example, need the ID of an order to figure out what the order number is because hopefully the label with the order ID number has a static name. Having this information though enables you to access the properties of the control at runtime to get the information you need about the control.

But, what do you do with that information when you have it? It is helpful to look at the updated (final version) of the CodedUITestMethod1, shown in Listing 6-12 (line numbers and breaks for readability and reference).

LISTING 6-12: Final Version of the CodedUITestMethod1 (from Listing 6-11)

```
  [TestMethod]
  public void CodedUITestMethod1()
  {
1   this.UIMap.LogonasJeffEditor();
2   this.UIMap.ClickAddEntry();
3   this.UIMap.EnterTestBodyforthebodyandclickSavePost();
    //Construct the URL and any related search properties
4   string year = DateTime.Now.Year.ToString();
5   string day = DateTime.Now.Day.ToString();
6   string month = DateTime.Now.Month.ToString();
7   string post = string.Format("/post/{0}/{1}/{2}/", year, month,
  day);
8   string controlDefinition = string.Format(
        "class=taggedlink href=\"{0}", post);
9   string absolutePath = string.Format("{0}New-Test-Post", post);
```

LISTING 6-12: Continued

```
10 string href = string.Format("http://tfs2010:8001{0}", absolute
Path);

11 this.UIMap.ClicktheLogoffbutton();
12 this.UIMap.ClicktheLogOnlink();
13 this.UIMap.EnterthepasswordasPssw0rdandclickLogin();
   //Replace the generated search properties with our own
14 HtmlHyperlink actualLink =
       this.UIMap.UIInternetExplorerEnhaWindow.
       UINameoftheblogShortdeDocument.
       UIPost0Pane1.UINewTestPostHyperlink;
15 actualLink.FilterProperties
       [HtmlHyperlink.PropertyNames.AbsolutePath] = absolutePath;
16 actualLink.FilterProperties[HtmlHyperlink.PropertyNames.Href] =
       href;
17 actualLink.FilterProperties
       [HtmlHyperlink.PropertyNames.ControlDefinition] =
       controlDefinition;
18 this.UIMap.ClicktheNewTestPostlink();
}
```

Lines 1, 2, and 3 are the original three test steps. Lines 4–7 were added to dynamically construct the URL to the post that was created in step 3. As mentioned earlier, in this case it is easy to know what the resulting value would be, so you could create it yourself. Lines 8, 9, and 10 are search conditions that will replace the generated search conditions. To determine which search conditions to replace, you need to drill into the code a bit. The best way to do it is to start with the method in which the link is clicked and drill down from there. In this case you would start at the ClicktheNewTestPostlink method; then go to the UINewTestPostHyperlink (which is found in this method) and then you see the search criteria. Not all the search criteria needs to be replaced, just the criteria dealing with the URL. In this case, those criteria are the Control Definition, Absolute Path, and Href values.

After these are constructed, the test continues at lines 11, 12, and 13. At line 14, you get the reference to the link. (This call was taken from the Clickthe-NewTestPostlink method.) If you look in the UINewTestPostHyperlink property, the first line checks to see if it is null, and if it is, it creates the link and associates all the generated search criteria to it. So, lines 15, 16, and 17 actually overwrite that search criteria. And because the hyperlink is created only on the first call, when the code in line 18 calls it, it uses the already created instance with the overridden search criteria and finds the link on whatever day you run this Test Case on.

This might be more complicated than it seems, but consider the alternative: If you did not have access to any generated code, you could not create tests that handle dynamic situations like this. So, although it is a bit of work to get right, when you do you can run the tests regardless of any dynamic values, and you can tailor it to any application and any scenario. Hopefully, this real-world type of example can make it easier for you to handle the dynamic values in your own applications.

Other Tips

In the previous example, the URL was constructed because the assumption is that the full path is needed to make sure you get the right hyperlink. The good news is that this not the case, and you can simplify this with a few caveats. To simplify it, you can use the `contains` method, as shown here:

```
actualLink.FilterProperties
[HtmlHyperlink.PropertyNames.Href].Contains("New-Test-Post");
```

Because you are searching for strings, this is easy to do and saves you the hassle you went through earlier. So, why did I show you the hassle? The reason is that `contains` will not always work the way you think it should. Imagine the situation in which you run this test multiple times and instead of this being the search criteria for a link in the post pane, what if it were the search criteria for the post pane itself? Then `contains` would find multiple matches so the first one the code finds would be used. In general, the rule is to always use the least amount of code possible but be prepared to use more if needed.

Some additional classes and methods help you manipulate the Coded UI tests. The `UITestControl` class (the base class for all controls) enables you to specify that execution should pause until certain conditions are met. These are embodied in `WaitForCondition`, `WaitForControlExists`, `WaitForControlNotExists`, `WaitForControlPropertyEqual`, `WaitForControlPropertyNotEqual`, `WaitForControlReady`, `WaitForControlCondition`, and `WaitForControlEnabled`. Using these wait methods, delays can be intelligently added into the test rather than a delay of time that might not work.

You can find more information about these and other methods of the `UITest-Control` class at http://msdn.microsoft.com/en-us/library/dd434055.aspx.

In addition to these settings, there is a static class called Playback that you can call any member on during the testing process. This class contains a method called `PlaybackSettings` that enables you to call methods such as `DelayBetweenActions` that set an overall wait period between steps or the `SearchTimeout` method. These two classes are key classes for manipulating the generated Coded UI test. More information is available at http://msdn.microsoft.com/en-us/library/microsoft.visualstudio.testtools.uitesting.playback.aspx and http://msdn.microsoft.com/en-us/library/microsoft.visualstudio.testtools.uitesting.playbacksettings_members.aspx. You can find the complete list of classes in the UITesting namespace at http://msdn.microsoft.com/en-us/library/dd405972.aspx. Get to know these classes and methods if you plan to spend any time manipulating Coded UI Tests.

Combining Multiple Tests

One feature of the automated testing is to combine multiple tests into one long test. For example, you might have one test that logs in to the application, another that posts a blog, and yet another that adds a comment or edits a post. You can combine all these into one long running functional test. Combining tests is easy; simply select Test, Generate Code for Coded UI Test, Use Existing Action Recording. Browse to the Test Case that contains the existing recording and select it. The actions generate additional code that is added to your existing code. Beyond that, you can take any number of different steps to increase the number of test steps in your code.

Associating Coded UI Tests and Test Cases

At this point, you might have created one or more Coded UI Test Cases, which might not be helpful. You can execute a Coded UI Test Case simply by taking the compiled assembly and executing it with MSTest or TCM from the command line. You can also continue to run them through Visual Studio. The problem with both of these approaches is that they require you to sit there and do nothing while the test executes. This is, as you may guess, an incredible waste of time. To get the full benefit of the automated test, you need to associate it with a Test Case. (This also lights up many of the reports.)

To associate a Test Case with an automated test, open the Test Case you want to make the association with and select the Associated Automation tab (Figure 6-13).

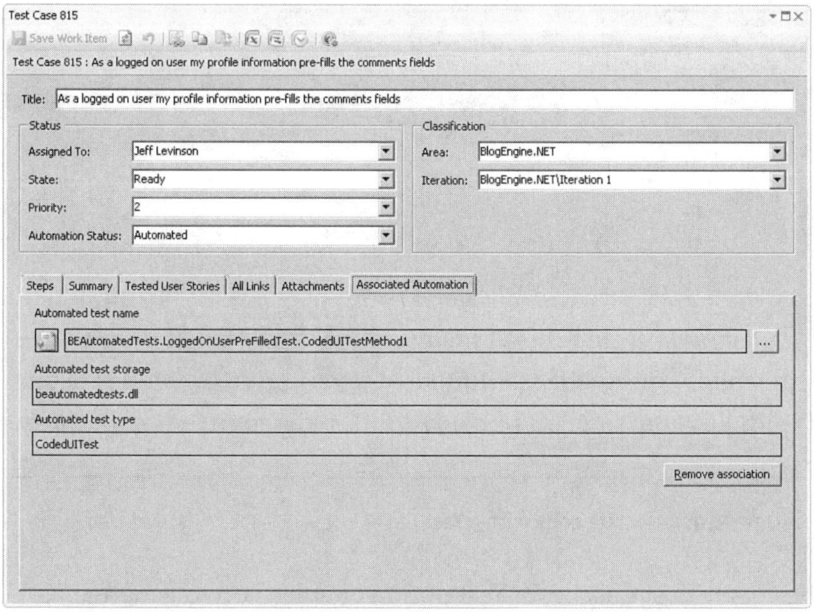

FIGURE 6-13: Associated Automation tab of the Test Case work item

Click the ellipsis in the upper-right corner, and select the code to associate with the work item.

> Before you do this, the solution that contains the automated test must be loaded.

After you click the ellipsis, select the automated test to associate the Test Case with, and click OK. The Automation Status value automatically changes to Automated, and you see the test information displayed on the Associated

Automation tab. Save the work item and you are ready to proceed. As a critical side note, the code that you associate to the Test Case must be stored in TFS or any attempt to execute the automated test will fail.

Another option, as mentioned previously, is in the Test List Editor: Right-click the test, and select Associate Test to Test Case; then find the Test Case and select it (Figure 6-14).

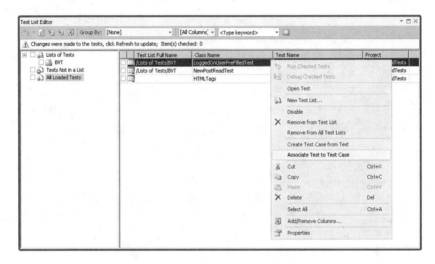

FIGURE 6-14: Associate code with a Test Case

The Create Test Case from Test option enables you to generate Test Cases so that if developers created a Coded UI test, they could create the Test Case to go with it. Also, because every test type displays in the Test List Editor, it means you can associate any type of test with a Test Case—including Unit Tests.

A third option is to use the TCM command-line tool, which you can get using the Visual Studio Command Prompt, or you can find it in %programfiles(x86)%\Microsoft Visual Studio 10.0\Common7\IDE. This tool has multiple features that make it easy to script getting information out of MTM (such as lists of test suites and test plans). You can find more information on this tool at http://msdn.microsoft.com/en-us/library/dd465192(VS.100).aspx. The more important aspect of it is that the tool has a *testcase* switch that can generate Test Cases for you from the tests that exist in a given assembly. (You can provide filters for which tests you want to create Test Cases from.)

After the first set of Test Case work items is generated, when you run this command again it merely updates the Test Case work items and suites with new information rather than duplicating the Test Cases. You can also use this tool to add these Test Cases directly to an existing suite; if this suite happens to be a requirements-based suite, you have succeeded in linking the Unit Tests to requirements with no additional work required.

ASSOCIATING UNIT TESTS

Use the same process to associate a Unit Test with a Test Case work item. For Unit Tests you generally need to take one additional step. After the Test Cases have been generated for a Unit Test, you need to associate the Test Cases with a requirement; this is not done for you (unless you use the /sync-suite switch). After you do this, the information available to you in reports becomes much better in terms of tracing Unit Tests to requirements. Be aware though that you should categorize your Unit Tests to make it easy to perform this operation in the minimum number of steps required; otherwise, it becomes too time consuming.

There is one consequence to associating automation; to manually run a test from MTM, you must select Run with options from the Test page. Therefore, if for some reason you want to execute the test manually more than once or twice going forward, you can create a copy of the Test Case before so that you can have one manual version and one automated version.

Finally, add the automated test solution to version control. Keep your test automation with your code because they are designed to go together for a given release. However, this depends on your situation. If you create automated tests that will be used for many releases and fairly insulated from changes to new releases of the code, you may want to create a separate branch for these Test Cases.

SUMMARY

This chapter taught you how to create and manipulate automated Test Cases. This includes the ability to add validation to the automated test using the Coded UI Test Builder and then to modify any generated code. At this point, you should handle more complex situations involving dynamic data values. Even though this chapter focused on dealing with Web Applications, the principles apply to WinForms and WPF applications equally.

You also know that you can associate Unit Tests with Test Cases and then with requirements to get requirements coverage information from Unit Tests using the tcm.exe command-line tool. Using this tool, testers can also execute Unit Tests as part of their automated test runs.

In Chapter 7, you learn how to execute automated tests using MTM and also using Team Build.

7

Executing Automated Test Cases

IN THE PREVIOUS CHAPTER YOU LEARNED how to automate Test Cases and associate automated tests with Test Case work items. You learned how to do this with both Coded UI tests and Unit Tests, but this is applicable to any automated test. In this chapter you take the next step and execute the automated tests. In this chapter you learn how to execute automated tests in four primary ways: manually through Visual Studio, from the command line, from Microsoft Test Manager, and as part of a Team Build.

In this chapter Unit Tests and Coded UI tests are treated differently for one major reason—to execute a Coded UI test, which interacts with the user interface, the agent that runs the tests must be running as a process (as opposed to a service). For the most part this means that certain configuration changes must be made to the various agents that execute the tests. You learn how to make the appropriate changes to the Test Agent and the Build Agent to accomplish the automated execution of a Coded UI test.

Executing Automated Tests Through Visual Studio

This is arguably the easiest way to execute an automated test and requires the least amount of setup. You can run tests within Visual Studio in three ways: local execution (default method), local execution with remote collection, and remote execution. Each has its place in the developer testing toolkit and all three ways are discussed here.

When running tests with Visual Studio, the tests are not reported against a build. Tests run through Visual Studio are designed to be developer-executed tests to verify functionality, not necessarily be the tests of record. Test results *can* be published to TFS and related to a particular build, but this must be done manually after the test execution finishes.

> ### DEVELOPER-FOCUSED TESTING
>
> This information is not covered in great depth because this is mostly focused on the developer testing experience rather than a tester-oriented experience. This section provides a good overview of what can be done, why it can be done, and how to do it, but it does not cover all the options available to a developer.

Local Execution

Whether you execute a Unit Test or a Coded UI test, the process for local execution is the same. This is because the user who runs Visual Studio is the user who runs the tests, and this user (you) has access to the Windows user interface. The default test settings are for the local execution of tests. You can access these settings by opening the local.test settings or Trace and TestImpact.test settings file in the solution node. Both of these settings are preconfigured to provide different levels of diagnostic information.

To set the active test settings file, from the main menu, go to Test, Select Active Test Settings, and choose the settings file you want to use. You can execute the test from the Test List Editor or Test View.

Local Execution with Remote Collection

This option enables developers to execute tests (such as load tests) from the local machine but gather data from a remote machine. The remote machine may be a system running SQL Server or Internet Information Services, or may be even a proxy server if the application connects to a data source outside of a corporate firewall. To perform a test with this structure, a Test Controller and a Test Agent need to be defined. Unlike the configurations used with MTM or Team Build (both of these options are discussed in more detail later) the Test Controller must not be registered with a Team Project Collection. The major reason for this is that as previously mentioned the testing process from Visual Studio is about developers verifying functionality rather than running authoritative tests. In addition, this enables tests to be executed without having TFS present because no data is reported back to TFS. The Test Agent is responsible for gathering the remote data and sending it back to Visual Studio. The steps for performing this configuration are discussed in the next section.

Remote Execution

Remote execution executes the test code on the remote machine. In this situation the code needs to be deployed to whichever remote machine needs to host the application before the test is executed. During test execution the Test Controller and Test Agent work to execute the test code on that remote machine as well.

RUNNING THE AGENT AS AN INTERACTIVE PROCESS

Remember that for a remote execution of a Coded UI test (this does not apply to Unit Tests because there is no user interface interaction) the Coded UI test must be set to run as an interactive process. The steps to do this are covered later in the section "Setting Up the Physical Environment."

To begin with, you need to configure the test controller.

To view the test controllers available to you, from the main menu select Test, Manage Test Controllers. This displays the Manage Test Controller screen, as shown in Figure 7-1.

All the available test controllers can be selected from the Controller dropdown. For the selected controller, all the agents associated with it are listed. As you can see from Figure 7-1, there are two agents associated with this controller.

FIGURE 7-1: Manage Test Controller dialog

Selecting an agent and clicking the Properties button enables you to apply settings specific to that agent as it relates to network switching, weighting (used in load testing to distribute test load), and attributes. Attributes enable you to specify tags that can be used to configure *roles*. Roles enable you to specify certain configurations that the test controller can then match to the appropriate machine. This abstracts the machines a bit so that machines can change or more than one machine can be used to fulfill a particular need. Figure 7-2 shows the Agent Properties dialog.

After the agents are configured, you can configure the test to execute on the remote machine. Figure 7-3 shows the Trace and Test Impact test settings configured for remote execution.

In Figure 7-3, you see that two roles have been added: Client and Web Server. You can specify multiple roles if the test executes on multiple machines, or if you are going to grab data from multiple machines. After you set some attributes, you can preview agents that match the criteria. This also shows you all data collectors installed on the machine.

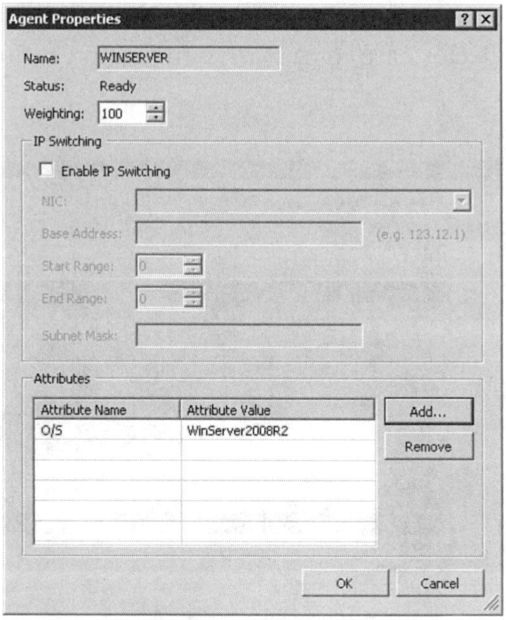

FIGURE 7-2: Agent Properties dialog

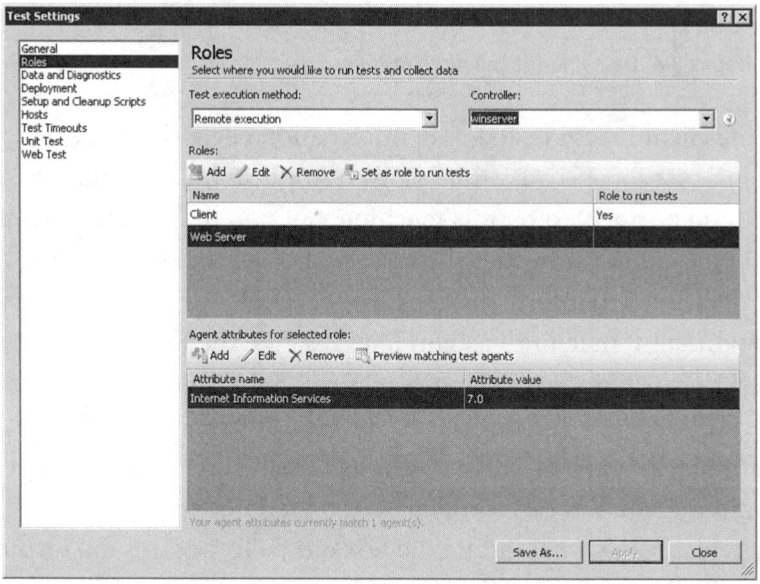

FIGURE 7-3: Visual Studio Test Settings

After the roles are set, you can select the Data and Diagnostics tab and set which data collectors are to capture information for each machine (see Figure 7-4).

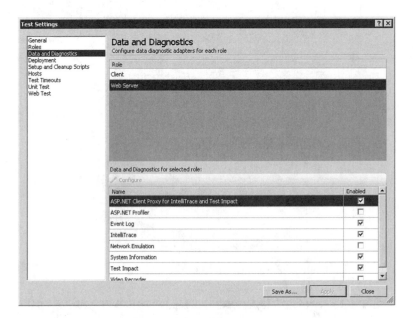

FIGURE 7-4: Data and Diagnostics settings

For the client machine, the only information needed is the event log and system information; because this is a Web Application, no actual code except the test code is executed on this machine. But you may want to set the Network Emulation that throttles the data sent to the web server. For the web server, more detailed information will be collected. You may collect data from as many different machines as you like. Execute the test as you would any other test from within Visual Studio. Figure 7-5 shows the results of a remote execution test.

After the test finishes, you can publish the results against a specific test run (assuming you have TFS and an automated build, discussed in the next section, which you can associate the test with). To publish the results, from the Test Results pane, select the Publish button (see Figure 7-6).

Result Summary

Test run name: jeff@TFS2010 2010-08-03 21:24:19
Run result: ✓ 2/2 tests passed, 0 failed, 0 skipped
Test settings: Trace and Test Impact
Submitted by: DEMO\jeff
Started on: 8/3/2010 9:24:36 PM
Completed on: 8/3/2010 9:27:09 PM

Debug Trace   Copy
V, 4928, 18, 2010/08/03, 21:24:40.265, WINSERVER\QTAgent32.exe, UnitTestExecuter.RunClassInitializeMethod: Acquiring m_runner.SyncRoot.
V, 4928, 18, 2010/08/03, 21:24:40.266, WINSERVER\QTAgent32.exe, UnitTestExecuter.RunClassInitializeMethod: Acquired m_runner.SyncRoot.
V, 4928, 18, 2010/08/03, 21:24:40.269, WINSERVER\QTAgent32.exe, UnitTestExecuter.RunClassInitializeMethod: Released m_runner.SyncRoot.
V, 4928, 21, 2010/08/03, 21:25:53.663, WINSERVER\QTAgent32.exe, UnitTestExecuter.RunClassInitializeMethod: Acquiring m_runner.SyncRoot.
V, 4928, 21, 2010/08/03, 21:25:53.663, WINSERVER\QTAgent32.exe, UnitTestExecuter.RunClassInitializeMethod: Acquired m_runner.SyncRoot.
V, 4928, 21, 2010/08/03, 21:25:53.664, WINSERVER\QTAgent32.exe, UnitTestExecuter.RunClassInitializeMethod: Released m_runner.SyncRoot.

Collected Files   Copy

TFS2010
    Event Log-TFS2010-20100803-212706.042-1.xml
    SystemInformation.xml   System Information from TFS2010
WINSERVER
    Event Log-WINSERVER-20100803-212705.413-1.xml
    SystemInformation.xml   System Information from WINSERVER

FIGURE 7-5: Remote execution test results

Test Results   ▾ ╫ ×
jeff@TFS2010 2010-08-03 21:24:19 ▾   ⚡ Run ▾ Debug ▾   🗔 🖉 ▾ 🔄 🗐   Group By: [None]   ▾
✓ No test runs were published   Results: 2/2 passed; Item(s) checked: 0

	Result	Test Name	Project	Error Message
☐	Passed	CodedUITestMethod1	BEAutomatedTests	
☐	Passed	CodedUITestMethod1	BEAutomatedTests	

Architecture Explorer   Error List   Output   Find Results 1   Pending Changes   Test Results

FIGURE 7-6: Test Results

In the Publish Test Results dialog, select the build number, flavor, and test runs you want to publish, and click OK (see Figure 7-7). The results are now available to you for reporting purposes.

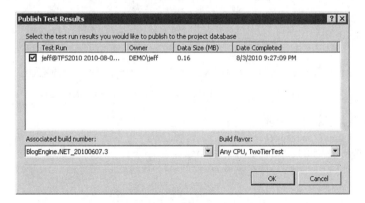

FIGURE 7-7: Publish Test Results

Executing Automated Tests from the Command Line

In the previous section, you learned how developers can execute tests from within Visual Studio and publish those results. You can also execute tests from the command line. You may want to do this for many reasons, but two of the most common reasons are to schedule the execution of tests outside of builds and to script tests along with various other commands (such as resetting data). You can use two tools to script test execution:

- Tcm.exe is a superset of mstest and actually calls mstest to perform the actual testing.
- MSTest.exe is a general purpose test execution engine that interacts with assemblies on the client rather than what is stored in TFS.

The major difference between these two tools is that tcm is designed to execute server tests and tightly aligns with MTM.

COMMAND-LINE TOOLS IN-DEPTH
Both tools have many options that can perform whatever tasks you need, including automatically publishing test results. For a comprehensive discussion of these tools, see http://msdn.microsoft.com/en-us/library/ms182489(VS.100).aspx (mstest) and http://msdn.microsoft.com/en-us/library/dd465192.aspx (tcm).

To execute the Test Cases shown in the figures, from the command line, use the following command from the Visual Studio Command Prompt:

```
Mstest /testcontainer:BEAutomatedTests.dll
/testsettings:TraceAndTestImpact.testsettings
/test:BEAutomatedTests.NewPostReadTest
/test:BEAutomatedTests.LoggedOnUserPreFilledTest
```

Figure 7-8 shows the output of this command.

The results of the output and all attachments are stored in the TestResults folder of the same directory where the command was executed. You can optionally specify a different location for the results.

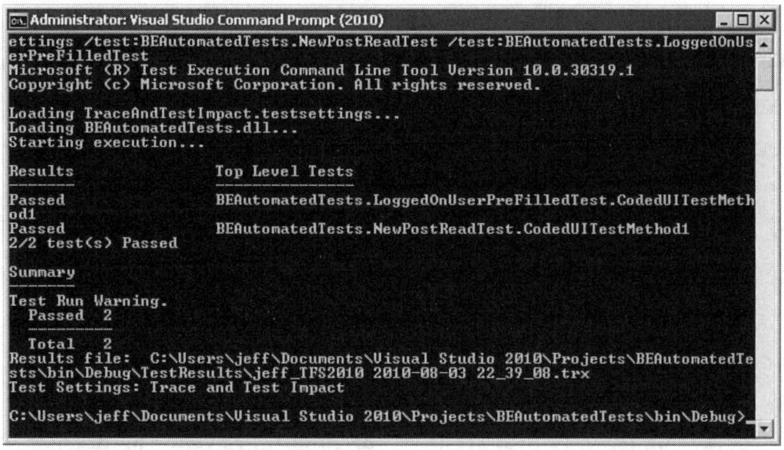

FIGURE 7-8: Command line test results

Executing Automated Tests in MTM

Before you can run an automated test in MTM, MTM needs to know where the code for the automated test is located. The Test Case knows the assembly that contains the code associated with it, but that's it. To let MTM know where the code is, an automated build needs to be associated with the test plan.

Creating an Automated Build

In the previous examples in this book, an automated build definition already existed for the BlogEngine.NET team project. This build is called DevOnDemand. However, when the build was created, it was building only the application solution and not the testing solution because it didn't exist at the time.

The first step is to edit the build definition. The key change that needs to be made is to change the Items to Build on the Process tab. Simply add the testing solution (or project) to the list of items to build. The next change that should be made is in the Advanced settings. Find the Disable Tests property and set it to True. Why?

If this is set to False, any tests found in the assemblies specified in the Basic, Automated Tests section will execute. For the moment, the build infrastructure is not set up to execute a Coded UI test. Later you see how to run Coded UI tests during a build but for this demonstration it is not necessary.

NAMING TEST ASSEMBLIES

One solution to this issue is to keep the Unit Test assemblies and Coded UI test assemblies separate. Doing this you can give the Coded UI assembly a name such as UIAutomated and just omit the word "tests." Another option is to call the Unit Test assembly [AppName]UnitTests and the Coded UI assembly [AppName]CodedUITests and then change the Automate Tests settings to ***UnitTests*.dll; then only your Unit Tests would be run as part of the build. This removes the assembly from the Automated Tests filter in the build definition (shown just below 2. Basic in Figure 7-9). Why you would want to do this is explained in the "Executing Automated Tests with Team Build" section.

After you make these changes, save the build definition, and queue a new build. Figure 7-9 shows the Process tab.

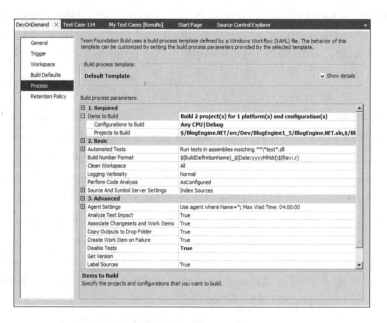

FIGURE 7-9: Automated Build Process tab

Setting Up the Physical Environment

If you have not set up your environment to execute automated tests, do this now. This section walks you through the setup that is not a best practice. This setup shows installing a Test Agent on the same machine as MTM. In general you would never do this because it defeats the purpose of running tests on remote machines, so testers can concentrate on manual tests. This assumes that as you read this book you may have only one machine to experiment on.

The Test Controller can be installed on the same server as TFS or another machine, but if possible, try to install it on another machine. The reason is that you can have only one Test Controller per machine; if you intend to have many Test Controllers, you probably do not want to have one on the actual TFS server because the Test Controller generates traffic to and from the test agents. This probably will not have an effect on the TFS server, but it makes sense to avoid the potential impact. Run the Test Controller install. (The Test Controller, Test Agent, and Lab Management Agent are all on the Agents media and not included with the TFS or VS media.) After the install is complete, run the Test Controller Configuration tool (shown in Figure 7-10).

FIGURE 7-10: Test Controller Configuration tool

You may run the Test Controller as a Network Service; however, if you run it as a discrete account, you have many more options from a security perspective. Register the controller with your Team Project Collection and optionally configure it for load testing (which is not covered in this book). Apply the settings, and close the Test Controller Configuration tool.

This install adds three security groups to the machine on which the Test Controller is installed. Table 7-1 describes these security groups.

TABLE 7-1: Test Controller Security Groups

Security Group	Description
TeamTestAgentService	Members of this group can connect to the Microsoft Visual Studio Test Controller 2010 service.
TeamTestControllerAdmins	Members of this group can run tests, view/delete results, create environments, and administer test controller/agents.
TeamTestControllerUsers	Members of this group can run tests and view results.

By default, the Test Controller account is added to the TeamTestControllerUsers group, the built in admins are added to the TeamTestControllerAdmins, and the account that the Test Agent runs under is added to the TeamTestAgentService.

Next, run the Test Agent (not Lab fManagement Agent) install. You need to install a Test Agent on every physical machine (or virtual machine).

WHAT IS A VIRTUAL OR PHYSICAL MACHINE?

In the context of MTM and Lab Manager, a virtual machine is any virtual machine controlled by System Center Virtual Machine Manager. Virtual machines not controlled by SCVMM or Lab Management are considered physical machines. The dividing line between physical and virtual is whether Lab Management controls it. This, for example, enables you to execute tests on VMWare virtual machines. The benefits of virtual environments controlled by Lab Manager are discussed in Chapter 8, "Lab Management."

After the install is complete, run the Test Agent Configuration tool (see Figure 7-11).

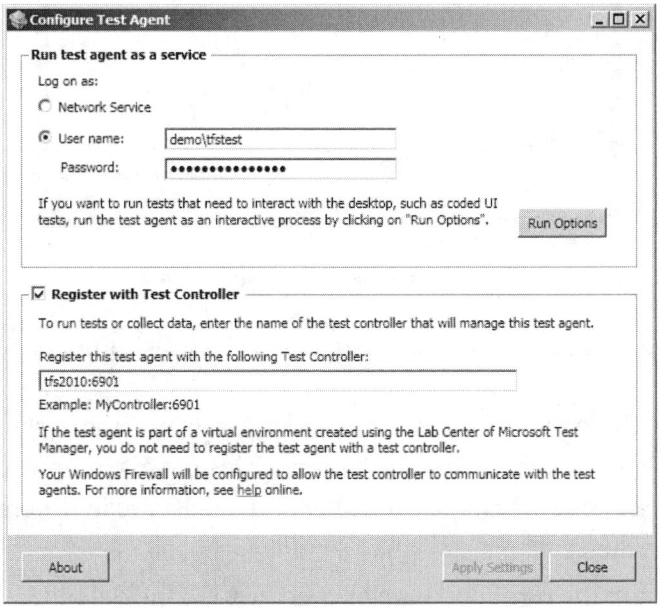

FIGURE 7-11: Test Agent Configuration tool

As with the Test Controller, you may run the test agent as a Network Service; however, the recommendation is to run it as a discrete account because it gives you more options from a security perspective but also, when running Web Applications, control over browser options. In the Run Options dialog, select Interactive Process, and click OK; then register it with a Test Controller.

This agent is configured to run as the tfstest service account. This is the normal configuration that you want. However, when running the test agent on a machine that you are logged onto (for example, you want to run automated tests on the same box that you are working on) you must use your account. (This limitation is mostly related to web applications because the web browser runs as the logged on account—if another account tries to open the browser, the browser will not start.) After you set up the test agent, you must reboot. Then, you see the Test Agent Status tray application, as shown in Figure 7-12.

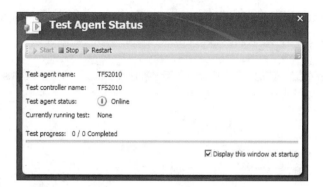

FIGURE 7-12: Test Agent Status tray application

If you see a status of Disconnected, check the following items:

- The machine the test agent is on and the machine the Test Controller is on can communicate with each other. (This means bidirectional and can be an issue when the controller and agents are in different subdomains.)
- Make sure the right ports are opened; 6901 is the default.
- Make sure that the account is in the right security groups as noted in Table 7-1.
- Make sure the Test Controller is running.

After you see the status as Online, you are good. You can also rerun the Test Agent Configuration tool and switch the test agent back to a Service as needed. You can find the tool on the Start Menu under Visual Studio 2010.

Running a Coded UI Test Through MTM

When the build is completed, you can head over to MTM and use this new build in two ways, which includes the automation code. The first—and probably best—way to handle this is to update the plan to use the new build. The other way to use this build is to select Run with Options on the Run Tests page. After you determine how you will use the build, you need to specify the automated run settings. As noted in Chapter 3, "Planning Your Testing," the automated run settings are the settings used when executing Coded UI (or any other automated tests for that matter). Typically these settings differ a bit from manual tests. A good example of this is that you typically won't record a video of the automated tests because these will be executed many times. The data will build up on the server because these are saved regardless of whether the tests pass or fail, unless you remember to update this setting so that only failed tests save videos.

To begin, from the top-left portion of MTM, select the Testing Center drop-down, and select Lab Center. The first item to check is that the Test Agent for a physical machine is available. When you installed the Test Controller, you registered it with a Project Collection. When you installed the Test Agent, you registered it with a Test Controller. Therefore, when you are on the Controllers page, you should see the controller and the agent, and the agent should be running, as shown in Figure 7-13.

FIGURE 7-13: Controllers tab, Test Controller Manager page

After this is verified, select the Lab tab to display the environments. To add a physical environment, select New, Physical Environment. This gives you the ability to add a new environment that you can use for automated testing.

PHYSICAL ENVIRONMENTS

In some cases virtual environments are not desirable. Most often this is true when testing hardware-based components or embedded software. In cases like these, adding many physical environments is a great benefit.

For a physical environment you need to specify the name of the environment, and optionally a description and the location of the environment. The location you specify is the test controller machine. A drop-down is available with all test controllers registered to the Team Project Collection (TPC). If no controllers are listed, refer back to the Controllers tab to see if any are listed there. If they are not, the next step is to check to make sure the controller service is running. Environment tags let you specify metadata about the environment that enables you to determine the suitability of the environment for specific situations.

The machines tab enables you to add the machines on which the automated tests will run. This tab is shown in Figure 7-14.

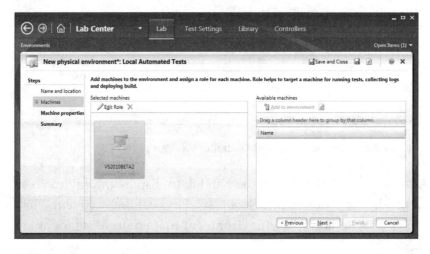

FIGURE 7-14: Machines tab

You must specify at least one machine (but you can specify more, which is common if the application is a multitier application) and specify the role that machine plays. To set the role, click Edit Role or click the server. The machine properties page enables you to specify tags that describe that machine. This is again used to specify whether the machine is suitable for certain tests; you can reference these during the build and deployment workflow. Figure 7-15 shows the completed physical environment in MTM.

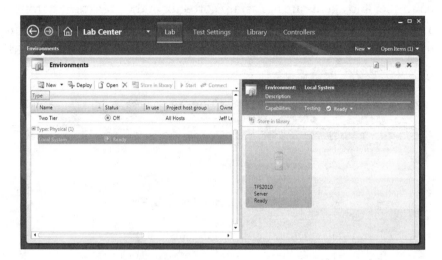

FIGURE 7-15: Environments page in MTM

Creating the Automated Test Settings

After the environment is set up, you can create the test settings for running automated tests.

CREATING TEST SETTINGS

Everything described here can be done from the automated test settings on the Plan, Properties page by selecting New. Any required items will be noted, and you are walked through what you need to set up.

The test settings for a manual test are identical to the test settings for an automated test with the exception that you can provide a few additional items that display on the Advanced tab.

On the General tab, you can specify the name and description of the test, and you must select either manual (the default) or automated so that MTM knows which settings to use for which tests. The Roles tab requires you to add the test system that contains a test agent. You are choosing a Role, and it chooses the matching environments. If no roles exist to select here, it means the controller and agents are not set up correctly or the physical environment has not been created yet. In addition, if you select an environment with multiple machines, you must select which machine the tests will be executed on (see Figure 7-16).

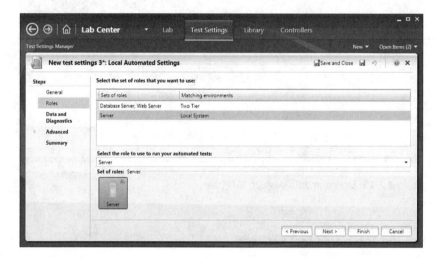

FIGURE 7-16: Roles tab of the Automated Test Settings

The Data and Diagnostics tab is the same for the manual test settings. It is typical to select only a few items such as IntelliTrace and to exclude items such as the video recording. In general you can use lighter diagnostics on automated runs; then if you do discover a problem, rerun it while gathering more detailed diagnostics.

The Advanced tab is unique to automated test runs in MTM. Here you can specify items to deploy that may be required for your test to run (data sources or other external dependencies that have not been added to the solution), set up and tear down scripts and hosts, set timeouts, and load add-ins for web tests. These add-ins are for protocol tests and not functional tests. When everything is configured, you see an additional entry with the Run type specified as Automated.

At this point, go to the Test Plan properties and set the automated run test settings and the test environment. Then, you have one final step before you can execute an automated test through MTM: Don't forget to set the build!

Running automated tests is now a routine matter of selecting the automated tests to run on the Test tab, Run Tests page and selecting Run. Typically, these runs are conducted on machines other than the machine that they are launched from. However, if you run these tests locally, make sure not to play with the keyboard and mouse.

Figure 7-17 shows the Automated Test Status page.

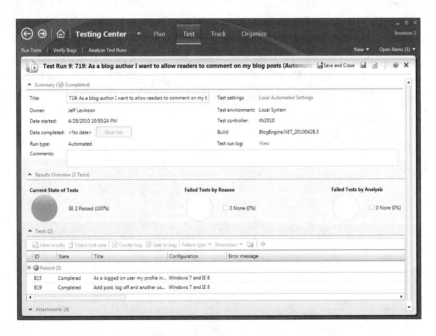

FIGURE 7-17: Automated Test Status page

This is the same page as the Test Run Results page (accessed from the Analyze Test Runs page). During the automated run, this page provides status on what is currently happening. However, this page does not update regularly to improve performance. You need to use the Refresh button to know what is currently happening. (If you are curious why this screen doesn't auto-refresh, in most situations you will set automated tests to run and check on them later.)

Executing Automated Tests with Team Build

Executing tests with Team Build (during the build process as opposed to using Lab Management) provides a certain elegance because Team Build calculates many metrics for you and outputs a nicely formatted report that you can run reports against. Specifically, it appears on the Build Success over Time report and the Quality Indicators report, both of which are valuable in tracking application quality.

Earlier, you saw how to create an automated build. Setting the automated build to execute your tests requires three specific changes: two in the build definition and one in the build host. The first two changes involve enabling the execution of tests. Ensure that the Disable Tests property of the build definition is set to False and that the assembly in which your tests reside matches the pattern in the Automated Tests property (see Figure 7-18).

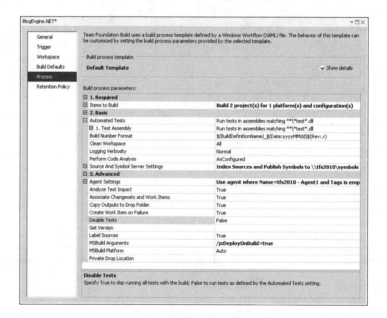

FIGURE 7-18: Build definition settings for executing automated tests

The final change involves the build host. By default the build host runs as a service; this means that it cannot interact with the desktop. To change this, log onto the server that has the build host installed on it that the build controller is registered with. Open the Team Foundation Server Administration Console, and select the Build Configuration tab (see Figure 7-19).

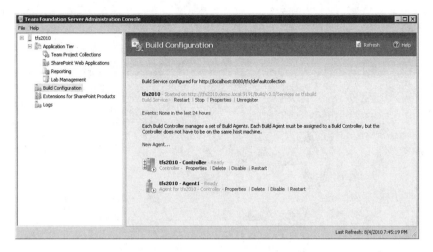

FIGURE 7-19: Team Build Configuration

The build host is the actual process under which the build agents run. For a Coded UI test to be executed during a regular build, this process must be set to run interactively. To set this, do the following:

1. Under the Build Host (shown as tfs2010 in Figure 7-19) click the Stop link.
2. Click the Properties link.
3. Select Interactive Process, and re-enter the build service password (see Figure 7-20).
4. Click Start.

When you finish, a command window opens with a note to press Esc when you finish running the interactive build. After you complete running the build, you need to reset the build service to run as a service. If you run this on a machine where you are logged on, the build service must run under the account of the user logged onto the machine. Typically, this is not an issue because the build executes on a dedicated build machine.

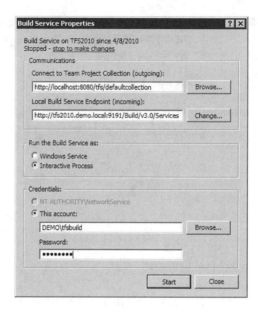

FIGURE 7-20: Team build properties

DEDICATED CODED UI TEST BUILD MACHINE

You may want to dedicate one build machine to do nothing but run Coded UI tests, so you do not need to constantly reset this service.

Figure 7-21 shows the results of the build with two Coded UI tests that have been executed.

BUILD WARNINGS

If you are curious about the build warnings, the first two are a result of the BlogEngine.NET application—one is that an XML comment is missing (the code is well commented, but the authors missed a spot) and the second is a variable declared but never used by the code. The third warning relates to the MSDeploy project added to the solution to handle the install duties for Chapter 8—it cannot be built by MSBuild.

FIGURE 7-21: Build results with automated testing

Automated Testing Gotchas

You need to be aware of a number of items while performing automated tests. (These issues do not apply to manual testing.) The biggest issue is the account you test under and whether you have run tests under that account and on that machine. These issues mostly apply to browsers and are not usually a problem with other clients.

Custom Dialogs

The first item to be aware of is the custom dialogs that pop up only in certain situations. The most obvious one is the Welcome to Internet Explorer dialog. Other browsers have their own ways to deal with a first time run, but consider how to handle IE. To get rid of this dialog, do the following (this applies to Windows 7):

1. Run regedit.exe.
2. Navigate to HKEY_LOCAL_MACHINE\Software\Policies\ Microsoft\Internet Explorer\Main.

3. Add a new key of type REG_DWORD, and call it **DisableFirstRun-Customize** and set the value to 1.

4. Exit the Registry editor.

To perform this same configuration on a server or in a domain, you need to edit the group policy. To do this, follow these steps:

1. From the command line or the run dialog in the Start menu, run gpedit.msc.

2. Navigate to the following branch: Computer Configuration, Administrative Templates, Windows Components, Internet Explorer.

3. Select the setting Prevent Performance of First Run Customize Settings.

4. Select Enabled, and set your choice to Go Directly to Home Page.

5. Click OK.

In the Group Policy Editor, some additional settings are available that may also make custom dialogs a little easier to handle in Internet Explorer:

- Turn off Reopen Last Browsing Session.

  If IE crashes, this dialog prompts you to restore your last session.

- Internet Control Panel, Security Page, Intranet Sites: Include all local (intranet) sites not listed in other zones.

  If you log into an application, for example, the login may not be successful depending on your network security settings. By adding the local sites to the Intranet security group automatically, this problem can be negated in most circumstances.

- Internet Control Panel, Security Page: Turn on automatic detection of the intranet.

  As with the previous setting, this can help eliminate the issues associated with applications being in the Internet zone instead of the Intranet zone.

- User Configuration, Administrative Templates, Windows Components, Internet Explorer: Turn on the auto-complete feature for usernames and passwords on forms.

  When you first enter a username or password on a form, IE prompts you to auto-complete and save usernames and passwords.

- User Configuration, Administrative Templates, Windows Components, Internet Explorer, Disable AutoComplete for forms.

  This disables the general pop-up dialog that occurs the first time you fill in any fields on a form (except the username and password fields) that prompts you to turn on auto-complete.

- Disable changing default browser check.

  By default IE checks to see if it is the default browser when you first run it. Enabling this setting disables that check. This is typically important when you have multiple browsers installed on a single machine, and they all want to be your "go to" browser.

It's also okay if you don't handle these settings, but that means that you need to log on once as every user on every test machine that will be executing the Coded UI tests. Typically, you should do this for both the TFS Build and TFS Test accounts; otherwise, your tests will fail the first time you run them because unexpected dialogs were shown that the test wasn't ready to handle.

Another tip here is that you should not generate a Coded UI test from any test that has one of these one-time dialogs because subsequent runs will fail when the test can't find the dialog.

Cleaning Up Your Tests

As a good practice, each test should be absolutely stand-alone. That is, it should not depend on any particular test running before it or any particular test running after it. During a manual test run, you can easily reset the system in between tests. This is not the case with a series of automated tests run as part of a regression suite, for example. You also can't make use of the pre- and post-scripts that can be run as part of the automated test run settings because you need to clean up after each test—not the run as a whole.

Because of this, make sure that you either record and integrate the steps necessary to clean up your Test Cases as part of the automation of the test or find some way to script the cleanup and include the script in the Test Cleanup method. Failure to do so will end with a lot of failed tests that didn't actually fail.

SUMMARY

This chapter taught you to execute automated tests from within Visual Studio, the command line, and Microsoft Test Manager, and as part of Team Build. As a tester, you now know how to set up a Test Controller and Test Agent and to put that Test Agent into an Interactive Process mode so that it can interact with the user interface. In addition you know how to set up a physical environment and create automated test settings. Having this knowledge means that you can execute functional tests and Unit Tests to verify application functionality. In Chapter 8, you learn about Lab Management.

8

Lab Management

L AB MANAGEMENT IS THE MOST exciting new feature to be released by
Microsoft for both developers and testers. Before explaining what this
chapter contains, it is important to define Lab Management because you may
have never heard of it. After reading this chapter, you will want to give
it a try!

Lab Management is Microsoft's Virtual Environment manager for developers and testers. One of the core concepts is the capability of a development
team to start up an environment that mimics production as closely as possible whenever it is needed. And not just one environment—as many environments as are needed with the minimal amount of work. You can use these
environments to run automated builds, automate tests, or to just provide
developers and testers a clean environment to run code on. In addition,
because it works on virtual machines (VM), you can "snapshot" the environments at a point in time and rollback to that point in time if necessary. This
helps find and fix bugs faster as you will see.

In this chapter you learn about the various scenarios that can be executed
with Lab Management, how to set up and manage VMs with Lab Management, and how to actually execute each scenario. You also learn how to
deploy applications to multiple tiers using the technology that Visual Studio
provides. By the end of this chapter, you will understand the concepts and
know how to handle many different situations you are likely to run into.

WHAT THIS CHAPTER DOESN'T COVER

This chapter does not cover the set up of an environment to support Lab Management nor does it cover configuring TFS to use Lab Management because these are administrative tasks and play no part in the actual testing process.

Managing Virtual Environments Through MTM

Before getting into the usage of Lab Management, you need to understand how to interact with the Virtual Environments through MTM.

PREPPED VMs

This chapter assumes that you have VMs prepped with the necessary agents stored in System Center Virtual Machine Manager (SCVMM). For more information on how to prep the VMs, see http://code.msdn.microsoft.com/vslab-mgmt for the lab prep tool that Microsoft provides to help simplify the process. Some of this chapter assumes you used this tool to configure your VMs.

Exercise 8-1 walks you through importing a VM into your project.

■ EXERCISE 8-1

Import a VM

This exercise uses a VM template instead of a stored VM. Some options will not exist for you (specifically items on the Hardware profile and OS Profile pages).

1. Open MTM and select Lab Center, Library tab, Virtual Machines, and Templates page.
2. Click Import (see Figure 8-1).
3. On the Name and Machine step, select Browse (see Figure 8-2).

4. Find an appropriate template or stored VM, and click Add (see Figure 8-3).

5. Enter the Name, Description (optional), and Default role, and click Next.

6. Set the amount of memory to use, and click the OS profile tab.

7. Fill in any relevant information. (For this chapter, the machines are joined to the external domain already.)

8. Click Finish.

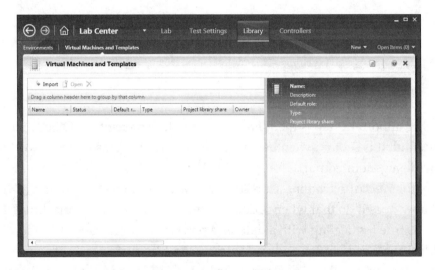

FIGURE 8-1: Import step 1

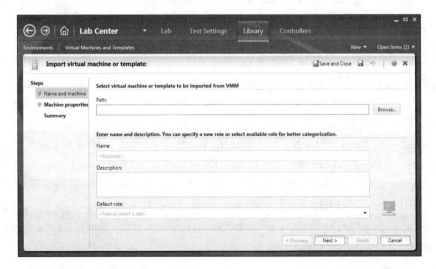

FIGURE 8-2: Import step 2

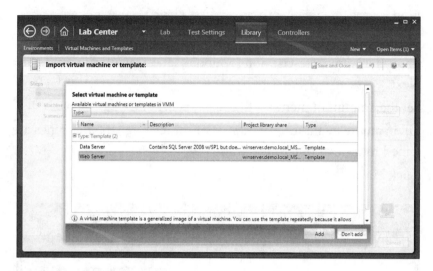

FIGURE 8-3: Import step 3

One important step is the Identity Information page of the OS Profile tab. By default it is set to * when using a template. That means that SCVMM can provide a generated name for the VM. This is probably a bad thing—especially for Web Applications. Consider that your script needs to enter a URL, but how does it do that when it doesn't know the name of the machine? The same is true for dealing with a database server; the connection string in your application needs to be updated, which can't be done easily if you don't know the name of the virtual machine. All is not as bad as it seems because there are ways to access this information during the deployment process, but it is extra work that you probably don't want to do.

When the VMs are imported, they are listed as Stored in MTM (see Figure 8-4). This process takes time, depending on your network speed. What is happening is that when you import a template to use in MTM, the VM template is copied so that the original is not touched in any way and can be reused.

After you have the VMs imported, select the Environments page. Here, you can compose your environments. (You can also compose them from the Lab tab by selecting New, New Virtual Environment.) Composing a new Virtual Environment lets you add any number of machines, override the machine properties that were set when you imported the templates, and most important, set Capabilities.

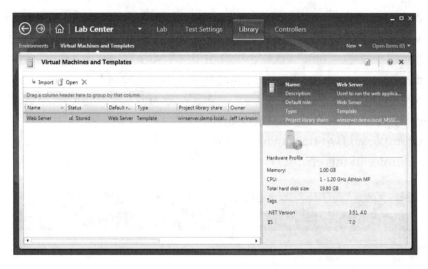

FIGURE 8-4: A stored VM

VIRTUAL MACHINES VERSUS VIRTUAL ENVIRONMENTS

You need to understand the distinction between a VM and a Virtual Environment. A VM is a single machine. A Virtual Environment is a set of Virtual Machines that work together and are treated as one. For example, you may have one VM that is a database server, another VM that is an application server, and another VM that is a client machine. These three individual VMs can be configured as a single three-tier environment consisting of a database server, application server, and client.

Capabilities describe what can be done with a VM. The three capabilities available are Run Tests, Run Workflows, and enable the environment for Network Isolation. The ability to run tests is obvious; Test Agent on the machine executes tests of any type, including Coded UI Tests, Web Performance tests, Unit Tests, and so on.

Run Workflows enables the machine to be used as a build machine and enables deployment workflows to be executed. This requires the Build Agent to be installed on the VM. Finally, the Network Isolation capability enables VMs to be reused. You can do this in two ways; both require that the template not be joined to an external domain. Network Isolation enables you to either create your own virtual domain (this requires that one of the machines in the environment be a domain controller) or the VMs are just in a workgroup. If the machines are joined to a domain, this option is not be available to you. This capability and general control of the VMs and environment as it relates to testing is provided by the Lab Agent.

A completed two-tier environment (the environment used for the rest of the examples in this chapter) is shown in Figure 8-5.

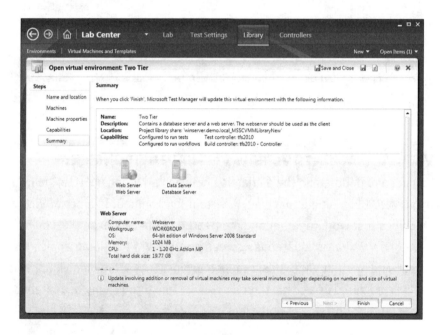

FIGURE 8-5: Completed two-tier environment

This environment contains a database server and a web server. The summary page shows information relating to each VM and the environment as a whole.

After an environment has been composed, you need to deploy the environment. (At this point an environment has been "created" but is just a series of configurations until the environment deploys.) To deploy the environment, go to the Lab tab, Environments page, and select the environment; click Deploy (see Figure 8-6).

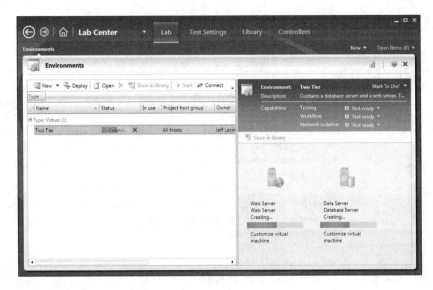

FIGURE 8-6: A deployed VM

During the deploy operation, the VMs are copied to the location specified in the Lab Management configuration settings. (This is transparent to you and is configured by the administrator.) The time it takes to perform this deploy is based on the network infrastructure, the number of VMs in the environment, and the size of the VMs.

After the environment deploys, you can then begin to use it. For each environment deployed you can choose the options shown in Table 8-1.

TABLE 8-1: Environment Options

Option	Description
Open	Opens the settings for the environment that enable you to change various hardware and OS properties, and the capabilities of the environment.
Store in Library	Copies all the machines in the environment to a library for reuse.
Start	Starts all VMs in the environment.
Connect	Opens the Virtual Environment Viewer that provides access to environment snapshots and remote connections to each of the machines in the environment.

TABLE 8-1: Continued

Option	Description
Shut Down	Shuts down each machine in the Virtual Environment. This is the equivalent of selecting Start, Shut Down from each machine.
Power Off	Shuts down each machine in the Virtual Environment. This is the equivalent of pulling the power cord out of the back of each machine; in general, do not use this method to shut down an environment.
Pause	Suspends each machine in the Virtual Environment. The state of the environment is stored, and resources the environment was using are released back to the operating system.

Because you may have created certain environments for certain uses on a project, you may want to mark that environment as "in use" so that other testers or developers do not use the environment. To do this, in the upper-right corner of the Environments page, select the In Use drop-down (Figure 8-7).

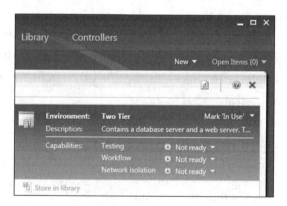

FIGURE 8-7: Mark 'In Use'

It does not lock the environment, but other users who may want to use it will be alerted that someone is already using it.

Finishing Virtual Environment Configuration

Before starting any types of builds, you need to finish the configuration of the Virtual Environment. This is actually a post-setup configuration done by the test team. To that end following are three critical tips:

1. Be sure to install any software needed for the deployment of applications before taking any snapshots.
2. Always take a snapshot of the Virtual Environment in its base state—that is, before you have made any changes to it and while it is in the Off state.
3. Always take a snapshot of the Virtual Environment in the running state with the account running the Test Agent as the logged on user.

Why these recommendations? The first recommendation is required, if, for example, you use MS Deploy to deploy applications. If you use Windows Installer XML (WIX) to create an MSI package, this is not necessary because Windows can execute an MSI package with no additional software, so it depends on your deployment mechanism.

The second recommendation simply enables you to go back to the base machine and change settings such as the amount of memory used, which cannot be done while the machine is in a running state or has been a snapshot in a running state.

WHAT IS A SNAPSHOT

If you are unfamiliar with VMs, a snapshot is what it sounds like; it is the VM as it exists at a given point in time. The power of snapshots is that you can roll back to that point in time, you can take multiple snapshots, or you can delete snapshots. You see snapshots discussed frequently throughout this chapter.

The third recommendation seems a bit odd because it violates one of the reasons for taking the first snapshot. This is an issue of configuration and speed. To run Coded UI Tests, you must be logged on as the account under which the TFS Test service runs. Taking a snapshot at this point means you don't need to log on. Another benefit is that when the environment runs and you roll back to that running snapshot, the environment does not need to spool up again; it simply resumes where it last was. This makes your testing process that much faster.

The first step is to configure the machine that will be executing the tests, for this example the Webserver (App Tier) server. Connect to the Virtual Environment which will open the Environment Viewer (see Figure 8-8).

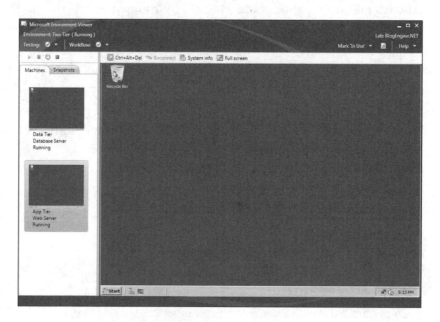

FIGURE 8-8: Microsoft Environment Viewer

In Figure 8-8, you can see both machines that have been logged onto. First, configure the Test Agent on the App Tier to run in interactive mode rather than as a service. Configure this according to the instructions in Chapter 7, "Executing Automated Test Cases." Then log onto the machine as the account that the Test Agent runs under.

Next, on the machine that is going to run the tests, if you test a Web Application that must work with Internet Explorer, make the updates as outlined in Chapter 7. Then shut down the environment and take two snapshots: the base and a running snapshot. Exercise 8-2 walks you through this process.

▪ EXERCISE 8-2

Snapshot of an Environment

To take a base and running snapshot of your environment, follow these steps:

1. In the Environment Viewer, click the Shut Down Environment button above the Machines and Snapshot tabs.

2. When all the machines in the environment have shut down, select the Snapshots tab.

3. Click the Take Snapshot button and name the snapshot **<environ-ment> (Base – Off)**.

   You do not need to give it this name, but it is worthwhile to come up with a standard naming convention as you will see when running an automated deployment.

4. Switch to the Machines tab, and restart the environment. (Make sure that all capabilities are running.)

5. Log on to the Web Server VM.

6. Switch to the Snapshots tab, and click Take snapshot.

7. Name this **<environment> (Base – Running)**.

At the end of the steps in Exercise 8-2, you should see something similar to Figure 8-9.

FIGURE 8-9: Snapshot tab of the Environment Viewer

On the Snapshot tab, you have a number of options to manage your snapshots. You can take a new snapshot, rename a snapshot, delete a snapshot, revert to the previous snapshot, or restore to a specifically selected snapshot. Another option discussed in the section "Manual Tests in a Virtual Environment" is sharing a snapshot that enables some easy troubleshooting of failed tests. If you are not familiar with Hyper-V, the Now node indicates the snapshot that the current state of the VM started from. In other words, the current state is the point in time at which the snapshot was taken plus any additional actions up to now. And the tree structure is not by accident; you can have a complex tree with different branches to meet a variety of needs. For example, looking at Figure 8-9, you could select the Two Tier (Base–Off) node and select Restore to Selected Snapshot, and you would end up with the situation shown in Figure 8-10.

FIGURE 8-10: Restored to a previous snapshot

At this point, the machine may or may not be running, but the Two Tier (Base–Running) snapshot is not affected by anything that happens at the moment because the base snapshot that the machine is running off of is the Two Tier (Base–Off) snapshot.

As a rule, because this can get complicated—even for people who know Hyper-V well, following are a few simple, recommend guidelines:

- If the tree is complicated, create additional Virtual Environments; it takes up only a little more space than numerous snapshots and is easier to navigate.

- Try to keep only three levels deep to the tree: the base (off), the base (running), and a snapshot for each build, and deploy to the Virtual Environment. There is a performance impact when you have large numbers of snapshots.
- Perform maintenance on the snapshots as you would for any environment, and remove unnecessary snapshots.

For the purposes of this chapter, everything depends on the Two Tier (Base–Running) snapshot.

Automated Test Settings

Before creating the lab build, you need to create the automated test settings (which are referenced during the lab build creation process). In MTM, select the Lab Center, Test Settings tab, and select New. Creating the test settings for automated tests is virtually identical to doing it for manual tests with one basic difference and a few more options. The first and most obvious difference is that you need to select Automated instead of Manual from the type of tests you want to run. The second difference appears on the Roles tab, as shown in Figure 8-11.

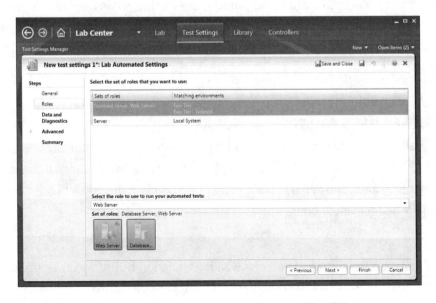

FIGURE 8-11: Roles tab of the automated test settings creation dialog

Here you can select the type of roles to execute the tests. Roles are things such as a database server or client or application server, or some other type of environment. The environments that match the required roles display. (Physical environments are also shown.) After you select the type of role for the automated settings, you have the option to choose any environment that matches the role (in the Test Plan properties, Automated Settings, Environment selection). The other key item, which was briefly noted in Chapter 7, is that you must select which role will execute the tests. In this case the tests will be executed from the Web Server role. The last difference, which was also noted in Chapter 7, is the Advanced page that enables you to execute scripts and select other items related to automated tests.

The last thing to take care of is to set the automated test settings for the Test Plan. In the situation in which you use the lab build template, you must set the environment to a Virtual Environment; otherwise, key options from the lab build will be unavailable to you, which defeat the purpose of using the lab build template. For this demonstration, the settings are Lab Automated Settings, and the environment is Two Tier.

Lab Management Workflow

Chapter 7 mentioned the need for automated builds in relationship to automated tests. Without automated builds, the testing tools don't know where the code that automates the test is located. So the assumption at this point is that you have an automated build. After you have an automated build, you can use a lab build.

OTHER USES FOR THE LAB WORKFLOW

In addition to using the Lab Management workflow to run automated tests, it can also be used as a build and deploy mechanism. In this usage the code would be built and deployed to a Virtual Environment; then testers can manually test the latest build.

For every Team Project you create, a folder called BuildProcessTemplates is added to source control. You can view this through the Source Control Explorer in Visual Studio. (Workflows cannot be edited in MTM.) This folder contains three build templates: DefaultTemplate.xaml, LabDefaultTemplate.xaml, and UpgradeTemplate.xaml. These are the Workflow (WF) 4.0 build definitions. You can reuse workflows as needed and simply supply different data. Double-clicking any file shows you the workflow (see Figure 8-12).

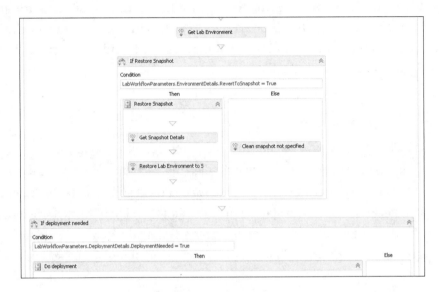

FIGURE 8-12: Partial view of the LabDefault template workflow

As you can see from the partial view shown in Figure 8-12, the flow through the process is straightforward to read but can be long. (The entire workflow could not fit readably onto two full pages in this book.) As you can see in this figure, part of the lab workflow enables you to roll back to a previous snapshot and then deploy your application.

Before covering the specific steps for using the lab workflow, look at the many workflow activities available out-of-the-box. Double-click any workflow definition file and view the Toolbox in Visual Studio. You can find more information on Windows Workflow 4.0 at http://msdn.microsoft.com/en-us/library/dd489396(VS.100).aspx.

Many options specifically handle builds and lab management. This list does not include the standard WF 4.0 activities. You can trace many of these activities back to the lab template that you will see now. In addition, you can also create your own activities. (Find more information on this at http://blogs.msdn.com/b/jimlamb/archive/2009/11/18/how-to-create-a-custom-workflow-activity-for-tfs-build-2010.aspx.)

For the purposes of this section, the BlogEngine.NET already exists. The actual creation of the Lab build is shown next. Open Visual Studio, and go to Team Explorer. Expand the Team Project, and right-click the Build node. Select New Build definition. Creating the build settings is the same for any build until you change the process template. On the Process tab, click the Show Details button next to DefaultTemplate.xaml, and select the LabDefaultTemplate.xaml from the list.

USING THE BUILT-IN TEMPLATES

The built-in templates have been thoroughly tested, so you should use them. Just don't change them. In this walkthrough the default templates are used but you need to branch them or otherwise copy them so that other builds in this Team Project can also start from the original version of these files and make changes as needed. If everyone starts editing the default templates, eventually (sooner rather than later) teams will start stepping on each other.

After you select the LabDefaultTemplate.xaml, the Process tab changes (see Figure 8-13).

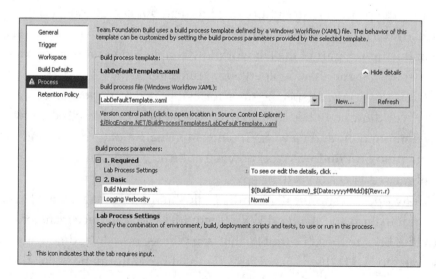

FIGURE 8-13: Process tab after selecting LabDefaultTemplate.xaml

Clicking in the Lab Process Settings gives you access to an ellipsis that brings up a lab-specific set of build options. These screens are covered in detail here. Figure 8-14 shows the Environment screen.

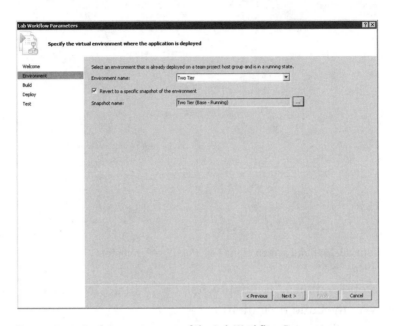

FIGURE 8-14: Environment screen of the Lab Workflow Parameters

You must select the specific environment in which the tests will be executed. (If you choose to execute them, you might also choose to just deploy to this environment.) The environment must already be deployed and running. The one option here to revert to a specific snapshot is one that is highly recommended. By starting with a known configuration, when issues are discovered it is easier to reproduce the issue. Select Next to move to the Build screen (Figure 8-15).

This screen lets you choose which build the tests will actually be executed against. The default is to create a new build (as shown in Figure 8-15). Another option is to use an existing build for the selected build definition. If the build definition is stable, selecting this option saves you the time of executing a whole new build. The amount of time you save is based on the amount of time it takes to complete the build, which can be from minutes to hours, so this is project-specific. If the build definition builds multiple configurations, select which configuration to actually deploy and test.

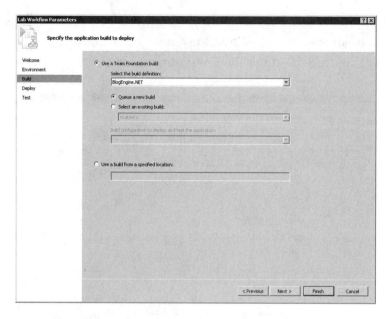

FIGURE 8-15: Build screen of the Lab Workflow Parameters

The second option is to simply point to a build in a specific location (regardless of the build definition).

Figure 8-16 shows the Deploy screen.

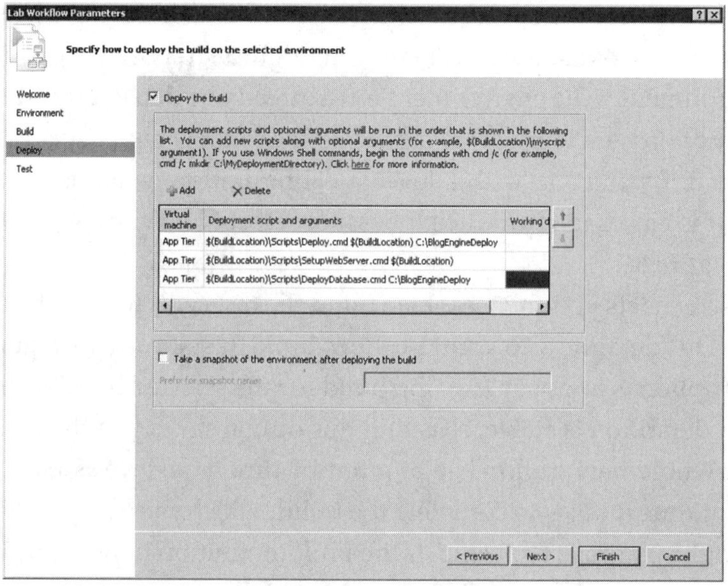

FIGURE 8-16: Deploy screen of the Lab Workflow Parameters

After you select the option to Deploy the build, you can provide pointers to scripts that execute to perform this deployment. Deploying applications via scripts is actually simple in Visual Studio 2010. In Figure 8-16 you can see three listed scripts: Deploy.cmd, SetupWebServer.cmd, and DeployDatabase.cmd. Two good options for creating these scripts are PowerShell or the Windows Shell command line. PowerShell provides the most options. The command line is used for this walkthrough. Also, although this deployment has been broken up into three scripts, these can all be in one script. You will probably like the granularity and reusability of scripts. Look at each of these scripts, starting with the Deploy.cmd script in Listing 8-1. (Line numbers are added for clarity.)

LISTING 8-1: Deploy.cmd Deployment Script

```
 1  set RemotePath=%1
 2  set LocalPath=%2
 3  if not exist %RemotePath% (
 4      echo remote path %RemotePath% doesn't exist
 5      goto Error
 6  )
 7  if exist %LocalPath% (
 8      rmdir /s /q %LocalPath%
 9  )
10  mkdir %LocalPath%
11  xcopy %RemotePath% %LocalPath% /s /y
12  @echo Copied the build locally
13  :Success
14  echo Deploy succeeded
15  exit /b 0
16  :Error
17  echo Deploy failed
18  exit /b 1
```

The first two lines simply assign the command line arguments to variables. The deployment script is passed two values: $(BuildLocation) (anything surrounded by a $(...) is called a macro) and C:\BlogEngineDeploy. Table 8-2 describes the available macros. This is the first critical item when constructing these scripts—the scripts are executed on the machine that you specify as the role that runs the automated tests (set when you create the automated test configuration settings). So, in this file the RemotePath points to the build machine, and the LocalPath points to the role that executes the tests.

TABLE 8-2: Macros and Their Descriptions

Macro	Description
$(BuildLocation)	The location of the build output or the specific directory selected if you chose to use an existing build.
$(InternalComputerName_ <VMName>	The name of the machine that you are referring to. In this chapter you have been using two systems: DataServer and WebServer. To reference them you use $(InternalComputerName_WebServer) or $(InternalComputerName_Dataserver).
$(ComputerName_<VMName>	The fully qualified domain name (FQDN) of the machine (for example webserver.demo.local). The reason for a second computer name macro is to support isolated environments. Isolated environments have one reference name when working inside the environment but communicate outside of the environment via the FQDN. How you reference the names depends on where the script that uses this macro is executed.

The next block of script (lines 3–6) check to see that the build location actually exists (and that you have permission to it) and if it doesn't, it throws an exception. It exits with a 1 (line 18). This triggers the build to fail and stops the execution of subsequent scripts.

Lines 7–10 check to see if the path provided (in this case C:\BlogEngineDeploy) exists on the VM. If it does, it deletes the folder and then re-creates it. Line 11 copies the entire contents of the build location to the VM. This is not necessary; you can simply copy only the files needed, which simplifies the script.

When the necessary files are on the VM, it's time to run the next script: SetupWebServer.cmd, as shown in Listing 8-2.

LISTING 8-2: SetupWebServer.cmd

```
1 %windir%\System32\inetsrv\appcmd add site /name:"BlogEngineWeb" /id:2
    /bindings:http://*:8001 /physicalPath:"C:\inetpub\wwwroot\BlogEngineWeb"
2 cmd /c %1\_PublishedWebsites\Package\BlogEngineWeb.deploy.cmd /Y %2
3 iisreset
```

Line 1 of the SetupWebServer script invokes the appcmd command-line tool (this is an IIS-specific command-line tool) to actually create the BlogEngineWeb site, set the appropriate bindings, and create the physical path where this site points to. You can find more information on this tool at http://technet.microsoft.com/en-us/library/cc772200(WS.10).aspx. There are many more options to appcmd, and if you haven't used it before, it can be a big help. Line 2 performs a neat trick; it executes the MSDeploy engine. You learned in the section on configuring the VM environment that you need to install any applications that are a prerequisite to installing your application. In this case MSDeploy is installed on the web server. The end result of this deployment is that the website content has been deployed to the physical directory, and all virtual directory settings have been set based on the BlogEngineWeb project. You can find more information on MSDeploy at http://blogs.iis.net/msdeploy/.

The last script, DeployDatabase.cmd does the actual work of deploying the database, which is shown in Listing 8-3. (Line breaks are for formatting purposes.)

LISTING 8-3: DeployDatabase.cmd

```
1 "C:\Program Files (x86)\Microsoft Visual Studio 10.0\VSTSDB\Deploy\vsdbcmd"
   /a:Deploy /dd+ /dsp:sql /model:%1\SharedDBServer.dbschema
   /manifest:%1\SharedDBServer.deploymanifest /p:TargetDatabase="master"
   /cs:"Server=%2;uid=SA;pwd=P@ssw0rd"
2 "C:\Program Files (x86)\Microsoft Visual Studio
10.0\VSTSDB\Deploy\vsdbcmd"
   /a:Deploy /dd+ /dsp:sql /model:%1\BlogEngineData.dbschema
   /manifest:%1\BlogEngineData.deploymanifest
   /p:TargetDatabase="BlogEngineData"
   /cs:"Server=%2;uid=SA;pwd=P@ssw0rd"
```

This script deploys the logins and other security associated with the BlogEngine.NET database; then the actual database is deployed. The usernames and passwords listed here are for the database on the Data Server VM. You could just as easily set this to integrated authentication and give the account that the test is running under the appropriate rights to the database server. This deployment script is made possible through the use of the Database Project in Visual Studio that simplifies deployments of any databases. The vsdbcmd command-line tool is installed with the build agent and does not need to be installed separately. The first command-line argument provides the path to the files, and the second argument provides the name of the database server to connect to.

One option you have is running different scripts on different machines. The first column of the script list enables you to select which machine the script is executed on, so many different scripts can be executed on many different machines. The limit is only your imagination.

So where do these scripts come from? They are part of the actual project and placed in a Scripts folder with the action set to Copy Always. These scripts can be part of the test project as well or even a separate project included as part of the build—it's up to you. The recommended method for doing this though is to version them as part of the actual project because they reference information contained in the project (such as the database project names and related information).

The final option on this screen is taking a snapshot after the deployment, which is highly recommended. The reason for this is because if a test fails, you want the developer to either re-execute the test or manually walk through the test on the machine starting in the state that it was in after the application was deployed but before any of the tests executed.

The last screen contains the testing options, as shown in Figure 8-17.

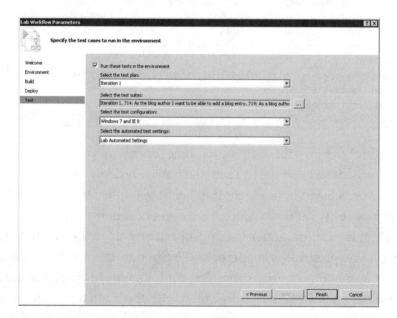

FIGURE 8-17: Test screen of the Lab Workflow Parameters

This screen enables you to select your test plan, tests to execute, test configuration, and the automated settings. The biggest gotcha here is making sure the automated test settings are created first. If you forget to create them, you will not have any options available to you in the final drop-down, and the tests will not execute. (You can save this build definition, create the test settings, and then come back and update the definition.) The settings here are self-explanatory. When you finish, click Finish and save the build.

Executing a Lab Build

When you execute the build, assuming everything is set up correctly, it just runs and executes the tests specified. That's it. No drama, no fuss, no muss. Okay, the reality is that the first time you go to execute any lab build you may have a lot of failed builds. You could get the paths and the filenames wrong or forget to set a value on the server for setup or to include the test data. You could forget many things when you do the first run. Don't worry. The builds execute rather quickly, and the following suggestions can help you avoid wasted time:

- Don't revert to a snapshot when you first execute your tests; manually do this outside of the environment because your first few attempts may not be successful—why waste the time of a restore?
- Don't take snapshots after the deployment until you get the build working correctly; it just wastes time with snapshots that most likely don't have the application deployed correctly.
- If you deploy a database, make sure the database server is configured correctly and that the usernames and passwords you provide are valid.
- As a corollary to the previous point, make sure you set the right username and password in the script executed by vsdbcmd or pass them in as a parameter to the script.
- Validate that you have passed the correct parameters to all the scripts.
- Make sure that all the Coded UI Tests pass on the machine on which they are created.

Figure 8-18 shows a completed lab build.

Figure 8-18: Completed Lab Management build

This build report is a bit different compared to a normal build report. First, selecting View Log opens the log for the lab build, not the application build. To view that log you need to select View Summary under the Compilation heading. You can also directly open the post deployment snapshot by clicking the link; you need to have MTM installed for this to work. Otherwise this report is the same as any other build report except that the test results shown here are not reported to TFS as part of the build. (But the results are published against that particular build number, and their results are available for reporting on.) That means that these results will not show up on the Build Success over Time report.

You can watch the tests execute by connecting to the server on which the tests are run during the build, but the usual rule applies: Don't play with anything while the test runs.

SERVER NAMES

Pay special attention to server names, especially when dealing with web applications. To make life easier, record the manual tests against a web server in the virtual environment against which the tests will be executed. This way the correct server name is recorded and output as part of the Coded UI test. If you forget to do this, do a search and replace in the .uitest file to replace the server name with the correct name.

Running Automated Tests Through MTM

After a build deploys to a Virtual Environment, running automated tests against the build is trivial. At this point, you have already created the automated run settings because they were required for the lab build. So it is simply a matter of updating the build that you run against. Remember that the build you run against serves two purposes: The first is from a reporting perspective so that you know the outcome of the tests, and the second is to locate the test assemblies.

DUAL PURPOSE BUILDS

In MTM the builds serve a dual purpose, which means you may need to make some adjustments to how you handle application code and test code. For now, this code must be tied together; that is, when you revise the test code, you must also rebuild the application code. They cannot move independently of one another, even though the test code can be executed against a different version of the application code. The critical report—which tests worked against which build—is what counts to the end users, so create your strategy around that notion.

To perform an automated run in MTM, make sure that the Virtual Environment is running, select the automated tests you want to execute, and click Run. This uses the automated test settings and performs the execution of the tests in the Virtual Environment, enabling you to work on other items. At this point, as with executing the build, it is all fairly well done for you.

SPEED UP YOUR TESTING

Adding lots of diagnostic data adapters to gather information takes time. It is worthwhile to keep multiple sets of automated (and maybe even manual) settings that you can use as needed. For example, one set may collect virtually no information (no IntelliTrace, no video recording, nothing) and another may gather detailed diagnostics because a bug was found in an earlier test run, and you need more data for the developer.

When the tests finish running, you can view them in the Analyze Test Runs page of the Test tab. Here you can drill into and see the results of the test and take the appropriate action (file bugs, grab environment snapshots—more on that in a moment—update the Failure Analysis, and add other comments).

Manual Tests in a Virtual Environment

Microsoft Test Manager and Lab Management have one last trick up their collective sleeve—handling manual test execution in a Virtual Environment. MTM does not need to be installed on the VM, although this is definitely beneficial because not having MTM installed means that you cannot record an action log.

WHY MANUAL TESTING IN A VIRTUAL ENVIRONMENT

This model provides many benefits. First, you can start up a VM with a build and let the user play with the application. Second, user acceptance testing can be done in an entirely controlled environment so that any bugs found can be more easily reproduced. Finally, performing manual testing in a Virtual Environment simply requires that the application be installed on the Virtual Environment. No builds or lab builds need to be created. (You should use automated builds, but the deployment does not need to be automated.)

To set up manual testing in a Virtual Environment from outside of the environment, create a new set of test settings, and on the Roles tab, select the Virtual Environment configuration you want (see Figure 8-19).

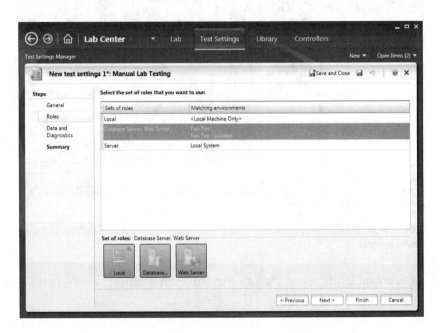

Figure 8-19: Configuring manual test settings in a lab environment

On the Data and Diagnostics tab, the one missing item is the ability to record an action log, although you still have the ability to gather other data and diagnostics.

GATHERING DIAGNOSTIC DATA

On the Data and Diagnostics tab, you can set different diagnostics to be run *for each machine in the environment.*

On the Test Plan Properties page, you can then select the test settings you created and an environment that matches the specified roles. When you start the test, Test Runner pops up next to the Virtual Environment viewer, as shown in Figure 8-20.

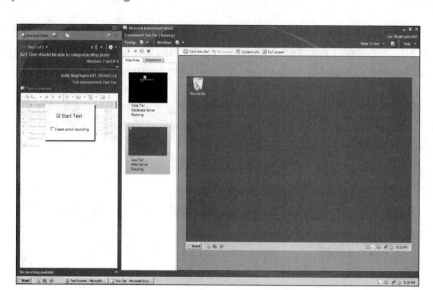

FIGURE 8-20: Manual testing in a Virtual Environment (MTM outside of the Virtual Environment)

This is a quick-and-easy way to run through manual tests when you do not have to record test steps.

When running manual tests in a Virtual Environment, you have the ability to snapshot the environment and have that snapshot automatically attached to a bug created during the test run. (You can also attach a snapshot to any work item at any time if you want.) To do this you would fail the test step, select the Snapshot Environment button (third from the right on the Test Runner toolbar) that not only snapshots the environment but also attaches the snapshot link (a .lvr file that stands for Lab Viewer) and then create the bug. Figure 8-21 shows the Repro Steps section of a bug created in this environment. To attach a snapshot to a work item at any time, select the Snapshots tab in the Microsoft Environment Viewer, select the snapshot you want to share, and click the Share snapshot button located directly above the list of snapshots. This creates a .lvr file that you can save to the machine and then add as a file attachment to any work item.

Two things are different about this particular set of steps: First, on step 5, there is a .lvr attachment. Clicking this opens the Microsoft Environment Viewer window and loads the snapshot this is associated with. There is one important warning here. When you click the link, Figure 8-22 appears.

FIGURE 8-21: Repro steps of a bug filed on a VM

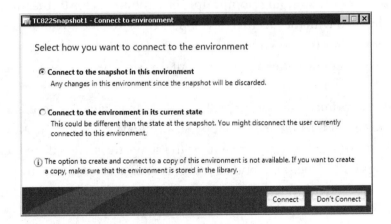

FIGURE 8-22: Connect to environment dialog

If you simply select Connect to the snapshot in this environment, whoever is working in this environment and has not made a snapshot of the environment will lose their work! You should put in place a process to make sure this does not inadvertently happen.

Second, data was captured from both agents.

The ability to execute manual tests in a controlled environment according to a set of scripts opens up several possibilities for managing software acceptance. Users can test the latest builds of software without impacting their day-to-day work and provide fast feedback to the team. Acceptance testing can also be performed in a controlled environment so that when a customer finds a problem it can be easily diagnosed.

SUMMARY

Whether you need a single machine or an entire farm of VMs, Lab Management provides an infrastructure to meet your testing and development needs. Regardless of whether you do only manual testing or a mix of manual and automated testing, Lab Management can create an environment that closely mimics your production environment at a fraction of the cost of physical machines.

Based on the value proposition of Lab Management, virtualization is the future of testing. Not only does it provide a huge cost savings from an infrastructure and maintenance perspective, but also from the time savings of quickly and easily spinning up multiple environments for test teams of any size. Combined with the fact that developers can also take advantage of these environments for their own development purposes or for testing purposes, Lab Management provides a powerful but easy-to-use solution for the entire team.

And, the primary reason for using Lab Management is to ensure that when a tester finds a bug, the developers can always reproduce it. Now there is no question. The environment will be the same, the state will be the same, the settings will be the same, and so will everything else because the machine the developers reproduce the bug on is the machine that the bug was found on!

■ 9 ■

Reporting and Metrics

T HIS BOOK PRESENTS YOU WITH the process of testing using the tools
provided by Visual Studio and Team Foundation Server 2010. Chapter 1,
"State of Testing," mentioned that metrics were one of the most important
items to come out of testing because without metrics, you can't prove, *or
improve*, quality. This chapter teaches you about the reporting capabilities of
Visual Studio and Team Foundation Server with a look at several different
aspects of reporting. The chapter concludes with a specific look at metrics:
what are good metrics, how you record them, and what actions you should
take based on them.

TFS includes a number of different mechanisms to make data available to
you, but at its core you report off of a SQL Server Analysis Services (SSAS)
data cube (described in the following section) through a number of different
user interfaces. These interfaces include SQL Server Reporting Services
(SSRS), Excel, and Excel Services (through Microsoft Office SharePoint Server
[MOSS]). You can also use PerformancePoint, PowerPivot, SQL Server Report
Builder, and Visio. Although all these interfaces are not covered, you learn
about the basic mechanics and see many examples that should provide guid-
ance when creating your own reports.

Understanding the Reporting Structure

Before discussing the details of the reports and data, you need to understand how the data is stored and transformed and some of the ramifications. Figure 9-1 shows the databases that the data passes through to get to the data cube.

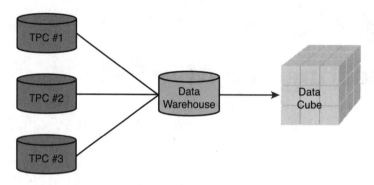

FIGURE 9-1: TFS data repositories

Team Project Collections (TPCs) are housed in individual databases in SQL Server. Every time a user makes a change to anything in TFS (work items, version control, test results, and so on) the changes are transformed and transferred to the Data Warehouse, which is a separate SQL Server relational database. Each TFS instance has one data warehouse. From here, every 2 hours (by default) the data is loaded into the SQL Server Analysis Services cube. The structure of these databases is beyond the scope of this book, but you can find additional information here:

- Relational Warehouse: http://msdn.microsoft.com/en-us/library/ms244691.aspx
- Analysis Services Cube: http://msdn.microsoft.com/en-us/library/ms244710.aspx

The cube is structured in *dimensions* and *measures*. Figure 9-2 shows this view.

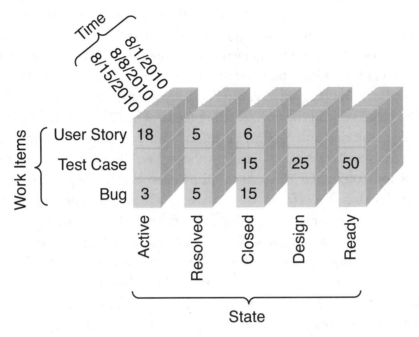

FIGURE 9-2: Visualizing the data cube

Figure 9-2 is a simplistic view of a cube but is illustrative of the structure. The Work items, State items, and Time items are dimensions. The values contained at the intersection of the dimensions are the measures. Looking at this cube, you can see that on August 15, 2010, there were three Active Bugs. Dimensions can be hierarchical. For example, here the Time dimension is represented in weeks, but you can navigate up the hierarchy to group information by Month, Quarter, or Year as well or navigate down to the specific date. Having this basic information it is helpful to examine another example. If you were to query the total number of work items, the value would be 142. Diving into a specific work item, say the Test Case work item, would lower that number to 90. Further querying on just the work items in the Design state would give you the value 25. Adding the date dimension would further reduce this number. In this way you can easily drill into specific information or view the information at any level.

When data is transferred from the TPC databases to the data warehouse, *time* is stripped out, which means that data based on date fields can be calculated for only full days and not hourly intervals. There is a good reason for this; to incorporate time as a dimension, there would have to be additional values for every minute or hour for every day of the year including a hierarchy. This has a negative impact on the performance of the cube. So, if you do need to report on time, you need to do it from the TPCs directly. There are other options, but they are advanced and beyond the scope of this book.

The cube is one of the most exciting features in TFS. Without the data it provides (historical and current) the information collected on the work items and in test results is wasted. Excel provides the ability to query directly on almost any data source. This makes it the easiest way for you to get information on that data and is far easier than using SQL Server Reporting Services. One drawback to using Excel is that you can't schedule report delivery and can't create composite reports. (You can have different reports on each tab, but that isn't quite the same.) These capabilities are available in SSRS. With this understanding the rest of the chapter talks about the data contained in the database, how to get to it, and how to create custom reports. This information is especially helpful when using Excel to report on data.

Built-In Reports

A standard set of reports provided for you highlight various pieces of information about your project. These reports are SQL Server Reporting Services (SSRS) reports. Depending on your installation of SharePoint, these reports are also available as Excel Services reports. Figure 9-3 shows the out-of-the-box Test Plan Progress report.

If you are familiar with the reports provided with TFS 2005 and 2008, you can notice many helpful differences. The salient parts of the report are the following areas:

- Related reports provide links to reports that further detail or provide a different perspective on the presented data.
- Questions This Report Helps Answer provides a link at the bottom that takes you directly to the MSDN documentation describing the information each report provides and what a good or bad report looks like.
- Parameter Values lets you know what parameters were provided to generate the report so that you can always re-create the report.

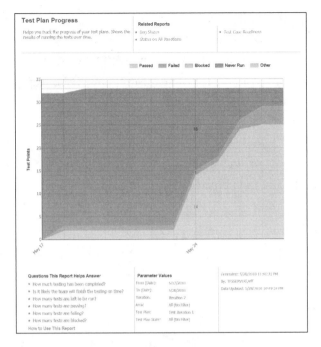

FIGURE 9-3: Test Plan Progress report

The How to Use This Report link provides the most valuable information, which isn't re-created here. Instead a few insights are provided on the trends and patterns to look for and some areas that the MSDN documentation does not cover. These reports and the additional information to consider are covered next.

SHAREPOINT VERSION AND REPORTS

Windows SharePoint Services (WSS) is the free version of SharePoint and includes dashboards composed of SSRS reports. The full version of Share-Point (Microsoft Office SharePoint Server) includes a feature called Excel Services that enables SharePoint to display data from an Excel file to the end user without the user having to open the file, as shown in Figure 9-13. The Excel Services reports, in most cases, are re-creations of the SSRS reports for use in creating custom dashboards.

Whether you use the Agile or CMMI template, the built-in reports are essentially the same. The reports related to quality are covered in some detail here. Additional information is available on the MSDN site. (Links are provided at the end of this section.) This is not an all-inclusive list of reports because the focus of this book is on providing only information about the quality reports.

Bug Status

The Bug Status report provides a timeline view of all bugs and their state over the lifetime of the bug (see Figure 9-4).

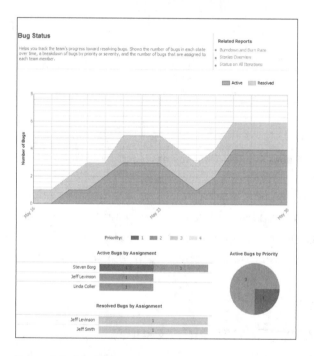

FIGURE 9-4: Bug Status report

At the beginning of a project there will be an increase in the active bug count because you are starting from no bugs at all; however, over time the number of active bugs should level off and then decrease as you approach a release. Following are a number of warning signs to look for on this report:

- Growing number of active bugs
- Bugs not being resolved

- Resolved bugs not being closed
- A large number of priority-one bugs

The last point is an important one. It is okay to ship with known bugs, but not usually with priority-one bugs still outstanding (maybe not even with priority-two bugs depending on how you classify each priority).

Another item to look for is a growing number of active bugs near the end of the iteration or the release, which are an indication that the team is struggling to get work done to meet a deadline and sacrificing quality. This is a common pattern at the end of a release cycle.

Bug Trends

The Bug Trends report provides information on the rate of arrival of new bugs and the rate of resolution and closure for existing bugs (see Figure 9-5).

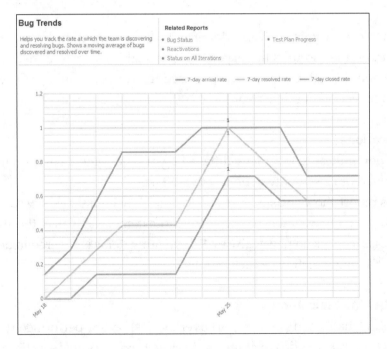

FIGURE 9-5: Bug Trends report

Notice the convergence (or rather divergence) of the trend lines. If the 7-day arrival rate is higher than the 7-day close rate, you will ship with bugs. The larger this gap is, the more problematic it will be for you. This also points to the philosophy teams use when dealing with bugs. Some teams have "bug bashes;" when the bug count gets to a certain point, they work on fixing bugs to the exclusion of all else. This is a key component of Technical Debt and can be an expensive approach to software development.

TECHNICAL DEBT

The concept of Technical Debt is not covered in this book but it is worthwhile to understand how bugs fit in with this. Technical Debt is a term coined by Ward Cunningham to describe the cost associated with not fixing problems when they occur but letting the problems build up.

Other teams (typically teams doing agile development) fix bugs and other problems as they occur. If this is your approach, this report is more important to you, and the active, resolved, and closed trend lines should be fairly close to each other and not divergent.

Reactivations

This report indicates how many times a bug or requirement has been marked as resolved or closed only to be reactivated (see Figure 9-6).

This report shows waste, pure and simple. Any item that shows up as red indicates that rework must be done. The more items reactivated, the less time a team has to work on new features. Reactivating items is covered in depth in Chapter 4, in the section "Reactivations."

Build Quality Indicators

The Build Quality Indicators report overlays test results performed during a build, code churn, code coverage, and active bugs to provide a comprehensive view of application quality over time (Figure 9-7).

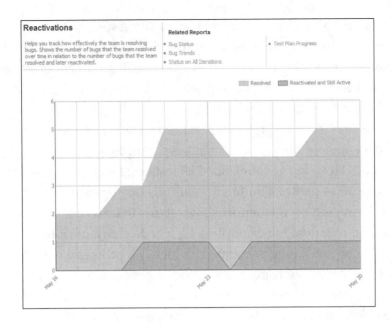

FIGURE 9-6: Reactivations report

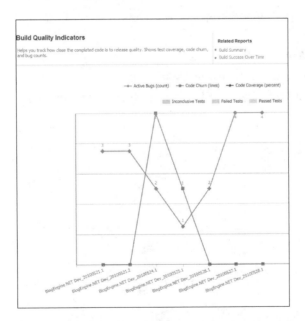

FIGURE 9-7: Build Quality Indicators report

The example shown here does not show the results of tests because no tests were run during these builds. This build report shows the lines of code that were changed for a bug fix and the corresponding number of active bugs. Over time the number of active bugs should decrease, and the code churn should decrease going into a release.

The tests that show up on this report are any tests executed during a normal build. In other words, tests executed as part of a Lab Build are not shown on this report. However, if your Coded UI tests are executed by the TFS Build service account as part of a build, those results display here as well.

The information on this report shows items that have a fairly tight and predictable correlation. For example, a high code churn most likely can lead to a smaller code coverage percentage (which is a bad sign) unless the team increases the number of tests in-line with the new and modified code. High code churn generally leads to a higher count of active bugs because of the increased likelihood of regression bugs being introduced. Over time, look at this report to show a downward trend in code churn and active bugs and an upward trend in code coverage and passing tests.

Build Success over Time

This report provides a heat map with build status, code coverage, and test result indicators for every build and platform over time (Figure 9-8).

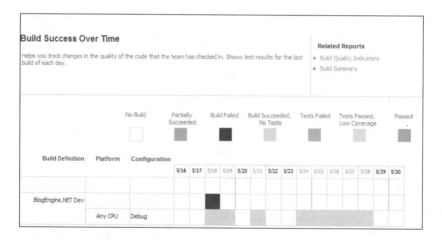

FIGURE 9-8: Build Success over Time report

Use this report to, at a glance, determine trends in your automated builds. Green and light-green are good; everything else is bad. Cases where the build passes (as in Figure 9-8) are good but that no automated testing occurs is generally something that should be rectified. In some cases this is not possible (Lab Build test results are not factored into this report) so yellow is actually a good sign.

You can drill into the Build Summary report by clicking the date link at the top of each column.

Build Summary

The Build Summary report provides the same information as the Build Success over Time report except the information is more specific with percentage of tests passed, percentage of code coverage, and actual code churn as opposed to generalities (Figure 9-9).

							Passed / Failed	Covered / Not Covered	Code Churn
Date	Build Name	Platform	Configuration	Progress	Build Quality	% Tests Passed	% Code Coverage	Code Churn (lines)
8/4/2010 8:54 PM	BlogEngine.NET_20100804.8	Any CPU	Debug	Succeeded	Ready for Initial Test	100 %		4242
8/4/2010 8:53 PM	BlogEngine.NET_20100804.7			Failed				
8/4/2010 8:45 PM	BlogEngine.NET_20100804.6			Failed				
8/4/2010 8:40 PM	BlogEngine.NET_20100804.5	Any CPU	Debug	Stopped				
8/4/2010 8:33 PM	BlogEngine.NET_20100804.4	Any CPU	Debug	Partially Succeeded				4226
8/4/2010 8:28 PM	BlogEngine.NET_20100804.3	Any CPU	Debug	Partially Succeeded				4226
8/4/2010 8:22 PM	BlogEngine.NET_20100804.2	Any CPU	Debug	Partially Succeeded				4226
8/4/2010 8:12 PM	BlogEngine.NET_20100804.1	Any CPU	Debug	Partially Succeeded				4225
6/7/2010 3:03 PM	BlogEngine.NET_20100607.3	Any CPU	TwoTierTest	Partially Succeeded				4169
6/7/2010 11:17 AM	BlogEngine.NET_20100607.2	Any CPU	TwoTierTest	Partially Succeeded				4166
	BlogEngine.NET Lab_20100607.2			Partially Succeeded				
6/7/2010 11:14 AM	BlogEngine.NET_20100607.1			Failed				
6/7/2010 11:13 AM	BlogEngine.NET Lab_20100607.1			Failed				

FIGURE 9-9: Build Summary report

The report is ordered by date with the latest builds at the top. Over time the percentage of tests passing should increase, and code churn should decrease. These builds show high code churn because the churn is calculated for each successful build, not partially successful builds. Any tests failing should be immediately addressed. As with other reports, code coverage should go up over time, and code churn should go down. One piece of information not shown on this report is the executed number of tests. For that look at the specific build log or the Build Quality Indicators report.

Stories Overview

Everything comes together on the Stories Overview report, which provides the percentage of work completed, number of hours remaining, total number of tests, test results, and bugs (and their status) for each requirement (Figure 9-10).

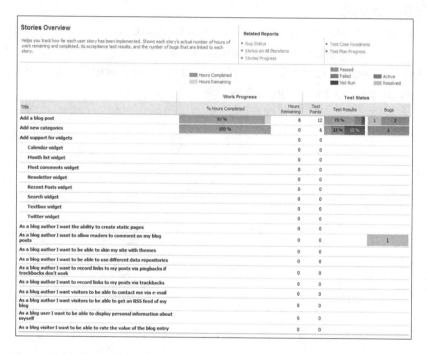

FIGURE 9-10: Stories Overview report

This is the information that customers want. Virtually all the other reports show things the team wants to know (there is value in customers knowing the information shown on other reports also) but this report speaks to the customers' requirements and the quality of those requirements. If I am a customer, I am monitoring this report. In particular it tells a customer how close to completion the team is, whether the requirement has a sufficient number of Test Cases, and if those Test Cases have been executed. For any bugs related to a requirement, this provides the status for those as well. This report combined with the Bug Status report gives a customer enough information to make a decision about the readiness of a feature for release. And because this is important to the customer, it is also important for the team to monitor because this is the visibility of your progress.

Test Case Readiness

The Test Case Readiness report indicates the number of Test Cases and the state they are in (Figure 9-11).

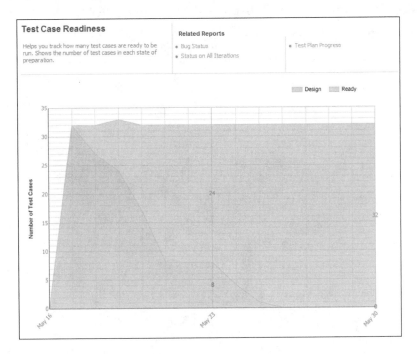

FIGURE 9-11: Test Case Readiness report

This report provides only general information. Remember to scope it to the right level (iteration or date range) but use it only as a guide. Test cases can also be executed in the design state, so this isn't necessarily indicative of whether the tests can be executed. (Although it can be inferred that any Test Cases that are Ready can be.)

What you should look for in this report is simple: The number of Test Cases in the Design state is dropping, and the number of Test Cases in the Ready state is increasing. One trend to watch for is the number of Test Cases increasing in any given period of time, which means that the iteration began without a good understanding of the acceptance criteria or that the team is working on writing code first without understanding how the features will be validated. This can be a dangerous situation that can lead to more bugs, not fewer bugs.

Test Plan Progress

The Test Plan Progress report displays the state of all Test Cases and results for one or more of the Test Plans (see Figure 9-12).

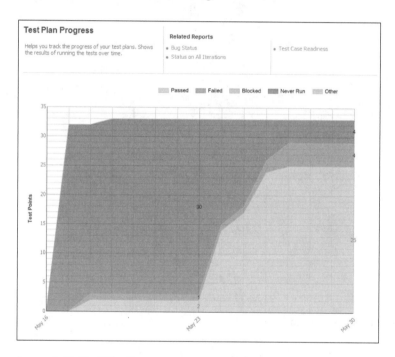

FIGURE 9-12: Test Plan Progress report

The information on this report is straightforward. You want to see a steadily decreasing number of Test Cases that have Never Run and a steadily increasing number of Passed Test Cases. Where you see Failed tests, there should be only a narrow band of failed tests. If the number of failed tests starts growing, you need to ensure that the bugs created from the failures are fixed quickly.

A growing number of failed tests indicate that you are in danger of shipping bugs. However, remember that it is the type of bug you ship that is critical, so use this report with the Bug Status report to ensure that the failures are something that the team needs to immediately work on. By itself this report can be misleading.

You can find more information on these reports on the Microsoft Developer Network (MSDN) documentation site:

- MSF for Agile v5.0: http://msdn.microsoft.com/en-us/library/dd380714(v=VS.100).aspx
- MSF for CMMI v5.0: http://msdn.microsoft.com/en-us/library/ee332487(v=VS.100).aspx

MSDN DOCUMENTATION

In past releases of Visual Studio and Team Foundation Server, the documentation was not complete; it didn't provide much key process information. In the 2010 release, however, the MSDN team completely revised the documentation, and the value of that documentation is fantastic. Included in the documentation are examples of good and bad reports, and the data required to "light up" the report. (The reports are shown as well; this is another new change, showing screenshots.)

Excel Services Reports (Dashboards)

The Excel Services reports largely follow the built-in SSRS reports except they are broken into smaller chunks because you can have only one graph per Excel Services report. An example of an Excel Services dashboard is shown in Figure 9-13.

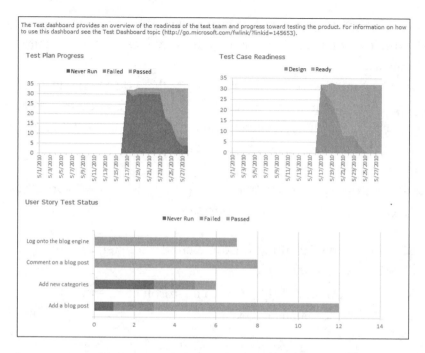

FIGURE 9-13: Partial view of the test dashboard (Agile template)

All the information from the related SSRS reports is shown on this dashboard. One difference between the dashboard and the SSRS reports is that you cannot set the filters without editing the Excel spreadsheet that these are based on. For that reason, using the dashboards is a starting point and drilling into additional data may be necessary. Because the dashboards are built from individual Excel graphs, building the individual graphs that make up the dashboards is the focus here.

Reporting with Microsoft Excel

Now that you have seen some of the built-in reports, it is time to create your own. Although you can build SSRS reports, they require a bit more work than building the reports with Excel. This section teaches you how to use Excel to quickly get to the data in the correct format. Excel is the primary means by which you create reports on the data stored in TFS. You can create these reports in two ways: have Visual Studio generate them for you and create them manually. In many cases starting with a generated report and then augmenting it is a good idea because the generated report takes care of several details.

Creating a Generated Report

You can generate reports through the results of a work item query in Visual Studio. Exercise 9-1 walks you through the basic steps. This works only with Flat queries and not with Directed Links or Tree queries.

■ **EXERCISE 9-1**

Generating Reports from a Work Item Query

The available types of graphs are based on the columns returned by the query. Selecting different columns can yield additional options.

1. Open Visual Studio 2010.

2. Expand the Work Items node for any team project.

3. Execute any flat work item query.

4. On the query results toolbar, select Open In Microsoft Office, and select Create Report in Microsoft Excel.

   At this point, Excel opens and you are prompted with the New Work Item Report dialog (see Figure 9-14).

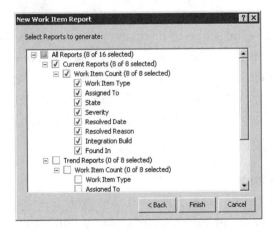

FIGURE 9-14: New Work Item Report dialog

5. Select one or more Current and Trend reports to create, and click Finish.

One graph from the generated report is shown in Figure 9-15.

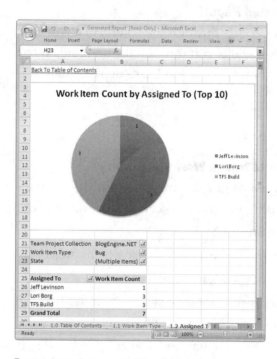

FIGURE 9-15: A generated Excel Report

At the bottom of Figure 9-15, a series of filters have been automatically created that narrow the scope of the query, and the fields that display have been created. At this point you can easily expand the scope of the query, narrow it down further, or just change it to fit your needs. This provides a head start for developing queries in Excel. Before creating your own reports in Excel, you need to understand one additional piece of information: Test Measures.

The Testing Measures

You will experience four testing measures in your test reporting endeavors: result count, result count trend, build result count trend, and point count trend. Selecting the wrong measure can result in data that looks valid but is not, so you need to understand what these measures are and how they manifest themselves. This applies to any reporting done from the cube. Table 9-1 defines these terms. The basic concept to understand is that the term *point* refers to a point in time. The term *trend* refers to data over time, and the absence of either of these terms refers to the current state.

TABLE 9-1: Test Measures Defined

Measure	Description
Point Count Trend	Provides a history of test outcomes and provides the latest result for each test point
Result Count	Shows the sum of all test results
Result Count Trend	Provides a history of test results over time
Build Result Count Trend	Provides the result count broken down by build
Result Transition Count	Shows results that have changed the outcome from one run to the next

With this understanding, Exercise 9-2 shows you how to create a Pivot Table report from scratch.

■ EXERCISE 9-2

Creating the Test Cases to User Stories Report

The data contained in this report is available to you in the Stories Overview report and also on an Excel Services report (the User Story Test Status shown in Figure 9-13) but this report can serve as the starting point for more detailed information that isn't available on those reports.

This exercise assumes that you use Excel 2007 or 2010. This works with Excel 2003, but the menu locations are different.

1. Open Microsoft Excel.
2. Select the Data tab, and choose From Other Sources, From Analysis Services.

3. In the Data Connection Wizard, enter the server name and click Next.

4. Depending on your version of SQL Server, you may see different items listed; select the database (Tfs_Analysis by default) and the Team System cube, and click Next.

5. After entering a description (optional) click Finish.

6. Click OK on the Data Import dialog. This displays the screen shown in Figure 9-16.

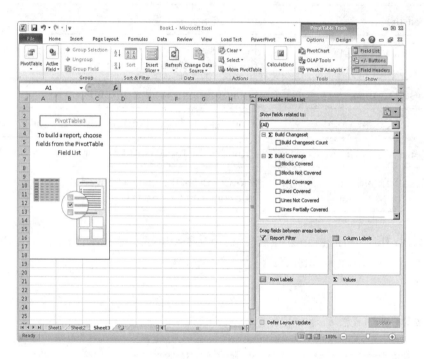

FIGURE 9-16: Excel Pivot Table reporting

7. From the Show Fields Related To (upper-right corner) select the Linked Current Work Item Test Case. This narrows your available selection to a more meaningful subset of data.

8. Scroll down this list to the Work Item Linked section, and drag the Work Item Linked.Work Item Type field to the Report Filter box below it. This places the field in the upper-left corner of the Pivot Table area (cell A1).

9. Select the drop-down in cell B2 (where it says all) and change it to either User Story or Requirement depending on the process template you are working with.

10. Next, select the Work Item Linked.Iteration Path, and drag that field to the Report Filter box as well. Set this filter to be the iteration you want to report on. (For this example, I use Iteration 2, but you can filter by Area, Team Project, or virtually anything else you want to filter on.)

11. Place a check mark in the Work Item Linked.Title field. This adds it to the Row Labels box. (You can also drag this field to the Row Labels box.)

12. Find the Test Case section in the PivotTable Field List, and check the Title field.

    This will blow out your list of fields in a way that doesn't make sense. What it does is add all Test Cases related to any User Story or Requirement to *every* user story or requirement listed. This is obviously not valid, but don't worry too much about what shows up while you are constructing the pivot table. Until you add the measures, all this is meaningless.

13. Select the Show fields related to Test.

14. Select the Point Count Trend measure from the Test measures (the Test measure has a Sigma [Σ] sign next to it) and then collapse all the requirements. (Do this by right-clicking a requirement and selecting Collapse Entire Field.)

15. Now that you have the data, you can create the graph. Select the Options Tab of the PivotTable Tools, and click PivotChart. (You need a cell selected that is part of the pivot table.)

16. Select the Stacked Bar in 3D. The results are shown in Figure 9-17.

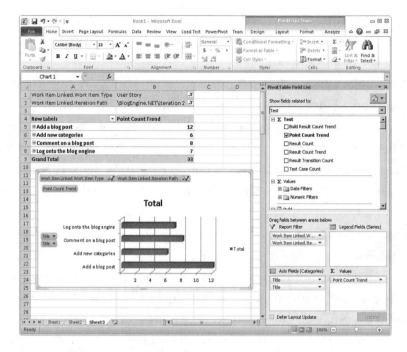

FIGURE 9-17: Test Cases with results per requirement

Now, what just happened? In this exercise you selected requirements, and then you selected Test Cases linked to requirements. When you selected the measures, the scope of that relationship was narrowed down so that you saw only Test Cases that had a result for the specific requirement that the Test Case was related to. When you start playing with the cube, there are many possibilities, and it is easy to end up with data that doesn't make sense. Always verify the information in the report the first time you create the report. In the next section there is a list of common structures that can provide a starting point for your reports.

With this basic chart, you can start adding additional information to it. For example, drag the Outcome field from the Test Results section field list to the Legend box; you get the graph shown in Figure 9-18.

This matches the current state of the test plan shown in Figure 9-13. You have many options, so included is a description of the various areas as they relate to testing and quality measures in Table 9-2. This is by no means exhaustive and obviously does not take into account any customizations you may make to the process templates.

FIGURE 9-18: Requirement test outcomes

TABLE 9-2: PivotTable Field Sections

Section	Description
Test Case	Represents a Test Case work item type. Although the Work Item section can also represent a Test Case work item type, this group of fields has specific test data associated with them. When possible, always use the fields in the Test Case section to display information on Test Case work item types.
Test Configuration	Represents the test configurations set up in Microsoft Test Manager.
Test Plan	Provides access to information on the test plan. This is usually used for grouping Test Cases and test results.
Test Result	Provides information on the result or status of a Test Case. This grouping provides information on Passed, Failed, Never Run, and so on. It also provides who executed the test that enables seeing test execution by tester.

TABLE 9-2: Continued

Section	Description
Test Run	Provides a more granular breakdown of the information in the Test Plan section.
Test Suite	Provides information for each suite in a test plan.
Work Item Linked	Enables access to work items linked to Test Cases. (In this particular case, although you can use it to provide information on any linked work items.) This enables you to discover if, for example, a Test Case failed and no associated bug was filed or to discover if multiple bugs were filed against the same test failure.

The graphs shown in Figure 9-19 through Figure 9-27, created from the test fields in the cube, show what you can accomplish; each graph could be part of a dashboard in Excel Services. The fields required and their locations (that is, how to construct the graphs) are also noted. Afterward, some of the information that the graphs display will be discussed.

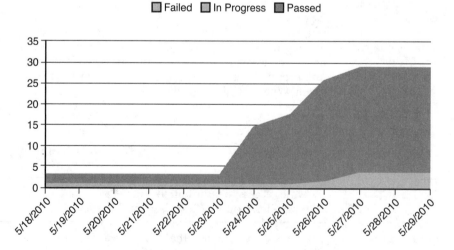

FIGURE 9-19: Test Results (Result Count Trend)

Test Results (Point Count Trend)

Never Run Passed Fail

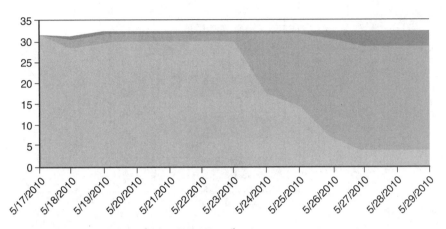

FIGURE 9-20: Test Results (Point Count Trend)

Test Case Count by Requirement

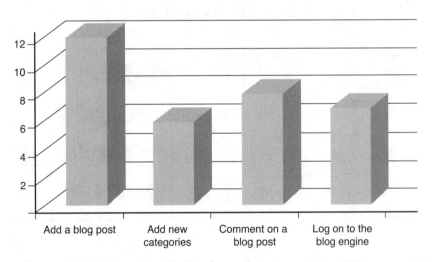

FIGURE 9-21: Test Case Count by Requirement

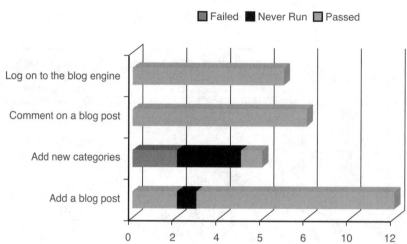

FIGURE 9-22: Requirements Status (1)

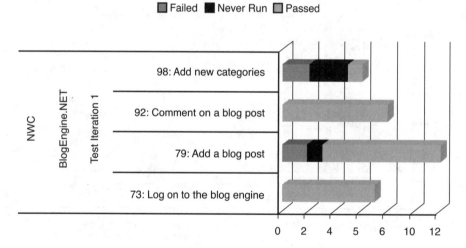

FIGURE 9-23: Requirements Status (2)

Execution by Tester and Date

■ Jeff Smith ■ Linda Collier ■ Rennie Arcturo

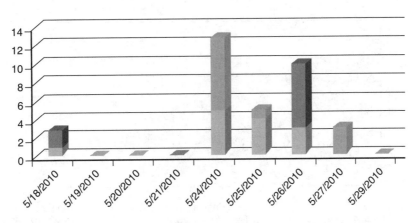

FIGURE 9-24: Execution by Tester

Test Failures by Type

■ Failed Known Issue   ■ Failed New Issue

■ Failed Regression   ■ Failed Unknown

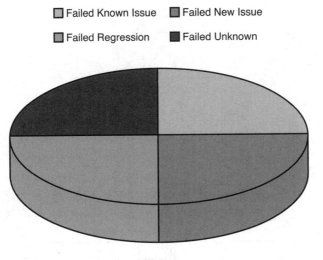

FIGURE 9-25: Test Failures by Type

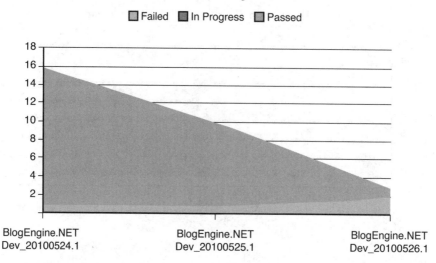

FIGURE 9-26: Test Results by Build

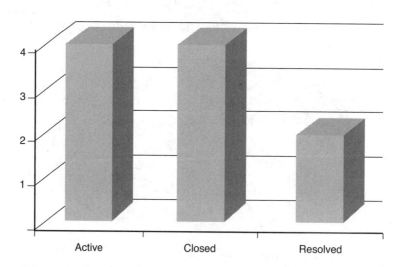

FIGURE 9-27: Bug Count by State

The information needed to create each of these reports is shown in Table 9-3.

TABLE 9-3: Fields and Placement to Create Excel Reports

Figure	Report Filter	Legend Field	Axis Field	Value
9-19	Test Plan Name	Outcome	Date, Test Run Title	Result Count Trend
9-20	N/A	Outcome	Date	Point Count Trend
9-21	Work Item Linked. Work Item Type, Work Item Linked. Iteration Path	N/A	Work Item Linked. Title, Test Case.Title	Point Count Trend
9-22	Work Item Linked. Work Item Type, Work Item Linked. Iteration Path	Outcome	Work Item Linked. Title, Test Case.Title	Point Count Trend
9-23	N/A	Outcome	Test Suite Hierarchy	Point Count Trend
9-24	Team Project Hierarchy	Test Result Executed By	Date	Result Count
9-25	Team Project Hierarchy	N/A	Outcome, Failure Type	Result Count Trend
9-26	N/A	Outcome	Build Name	Build Result Count Trend
9-27	Work Item Type (bug)	N/A	State	Work Item Count

Some of these reports look almost identical—and they are. This shows you some of the different information available and that some ways are a bit easier than others to get to the same data. In addition, some of these charts make a good demonstration for the test measures discussed earlier.

The difference between Figure 9-19 and Figure 9-20 is a perfect example of the difference between the Point Count Trend and Result Count Trend. Figure 9-19 provides information on just the Test Cases that have been executed, so the Result Count Trend gives you that information. But, if you want to know information about the number of Test Cases that have not been executed (that is, they have no results) the Point Count Trend provides that information.

Figures 9-21 and 9-22 are actually closely related. The only thing that separates them is the addition of the Outcome dimension on Figure 9-22. And Figure 9-22 is simply a refinement of already existing data but shows so much more information. Figure 9-23 is another way to present the same information shown in Figure 9-22 but in a far simpler manner. Figure 9-23 uses the Test Suite Hierarchy dimension to represent the information; you can see that hierarchy in the label (NWC\BlogEngine.NET\Test Iteration 1). It is easy to remove this label after the fact. This report required only three fields to create, whereas the reports shown in Figures 9-21 and 9-22 required six fields.

Figure 9-24 is a simple way to determine which tester executed how many tests with what outcomes on a given day. It helps keep track of the amount of Test Cases each tester is actually executing and whether some testers find more or less bugs than other testers. In practice this information isn't particularly helpful except to ensure that testers are testing. (Although I don't like reports used for this purpose, management most assuredly will.) This report can be refined further by adding test configuration information, or test plan information to note how many different plans testers are working in.

In addition to reporting with Excel, you can create many more powerful reports and Scorecards with other tools in the Microsoft family of products from PowerPivot (an Excel add-in) to PerformancePoint and Visio and SQL Server Reporting Services. Explore the different platforms to see what fits your organization's needs best.

Metrics

Up to this point, you have learned how to create test plans, create tests, and execute tests. You also gained hints and tips for the types of information you should look for. This section brings that information together in a discussion about what makes a quality metric and what you can do with it.

Before discussing metrics, determine what metrics are important and relevant in the testing context. Metrics can best be defined as "measurements taken of specific processes with the intention of improving those processes over time." If you take measurements and do not compare them to previous measurements, they are useless. If you take measurements of all processes, the value of the measurements is useless because you have no clearly defined purpose for gathering those measurements. There are many great quotes from people of all walks of life that apply. Some of those that apply are listed here.

> "Where you cannot measure your knowledge is meagre and unsatisfactory."
>
> —Lord Kelvin (Sir William Thomson)

> "I believe in evidence. I believe in observation, measurement, and reasoning, confirmed by independent observers. I'll believe anything, no matter how wild and ridiculous, if there is evidence for it. The wilder and more ridiculous something is, however, the firmer and more solid the evidence will have to be."
>
> —Isaac Asimov

> "If it can't be expressed in figures, it is not science; it is opinion."
>
> —Robert Heinlein

> "It is really just as bad technique to make a measurement more accurately than is necessary as it is to make it not accurately enough."
>
> —Arthur David Ritchie

> "The progress of science is often affected more by the frailties of humans and their institutions than by the limitations of scientific measuring devices. The scientific method is only as effective as the humans using it. It does not automatically lead to progress."
>
> —Steven S. Zumdahl

These quotes all convey different ideas about measurement—what it means to have a measurement and what it means to not have a measurement. Probably the most important of all the quotes about metrics is the last one by Steven Zumdahl. His point is elegantly stated—just because you are given the information with which to make improvements, it is up to you to act on that information—information without action is wasted information.

When trying to improve a company's process, the company must start with a desire to make a change. If a company does not want to change, gathering metrics is not useful and a further waste of time on top of the time already wasted. For those organizations that do want to make a change, that is the first step. It is exactly like any 12-step program: You can't get help until you admit you have a problem. But when you do, and are willing to make a change, the possibilities are almost endless. This is not a simple decision. Not because companies don't want to make a change but because there is a cost associated with gathering metrics, reviewing them, and then improving the process—it is not free. But the reality is that if an organization spends the time and money to do it correctly, it can get a ROI by improving efficiency, increasing quality, and increasing customer satisfaction.

In general two areas exist in which people want to make improvements: time management (tracking time, schedule, resources, and so on) and quality. Although separate, these two areas are inextricably linked. Why? You cannot manage time, schedule, and resources without understanding the effects of poor quality. And you cannot become more efficient unless you reduce the number of defects. This is why testers are so critical to any strategy to improve process.

CUSTOMIZING THE PROCESS TEMPLATES

The process of customizing work items is beyond the scope of this book because although it is generally a simple process, so many options exist. For more information on customizing process templates, see http://msdn. microsoft.com/en-us/library/ms243849(VS.100).aspx. Again, the MSDN documentation team has done an excellent job with the 2010 release, and this topic links you to all the information you need to know to perform a customization.

As you read this information, be aware that this is not a full-blown discussion of how to implement a metrics gathering program in an organization. Many steps are involved in that process and many organizational challenges. Rather, read this with an eye toward understanding what you should be gathering and work to apply it on a project-by-project basis. (Or augment an organizational plan if these ideas are relevant to you.)

What to Measure

The first question to ask is, "What should I measure?" To answer that you need to ask another question, "What am I having problems with?" This may be a bit more difficult to answer. What are you having problems with right now, or what areas do you want to improve efficiency and quality in? You've probably identified some items you want to improve—even if you don't have hard data on what the specific problem is, you "know" a problem exists. After you identify what you want to change, cut the list down to just one or two items. Trying to measure everything at one time can throw up too many variables for you to adequately determine root cause and also cause you to not measure the results of changes easily. (That is, what change did I make that changed the results?) Also, too many changes at one time can overwhelm the development team—a team that probably already has enough work to do that concentrating on many additional changes at one time would be detrimental to its productivity.

After you have the order of items you want to improve, you need to determine how to quantify the problem because if you can't measure it, you can't determine improvement. In any organization, management will not authorize a dime being spent if you can't prove that you are having a problem and don't have a plan to show improvement. So before you start making changes, make the case in an objective way. To do this you need to determine what measure (or measures) to use—don't worry about the solution to it now. Depending on the issue, you may want to track different aspects.

Look for several basic aspects of software development that relate directly to quality. These are the "low-hanging fruit" and can be easy to fix with the right plan, resources, and tools:

- First-time defect rate
- Bug reactivations (bad bug fixes)
- General bug counts

These serve as the basic high-level metrics and lay the groundwork for all other quality metrics. These may be too high level for you if you want to solve a specific problem but are discussed toward the end of this section. Now look at each of these items to determine how to measure them, the cause, and the solution.

How to Capture a Metric

When you first set out to gather a measurement, you need to do a little bit of upfront work. Worry about how to fix it after you have proven it. This work starts with defining the problem that you want to prove. (Assuming that you don't already have a baseline, you need to create one first.) Maybe the problem is a high number of defects with a certain feature in the application.

After you define the problem, determine the measurement that you want to use. In this example, you may determine that comparing the bug count in this particular feature with the bug counts in the other features is the way to go. Possibly you could simplify this by measuring the percentage of bug counts in this feature versus the rest of the application, to save on some overhead.

Having done this, you need to determine what pieces of data are required to calculate the metric. In this case you need a way to map the bug that was filed against a specific feature. Guess what? If you correctly use TFS and file bugs against a requirement, the information is automatically captured and calculated.

But maybe the team is not associating bugs with requirements. You need to document the process change so that the team understands how to do this. And this is a critical point that you must not underestimate: One of the key barriers to capturing valid data is the culture. If developers and testers don't follow the process, any data you gather is, by extension, invalid. You must socialize the information you are trying to gather. Explain to the team why this process must be followed, what data you are trying to gather, and what you will use it for. If there isn't a business decision at the end of the tunnel, why bother? So what's the explanation?

In this particular case, you want the team to be proactive about finding and fixing the bugs because of poor customer satisfaction or lost sales due to the product not working properly.

You may need to determine the accuracy of this perception.

Whatever you do, realize that the development team must be your ally, and you cannot gather information that does not somehow benefit the team. At the end of the day, people do what makes things better for them. That may sound cynical, but if you do not approach the process like this, you can have an uphill battle.

First-Time Defect Rate

The first-time defect rate is a popular metric that people like to look at, which tells how many defects are filed against requirements after the developer says, "I'm done." Usually first-time defect rates are quite high. The downside of this is that it means testers and developers (and maybe users) are wasting a lot of time.

Causes of First-Time Defects

The two major causes of first-time defects are coding errors and expectations. The first item, coding errors, is straightforward. The developers made a mistake and didn't catch it while they were testing. This happens all the time, even though we wish that were not the case. The second item is a bit more insidious but actually easier to solve than the first item. So let's look at the second item first.

What do I mean by expectations? I mean that what the tester expects the application to do and what the developer thought the application should do are different. If this is the case, teams are setting up for a high first-time defect rate. The solution is easy: Make sure the developers and testers have the same expectations from the beginning.

The second problem, coding errors, usually occurs because not all possible paths were thought through or the developers were rushing to get code done and overlooked something. The solution to this is also simple: code reviews and in many cases Unit Testing.

Measuring the Defect Rate

Measuring the problem is fairly easy if you use the process templates correctly. But it can still be a little tricky. Following is the process: Developers have a requirement in the Active state and a series of tasks also in the Active state. As the developers finish each task, they set the state to Closed. (Even if you use the CMMI template, you can simply skip the Resolved state for Task work item types.) After all the tasks related to the requirement are closed, the developers set the requirement to Resolved. This is the indicator to the testers that they can test the requirement. During testing, if they find bugs, they will do a couple of things. First, they file a bug that by default is associated with the Test Case. The next step the testers perform is more difficult. They assign the bug to the developers. Why is this more difficult? Because, if they simply assign bugs to the developers as they file them, you can't determine a first time defect versus a reoccurring defect. With a constant flow back and forth, it is difficult to determine.

This is one of the lessons you should take away about metrics: You must figure out how the process affects the measurements. If you don't, everyone can still follow the process, but you can end up with measurements that you can't parse to come up with valid information. How do you get around this? You can set a time frame. For example, maybe you create a test plan for "newly completed requirements" and test only on first-time finished require-ments as part of this plan. Then it's fairly straightforward because you can look at the plan and say how many bugs were filed against it. You can clone the test suite to another plan that can be the "fixed requirements" plan. To report on first-time defects, list the bugs created based on Test Cases in the "newly completed requirements" test plan. And to compare first-time defects with the rest of the defects, compare this to the total number of defects in all other plans. Simple. But it requires planning.

Lowering the First-Time Defect Rate

As mentioned previously, lowering these defects is straightforward if the commitment is there. To start with, have customers sign off on Test Cases in addition to requirements *before* developers start coding. Right now you are thinking, "No way will that ever happen." That's why you need to have a commitment. But if you think about it, it isn't that hard to make happen.

The Test Cases don't need to be fantastically detailed. The more detailed the better, but you want to create a baseline that makes sense: Look at certain agile techniques such as writing Acceptance Test Cases on the back of the user story index card. Keep it simple. What you need to do in this situation is to get a common understanding between the customer, developers, and testers.

It won't be perfect because customers change their mind all the time, but at least you can tell when it was the customer changing its mind versus the developers making a mistake.

WHAT TO TEST

Chapter 3, "Planning Your Testing," started this discussion. When time is short you must ensure that you test 100% of the normal path activities. That is, you want to test the parts of the system that will be most used by the customer. Test as many of the alternative and exception paths as you can, (Obviously, if you can, test all of them 100%, but that is rarely the case.) If you can't wait for testers to create every Test Case, make sure they create the important ones first. Tests such as boundary conditions and other nuanced technical tests can be created while the developers are writing code. It is the business-oriented Test Cases that are most important in this situation.

This next recommendation applies to both causes of first-time defects: Make sure the developers' work goes through a formal code review. Only in this case you need to add one more twist: The developers execute the Test Case before they give it to the testers. What are the odds of the testers finding a defect? The answer is a lot less than if the developers didn't first run the testers' Test Case.

Comparing Measurements

This metric can be easy to measure if you work on an agile project in which the team is working on a certain number of features each iteration. You can baseline it by not making any changes to how you normally do work the first few iterations and then compare the first-time defect rate every iteration. This is a good example of the time box style of measurement previously mentioned. For longer running projects with larger iterations or no iterations, you need to create artificial time boxes to perform measurements and break up requirements in such a way that you can measure them accurately.

Comparing this metric between projects is valid. It is not team-dependent; it is process-dependent. Some metrics, such as estimating accuracy, are team-dependent, but this isn't one of those metrics.

Related Metrics

This is a list of metrics that can have some type of impact on the first-time defect rate metric. Although this metric appears be fairly easy to capture and reduce, other data is pertinent to this metric:

- **Requirement complexity**—The more complex the requirement, the greater likelihood of first-time defects. Try breaking the requirements down into smaller requirements.

- **Number of external systems involved**—Some things are beyond your control. At a certain point, you need to accept it, but you should account for it if possible.

- **Defects versus change requests**—Customers can and do change their mind. This leads to what looks like defects but in reality are not. Having Test Cases available to verify functionality should enable you to account for these changes as actual change requests rather than defects.

Bug Reactivations

A bug reactivation is just what it sounds like. The bug was "fixed" before but wasn't actually fixed. This is just straight waste, and teams must eliminate this almost entirely.

Causes of Bug Reactivations

Only one cause for reactivating a bug exists: The bug was not well documented the first time. This causes the developer to have to guess at the solution, or the developer cannot reproduce the bug in the first instance and closes it; then a tester or user finds it.

Measuring Reactivations

TFS tracks reactivations—that is, how many times bugs and requirements transition from the Resolved or Closed state back to the Active state. This requires some diligence on the part of the team. Every time a bug is filed against a resolved requirement, the tester must reset the requirement back to the Active state. When a tester goes to verify a bug, if the bug is not resolved, the tester must set the bug back to Active. Typically, every time a bug is reactivated, a requirement must also be reactivated, but this largely depends on your teams' strategy. (The built-in reports can give you information on either work item type, but the Bug work item type is more important.) If testing occurs on unresolved functionality, this does not apply. For this reason, what appears on the Reactivations report may give you different information depending on your process.

Lowering the Reactivation Rate

Fortunately, the tools available in MTM and Visual Studio should reduce reactivations. Where the tools won't help as much is when customers file bugs. This is where process is important and somewhat independent of any tool suite that you use. But assuming that you are reading this book because you are using MTM and VS, you have an advantage over everyone else.

From a process perspective, take the time to have testers reproduce the bug, and have testers close the bug if it can't be reproduced. Do not assign the work to developers when you haven't verified the bug and provided detailed instructions on how to re-create it. That just annoys everyone. Using testers as the gatekeepers to the developers keeps the developers doing what they should be doing—writing code.

Comparing Measurements

You probably want to compare measurements against your current project because fewer reactivations mean less wasted time and higher productivity. Your best bet is simply to trend the reactivations using the built-in reactivations report.

General Bug Counts

Chapter 1 mentioned four bug count metrics: Total Bug Count, Bug Count per Phase, Bug Count per Feature (bug density map), and Regression Bug Count. Each of these numbers provides information about waste but also about how to prevent future problems. This information is actually some of the easiest information to capture but might be a bit tricky.

A NOTE ABOUT GENERAL BUG COUNTS

Often there is a big push to lower the total bug count. This is obviously a good idea if the time is available. But a key focus is on making sure that the right bugs are fixed. Recognizing that there will always be bugs, you want to make sure you get rid of the bugs that customers are most likely to find. Therefore, use general bug counts as a guide but work to understand which bugs are the highest priority and fix those first.

Measuring General Bug Counts

Let's look at the Total Bug Count. Are you capturing it right now? Are you sure? You may not be because the Total Bug Count *includes bugs found in production.* Where this becomes tricky is if there is no integration with the help desk. Every bug that comes in from the help desk, and bugs found in testing must be entered into TFS. The obvious goal of counting bugs is to know the quality of the software and to improve that quality.

Bug Count per Phase is an interesting metric because it is designed to measure the effectiveness of the testing process and also the developer/tester relationship. At the Bug Count per Phase (this metric applies only to a waterfall structure) look for a steady reduction in Bug Counts per Phase. In other words, if you find bugs earlier, there will be fewer bugs later. And this makes perfect sense. Bugs not found earlier in the process lead to an increased number of bugs later in the process. Improving this number involves introducing testers early in the process, including peer reviews of requirements, design, and functional specifications. If formal testing is not done early in the process (and yes, peer reviews are a form of testing) the reduction of bugs in later phases can never be accomplished. It is almost impossible to code around a requirement or design defect, and if you do, it will simply come back to haunt you later. This information can be captured by TFS in a variety of ways. As mentioned in Chapter 5, "Resolving Bugs," there is a Found In field in the Bug work item type for the CMMI template but not for the Agile template. One easy way to solve this without customizing the work item type is to use areas. Set up one area for Testing, User Acceptance Testing, and Production, and simply classify the bugs based on when they are discovered.

Bug Count per Feature has a different focus. The goal of this metric is to identify weak features—those features likely to produce more bugs in the future. The effect of gathering the number of bugs per feature enables you to classify the highest risk features and to implement additional testing against those features. There should be a correspondingly high number of Test Cases against a feature that has a high number of bugs. This enables teams to get ahead of the problem. Maybe this also includes doing additional code reviews and being proactive about the feature quality. This information can be captured in one of two ways: by using areas to classify bugs as belonging to a feature or by simply linking bugs to the requirement. (I would argue for the latter.)

Regression bugs are the last of the bug count totals. Regression bugs indicate two items: The testing process is inadequate when dealing with bug fixes (reactivations) or change requests and that some code may be more fragile than other pieces of code. When a bug is discovered in an area that has already been tested, the information must be captured in a way that facilitates reporting these bugs as regressions. The Reactivations section describes resetting bugs from Closed back to Active, which is a way to capture a regression bug as well. Another way to handle this is to simply set the Failure Type in the test result to Regression, which provides a clean, easy way to report on it.

HOW TO REPORT THEM

How you report a regression is up to you. You need to take proactive steps to ensure that regression bugs don't occur. Whether these are reactivations, you need to recognize the issues and make changes. Or you can record them as both reactivations and regressions; just don't look at the reports with each other because they can give an inflated and incorrect view of application quality.

Reducing General Bug Counts

Following are a couple of general suggestions for reducing bug counts: formal reviews and testing the 20% of code used 80% of the time.

Formal Reviews

Formal reviews, or the lack of, are one of the key issues when looking at quality. So how do you track reviews and what does this have to do with testers? The MSF for CMMI template includes a Review work item type. One thing that works is to attach one or more Review work items to each feature that needs to be reviewed (maybe a design review, in-progress review, and final review). This enables you to schedule reviews. But how effective are your reviews? A review requires a couple of key items. A formal agenda is absolutely required; if you perform informal reviews, they cannot provide as many benefits. You also need to provide a list of items that will be reviewed and what the expectations of those items are. You must have the code metrics, the results of a static code analysis run, code comments, and so on. You also must give individuals who will be involved in the review some time to read the documentation related to the feature so that they are prepared.

How much money does it cost to hold a review? The costs depend on the salary of the people involved, but you can do a basic cost calculation with a burden of $100 per person. Say there are four people involved in the review (the developer who wrote the code, another developer, a tester, and a note taker). Each of these people prepares for the meeting for 1 hour for a total of 4 hours. The review is 1 hour for a total of another 4 hours. This is a total of 8 hours, $800 dollars. Now, contrast this against finding a bug. The bug is filed, and the developer talks to the tester about the bug—or even worse they must figure out what is causing the bug. This takes maybe 2 hours. The developer then fixes the bug. There is no easy way to determine how long it takes to fix it, but let's say it's a simple 3-hour fix. Next, the tester needs to test the feature again—the time it takes is unknown but say 1 hour. So this is 6 hours of rework plus the developer can't work on new features for those 3 hours and the tester for that 1 hour. So finding a single bug would cost more than a single review. The truth is that code reviews almost always find more than one issue before it becomes a bug. When applied to documentation reviews, the number of potential issues found will probably be much higher.

Now how do you track reviews? The first rule is that you do not fix problems during the review; you'll never finish the review if you do. The second rule is that you do not file bugs during a review. Because you are supposed to find things during reviews, the developers' work should not be "complete" at this point, so don't penalize them. And the third rule is that the review is to provide constructive criticism—not beat the person who made the mistakes over the head. This is where the old axiom of not throwing stones in glass houses applies. But what should you do? You can do a few things that give you the ability to report on reviews. The first is to simply create child tasks for the review—one for each issue discovered. This enables you to track the status of all the items found during the review and does not penalize the developer but provides a list of what needs to be fixed. This also enables you to determine the effectiveness of the review process. If you hold a review and no tasks are created from the review, you aren't doing the review correctly. The reality is that you will almost always find something to fix. So a lot of reviews with no associated tasks mean the process needs to be examined. The second solution is to associate tasks with the Review work item and the Requirement for which the review was done. If you do it this way, the tasks created from the review would be linked to the review with a Related link type and would be a child of the Requirement.

Test the Normal Path First

In every development project, a limit exists on time and resources. The practical effect of this for testers is that they cannot test everything. You should have thorough coverage of all requirements, but reality almost always gets in the way. This means that you need to be selective in what you test. The problem occurs when testers feel like they have to test everything with no time or software that isn't ready for testing. This leads to lower quality tests that have broad coverage but no depth. The solution is to focus on the normal path, which means 100% test coverage of the normal path. This actually has a positive effect on the metrics. The number of bugs found by users can decrease because the part of the application used most by users has the highest amount of test coverage. The key to using this technique is that when bugs start to get filed against alternative path scenarios that you jump on them with a vengeance. If users find one bug, okay. If they find two bugs, you better work up and execute Test Cases quickly for those scenarios. Determining the bug density count by feature can help you track this trend.

How do you track this coverage? The easiest way is to add an area for Normal Path and an area for Alternative Path and simply classify the Test Cases in the appropriate area. This may not always be acceptable because areas may be used for some other specific purpose. Another way to handle this is to modify the Test Case work item type and add a field that enables you to specify normal or alternative paths. Either of these simple changes can enable you to run reports that determine what percentage of the normal path tests have been executed against a requirement and what percentage of alternative path tests have been executed against a requirement. You can then correlate bugs found with test coverage of the requirements and make an informed decision about when to increase the test coverage of alternative path tests.

SUMMARY

At the end of the day, teams write Test Cases to validate requirements and execute tests to verify quality. Doing this is not helpful if the information cannot be quickly and easily examined for trends and forecasting, which is exactly what the TFS Cube lets teams do. By using the innate capabilities of TFS, teams have an in-depth understanding of their applications in a way that was previously unavailable. You can use this information to apply resources to resolve problems before they start to affect the team.

Stakeholders can use this information to make informed business decisions based on accurate data. Is a requirement ready for release? Should the requirement be delayed because too many problems exist? The additional information provided by the reports enables businesses to make better decisions.

This chapter introduced you to the TFS Cube, how data is processed, and how to report on that data to meet your needs. It also brings you full circle in your understanding of the testing tools in Visual Studio 2010, Microsoft Test Manager 2010, and Team Foundation Server 2010. You have the ability to plan the testing process, write and execute Test Cases, file and resolve bugs, and report those results to your users. Over time Microsoft will evolve the platform to include even more capabilities and further reduce the cost of finding and fixing bugs.

Index

A

Acceptance Test Driven Development (ATDD), 26

acceptance testing, 25

  ATDD (Acceptance Test Driven Development), 26

access to Test Cases, 6

active state, 93

adding

  recorded steps, 164-165

  validations, 157-164

advantages of Microsoft Visual Studio 2010, 5

  automated tests, 9-10

  communication, 5-6

  development and testing process flow, 7-9

  metrics, 10-12

  project visibility, 6

agents, running as interactive processes, 185

Agile, updating bugs, 114

agile practices, 23

agile testing, 20

Agile Testing: A Practical Guide for Testers and Agile Teams (Crispin and Gregory), 20

ALM (Application Lifecycle Management), 19

analysis categories, 42-43

analysis phase (Test Cases), 56-61

Analysis section, detailed test results, 95

Application Lifecycle Management (ALM), 19

applications

  BlogEngine.NET. *See* application, xxiv

Asimov, Isaac, 269

ASP.NET, MSAA, 162

assigning

  builds, 127-129

  test configurations, 51-53

  testers, 53-54

Associated Change sets, 124

Associated Work Items, 124

associating

  Coded UI Tests and Test Cases, 178-181

  Unit Tests, 181

ATDD (Acceptance Test Driven Development), 26

Attachments section, detailed test results, 98-100

attributes, 186

automated builds, creating, 191

automated builds (Test Plans), 40-41

automated test settings, 221-222

  Lab Management workflow, 222-231

automated testing, 24

automated testing framework, 139-141

automated tests, 9-10

  creating from manual tests, 141-142

    coded UI tests, 144-157

    examining generated web application coded UI tests, 142-144

  executing, 183-184

    from command line, 190

    local execution, 184

    local execution with remote collection, 184

    in MTM, 191-196

    remote execution, 185-189

  executing with Team Build, 202-203

  issues with, 205

    custom dialogs, 205-207

  running through MTM, 233-234

automating manual Test Cases, 142

automation, choosing to automate, 136-138

B

best practices for parameterized tests, 88

binaries, 82

black-box testing, 21

Blocked field, 113

blocked test cases, 101

BlogEngine.NET application, xxiv

BlogEntryHTMLBasicTestCodedUI-TestMethods, 167

boundary cases, 21

Browser Window class, 150

bug count per feature, 11, 279

bug count per phase, 11, 278

bug reactivations, 276

  comparing measurements, 277

  lowering, 277

  measuring, 276

Bug Status reports, 244-245

Bug Trends reports, 245-246

Bug work item type, 107-110

  customer reported bugs, 110

  reactivations, 111

  test team reported bugs, 110

  triaging bugs, 110

Bug work item type, generated bugs, 116-119

bug workflow, 113

bugs

  bug count per feature, 11

  bug count per phase, 11

  differences and modifications, 112-116

  finding and filing, 88-89

  fixing, 122-124

    Associated Change sets, 124

    Associated Work Items, 124

    impacted tests, 125

  regression bugs, 11, 16, 138

  total bug count, 11

  triaging, 116

  updating in Agile, 114

  verifying fixes, 129-131

$(Build Location), 228

Build Quality Indicators reports, 246-248

build reports, 232
Build Result Count Trend, 257
Build Success over Time reports, 248-249
Build Summary reports, 249-250
build warnings, 204
building quality at the beginning of projects, 17
builds, 82
  assigning, 127-129
  automated builds, creating, 191
  dual purpose, 233
  lab builds, executing, 231-232
  quality, 125-127
  retention, 130
  work items, 125
builds (Test Plans), 40-41
built-in reports, 242-244
  Bug Status, 244-245
  Bug Trends, 245-246
  Build Quality Indicators, 246-248
  Build Success over Time, 248-249
  Build Summary, 249-250
  reactivations, 246
  Stories Overview, 250-251
  Test Case Readiness, 251-252
  Test Plan Progress, 252-253
built-in templates, 224
business value of software quality, 14

C

capturing metrics, 272
challenges of software testing, 1-3
Cigna Corporation, 4
cleaning up tests, 207
closing IE Browser window, 165
Code Complete (McConnell), 13

code coverage, 11
Coded UI Test builds, 159
Coded UI Tests, 24, 144-147
  associating with Test Cases, 178-181
  maintaining, 154
  recording from scratch, 165
  running through MTM, 196-199
  searching for controls, 148-157
CodedUITestMethods, 170, 175
combining tests, 178
command line, executing automated tests, 190
communication, improving, 5-6
$(ComputerName_), 228
Computer Science Corporation, 4
configurations (Test Plans), 41
configuring virtual environments, 217-218
connecting to Team Foundation Server, 33-34
construction phase (Test Cases), 61-62
Contents section (Test Plans), 43
  query-based suites, 45
  requirements-based suites, 44-45
  static suites, 46
Continuous Integration builds, 40
Control Specific section, validations, 161
controls, searching for (Coded UI Tests), 148-157
corner cases, 21
cost of poor software quality, 3-5
costs, defect cost, 11
Covey, Stephen R., 26
Crispin, Lisa, 20
cube (SSAS), 240-242
Cunningham, Ward, 246
custom dialogs, automated tests, 205-207

customer reported bugs, 110
customizing
  process templates, 115, 270
  work items, 61

D

cashboards, 254
data, gathering diagnostic data, 235
data driven test cases, 77
data sources, Test Cases, 168
database unit testing, 22
default diagnostic data adapters (Test Plans), 40
defect cost, 11
defect root cause, 11
Deploy.cmd, 227
DeployDatabase.cmd, 229
deployed products, testing, 27-28
deployed VMs, 214
deploying test code, 127
detailed test results, 95
  Analysis section, 95
  Attachments section, 98-100
  Links section, 100
  Result History section, 100-101
  Test Step Details section, 96-97
developer-focused testing, 184
developers, testing, 136
development
  ATDD (Acceptance Test Driven Development), 26
  FDD (feature-driven development), 65-66
  moving from one iteration to another, 67-68
development of Lab Management, xviii-xix

development of Microsoft Visual Studio Test Professional 2010, xvii-xix
diagnostic data, gathering, 235
diagnostic data adapters (Test Plans), 40
differences, bugs, 112-116
documentation, MSDN, 253
done, definition of, 18
dual purpose builds, 233
dynamic values, 172-178

E

edge cases, 21
editing test steps, 73
encrypted passwords, 148
end of projects, building quality at, 17
environments, setting up (executing automated tests), 193-196
examining test results, 92-93
  detailed test results, 95-101
  test run results, 93-94
Excel Services, 243
Excel Services reports, 253-254
Exception Data, 120
executing
  automated tests, 183-184
    from the command line, 190
    in MTM, 191-196
    local execution, 184
    local execution with remote collection, 184
    remote execution, 185-189
    with Team Build, 202-203
  lab builds, 231-232
  tests, 85-86, 159
    parameterized tests, 87
expectations of software quality, 15

exploratory testing, 23
  MTM, 101-104
external software quality, 13-14

F

failures, failure categories, 42
FBI's Virtual Case File system, 4
FDD (feature-driven development), 65-66
feature-driven development (FDD), 65-66
filing bugs, 88-89
finding bugs, 88-89
first-time defect rate, 273
  causes of, 273
  comparing measurements, 275
  lowering, 274-275
  measuring, 273-274
  related metrics, 276
fixing bugs, 122-124
  Associated Change sets, 124
  Associated Work Items, 124
  impacted tests, 125
formal reviews, reducing general bug
  count, 280
Found in Environment field, 114
FQDN (fully qualified domain
  name), 228
frameworks, automated testing, 139-141
functional testing, 24

G

general bug counts, 277
  measuring, 278-279
  reducing, 279-282
Generate Code dialog, 164
generated bugs, 116-119

generated control class, 174
generated web application coded UI
  tests, 142-144
generating
  reports from work item queries, 255-256
  ValidateHTMLInfo code, 171
goals of software testing, 19
gray-box testing, 22
Gregory, Janet, 20
Group Policy Editor, 206

H

Heinlein, Robert, 269
How Found field, 114

I

IE Browser windows, closing, 165
IE DOM (Internet Explorer Document
  Object Model), 136
IEFrame properties, 162
impacted tests, 125, 131-132
importing
  Test Cases, 77
  VMs, 210-212
improving communication, 5-6
inconsistency issues, parameterized
  Coded UI Tests, 168-169
  resolving, 169-170
increasing project visibility, 6
initial design (Test Cases), 56-61
integration testing, 23-24
IntelliTrace, 119-122
Intellitrace Settings, 80
internal software quality, 13-14
$(InternalComputerName_ring, 228

Internet Explorer Document Object Model (IE DOM), 136

iterations, moving from one iteration to another, 67-68

K

Kelvin, Lord, 269

Kristensen, Mads, xxiv

L

lab builds, executing, 231-232

Lab Management, 194, 209
  development of, xviii-xix

Lab Management workflow, 222-231

Links section, detailed test results, 100

load testing, 24

local execution, automated testing, 184
  with remote collection, 184

LoggedOnUserPreFilledTestClass, 142-143

lowering
  bug reactivations, 277
  defect rates, 274-275

M

macros, 227-228

maintainability, 16

management, test management, 27

manual black-box testing, xvii-xviii

manual Test Cases, creating, 74-75

manual tests in virtual environments, 234-238

McConnell, Steve, 13

mean time between failures (MTBF), 16

measuring
  bug reactivations, 276
  defect rates, 273-274
  general bug counts, 278-279

metrics, 268-271
  bug reactivations, 276-277
  capturing, 272
  explained, 10-12
  first-time defect rate, 273
    causes of, 273
    comparing measurements, 275
    lowering, 274-275
    measuring, 273-274
    related metrics, 276
  general bug counts, 277
    measuring, 278-279
    reducing, 279-282
  what to measure, 271-272

Microsoft Active Accessibility. *See* MSAA

Microsoft Environment Viewer, 218

Microsoft Excel
  fields and placement, 267
  reporting with, 254
    creating generated reports, 255
    testing measures, 256-257
  reports, creating Test Cases, 257-268

Microsoft Team Foundation Server 2010, Lab Management, 194, 209

Microsoft Test Manager. *See* MTM

Microsoft Visual Studio Test Professional 2010, development of, xvii, xix

middle of project, building quality at, 17

modifications, bugs, 112-116

MOSS (Microsoft Office SharePoint Server), 239

MSAA (Microsoft Active Accessibility), 136
  ASP.NET, 162

MSBuild, 8

MSDN (Microsoft Developer Network), documentation, 253

MSF for Agile Bug work item types, 108

MSF for CMMI Bug work item type, 109

MSI packages, 217
MSTest.exe, 190
MTBF (mean time between failures), 16
MTM (Microsoft Test Manager), 8
  connecting to Team Foundation Server, 33-34
  executing automated tests, 191-192
    setting up physical environment, 193-196
  explained, 30
  exploratory testing, 101-104
  managing virtual environments, 210-216
  navigation controls, 30
  navigation layout, 31
  running automated tests, 233-234
  running Coded UI Tests, 196-199
    creating test settings, 199-201
  selecting team projects, 34
  table of components, 31-33
  Test Plans. *See* Test Plans
  Tool Center, 33

N

NameoftheblogShortdeDocument, 163
naming test assemblies, 192
navigation controls (MTM), 30
navigation layout (MTM), 31
need for testers, 3-5
nightly builds, 40
nonfunctional requirements
  explained, 15
  maintainability, 16
  reliability, 16
  security, 16
  usability, 16
Nyveldt, Al, xxiv

O

Original Estimate field, 114

P

parameterized Coded UI Tests, 166-168
  inconsistency issues, 168-169
  resolving inconsistency issues, 169-170
parameterized test cases, creating, 78
parameterized tests
  best practices, 88
  executing, 87
passwords, encrypted, 148
pausing test runs, 89-90
PeopleSoft, 4
physical environments, 198
physical machines, 194
PivotTable field sections, 261
plans. *See* test plans
Point Count Trend, 257
poor software quality, cost of, 3-5
PowerShell, 227
pre-user acceptance testing, 25
process, impact on quality, 19
process flow, 7-9
process templates, customizing, 115, 270
project visibility, increasing, 6
projects
  relationship with test suites, test cases, and Test Plans, 36
  selecting in MTM (Microsoft Test Manager), 34
properties of Test Plans, 38
Proposed Fix field, 115
purpose of software testing, 19

Q

quality
  as team effort, 18
  building at beginning of project, 17
  builds, 125-127
  business value, 14
  cost of poor software quality, 3-5
  definition of done, 18
  expectations, 15
  impact of process on, 19
  internal versus external, 13-14
  maintainability, 16
  reliability, 16
  requirements, 14
  security, 16
  usability, 16
query-based suites, 45

R

Range Selector, 102
reactivations, 111, 246
recorded steps, adding, 164-165
recording Coded UI Tests from
    scratch, 165
reducing general bug counts, 279-281
  test normal pathfirst, 281-282
regression bugs, 11, 16, 138, 279
regression testing, 25
related metrics, defect rates, 276
reliability, 16
remote collection, local execution
    (automated tests), 184
remote execution, automated testing,
    185-189
replaying test steps, 90-91

reporting with Microsoft Excel, 254
  creating generated reports, 255
  testing measures, 256-257
reporting structures, 240-242
reports
  built-in reports, 242-244
    Bug Status, 244-245
    Bug Trends, 245-246
    Build Quality Indicators, 246-248
    Build Success over Time, 248-249
    Build Summary, 249-250
    reactivations, 246
    Stories Overview, 250-251
    Test Case Readiness, 251-252
    Test Plan Progress, 252-253
  Excel Services, 253-254
  generating from work item queries,
      255-256
  User Stories, creating Test Cases,
      257-268
requirements for software quality, 14
requirements coverage, unit tests, 141
requirements-based suites, 44-45
resolution types, 42-43
resolving data inconsistency,
    parameterized Coded UI Tests,
    169-170
Result Count, 257
Result Count Trend, 257
Result History section, detailed test
    results, 100-101
resuming test runs, 89-90
Ritchie, Arthur David, 269
Root Cause field, 115
Run settings (Test Plans), 38-40
Run Tests page, 92

running
  automated tests through MTM, 233-234
  Coded UI Tests through MTM, 196-199
  tests, 79-80
    Test Runner, 80-84

S

SAP, 3
Scheduling Test Cases, 64-65
Science Applications International
    Corporation, Virtual Case File
    system, 4
SCRUM, 20
SCVMM (System Center Virtual Machine
    Manager), 210
search conditions, 176
searching for controls, coded UI tests,
    148-157
security, 16
security groups, test controllers, 194
server names, 233
servers, Team Foundation Server
    (connecting to), 33-34
service level agreements (SLAs), 16
SetupWebServer.cmd, 228
Share-Point, 243
Shared Step, executing tests, 86
shared steps
  creating, 76-77
  Test Case work item type, 75
shipped products, testing, 27-28
Siebel Systems, 4
SLAs (service level agreements), 16
smoke tests, 23
snapshots, 217
  of environments, 219-221

software quality
  as team effort, 18
  building at beginning of project, 17
  business value, 14
  definition of done, 18
  expectations, 15
  impact of process on, 19
  internal versus external, 13-14
  maintainability, 16
  reliability, 16
  requirements, 14
  security, 16
  usability, 16
software testing, need for testers, 4
speeding up testing, 234
SSAS (SQL Server Analysis Services), 239
  cube, 240-242
SSRS (SQL Server Reporting
    Services), 239
  built-in reports, 242-244
    Bug Status, 244-245
    Bug Trends, 245-246
    Build Quality Indicators, 246-248
    Build Success over Time, 248-249
    Build Summary, 249-250
    reactivations, 246
    Stories Overview, 250-251
    Test Case Readiness, 251-252
    Test Plan Progress, 252-253
static suites, 46
  Test Cases, 80
Stories Overview reports, 250-251
suites. See Test Suites
Symptom field, 115
System Center Virtual Machine Manager
    (SCVMM), 210
system testing, 21, 25

T

Tcm.exe, 190

Team Build, executing automated tests, 202-203

Team Foundation Server. *See* TFS

  connecting to, 33-34

Team Project Collections. *See* TPCs

teams, involvement in building software quality, 18

Technical Debt, 246

templates

  built-in, 224

  process templates, customizing, 115, 270

  Test Approach Word template, 30

test approach, 30

Test Approach Word template, 30

test assemblies, naming, 192

test attachments, 119

Test Case Readiness reports, 251-252

Test Case work item type, 72-74

  data driven test cases, 77

  shared steps, 75

    creating, 76-77

Test Cases

  access to, 6

  adding to Test Plans, 46-47

  assigning testers to, 53-54

  associating with Coded UI Tests, 178-181

  automating manual Test Cases, 142

  blocked, 101

  creating manual, 74-75

  data sources, 168

  FDD (feature-driven development), 65-66

  handling different test, configurations, 68

  importing, 77

  moving from one iteration to another, 67-68

  parameters, creating, 78

  relationship with team projects, test suites, and Test Plans, 36

  scheduling and tracking, 64-65

  static suites, 80

  testing workflow, 55-56

    analysis and initial design, 56-61

    construction, 61-62

    user acceptance testing, 62-64

  User Stories Report, 257-268

test code, deploying, 127

Test Configuration Manager

  accessing, 49

  adding configuration variables, 50

  assigning test configurations, 51-53

  creating test configurations, 51

test configurations

  accessing Test Configuration Manager, 49

  adding configuration variables, 50

  assigning, 51-53

  benefits of, 49

  creating, 51

  explained, 48

  handling different test configurations, 68

Test Controller Configuration tool, 193

Test Impact Analysis (TIA), 7, 125

Test List Editor, 158

test management, 27

Test Manager. *See* MTM (Microsoft Test Manager)

test parameters, 77

Test Plan Progress reports, 252-253

Test Plan Status section (Test Plans), 42
  analysis categories, 42-43
  failure categories, 42
Test Plans, 55. *See also* testing workflow
  builds, 40-41
  configurations, 41
  Contents section, 43-44. *See also* Test
    Suites
    static suites, 46
  creating, 37
  default diagnostic data adapters, 40
  properties, 38
  relationship with team projects, test
    suites, and test cases, 36
  Run settings, 38-40
  Selecting, 35
  Test Cases
    adding to plans, 46-47
    assigning testers to, 53-54
    FDD (feature-driven development),
      65-66
    handling different test
      configurations, 68
    moving from one iteration to another,
      67-68
    scheduling and tracking, 64-65
  Test Plan Status section, 42
    analysis categories, 42-43
    failure categories, 42
  Test Suites
    adding to plans, 46-47
    creating, 47
    query-based suites, 45
    requirements-based suites, 44
    static suites, 46
test results, examining, 92-93
  detailed test results, 95-101
  test run results, 93-94

Test Results, test attachments, 119
test run results, 93-94
Test Runner, 80-84
  bugs, finding and filing, 88-89
  pausing and resuming test runs, 89-90
  replaying test steps, 90-91
Test Runner (TR), 71
test runs, pausing and resuming, 89-90
Test Scribe tool, 33
test settings, creating, 199-201
Test Step Details section, detailed test
    results, 96-97
test steps
  editing, 73
  replaying, 90-91
Test Suites, 43-44
  adding to Test Plans, 46-47
  creating, 47
  query-based suites, 45
  relationship with team projects, test
    cases, and Test Plans, 36
  requirements-based suites, 44-45
  static suites, 46
test team reported bugs, 110
testers
  assigning, 53-54
  need for, 3-5
  testing mindset, 20
testing
  automated testing framework, 139-141
  developer-focused testing, 184
  exploratory testing with MTM, 101-104
  manual black-box testing, xvii-xviii
  speeding up, 234
testing measures, Microsoft Excel,
    256-257
testing mindset, 20

testing workflow, 55-56
  analysis and initial design, 56-61
  construction, 61-62
  user acceptance testing, 62-64
tests
  automated tests. *See* automated tests
  cleaning up, 207
  Coded UI Tests. *See* Coded UI Tests
  combining, 178
  executing, 85-86, 159
    parameterized tests, 87
  generated web application coded UI
    tests, 142-144
  impacted tests, 131-132
  manual tests in virtual environments,
    234-238
  parameterized Coded UI Tests, 166-168
    inconsistency issues, 168-169
    resolving inconsistency issues,
      169-170
  parameterized tests, best practices, 88
  running, 79-80
    Test Runner, 80-84
  Test Runner
    finding and filing bugs, 88-89
    pausing and resuming test runs, 89-90
    replaying test steps, 90-91
  Unit Tests
    associating, 181
    requirements coverage, 141
tests coded UI tests, 144-147
  searching for controls, 148-157
TFS (Team Foundation Server), 12, 239
  automated tests, 9-10
  metrics, explained, 10-12
TIA (Test Impact Analysis), 125, 132
  explained, 7-9

time, 241
Tool Center, 33
tools, Test Controller Configuration
  tool, 193
total bug count, 11
TPCs (Team Project Collections), 240
tracking Test Cases, 64-65
transparency, 6
triaging bugs, 110, 116

U

UAT (User Acceptance Testing), 21, 63
UI test files, 154-155
UIA (User Interface Automation), 136
UISigninDocument class, 150-152
UISigninWindowsInterneWindow
  class, 148
unit testing, 22
Unit Tests, associating, 181
  requirements coverage, 141
updating bugs in Agile, 114
usability, 16
User Stories reports, Test Cases
  (creating), 257-268
user acceptance testing, 62-64
User Acceptance Testing (UAT), 21
User Interface Automation (UIA), 136
users, expectations of software quality, 15

V

ValidateHTMLInfo code, generating, 171
validations
  adding, 157-158, 160-164
  multiple validations, 158
values, dynamic values, 172-178
variables, adding to test
  configurations, 50

verifying bug fixes, 129-131

videos, 97

Virtual Case File system (FBI), 4

virtual environments

  configuring, 217-218

  managing with MTM, 210-216

  manual tests, 234-238

  options, 215

  snapshots, 219-221

  versus virtual machines, 213

virtual machines, 194

  versus virtual environments, 213

virtualized testing, 90

visibility of projects, increasing, 6

Visual Studio Test Professional 2010, development of, xvii, xviii

VMs (virtual machines), importing, 210-212

VMWare virtual machines, 194

vsdbcmd command-line tool, 229

W-X-Y

Waste Management, Inc., 3

white-box testing, 21

Windows SharePoint Services (WSS), 243

work item queries, generating reports, 255-256

work items

  builds, 125

  customizing, 61

workflow, 55-56

  analysis and initial design, 56-61

  bugs, 113

  construction, 61-62

  user acceptance testing, 62-64

WSS (Windows SharePoint Services), 243

Z

zero defect releases, 3

Zumdahl, Steven S., 269

THIS PRODUCT

informit.com/register

Register the Addison-Wesley, Exam Cram, Prentice Hall, Que, and Sams products you own to unlock great benefits.

To begin the registration process, simply go to **informit.com/register** to sign in or create an account. You will then be prompted to enter the 10- or 13-digit ISBN that appears on the back cover of your product.

Registering your products can unlock the following benefits:

- Access to supplemental content, including bonus chapters, source code, or project files.
- A coupon to be used on your next purchase.

Registration benefits vary by product. Benefits will be listed on your Account page under Registered Products.

About InformIT — THE TRUSTED TECHNOLOGY LEARNING SOURCE

INFORMIT IS HOME TO THE LEADING TECHNOLOGY PUBLISHING IMPRINTS Addison-Wesley Professional, Cisco Press, Exam Cram, IBM Press, Prentice Hall Professional, Que, and Sams. Here you will gain access to quality and trusted content and resources from the authors, creators, innovators, and leaders of technology. Whether you're looking for a book on a new technology, a helpful article, timely newsletters, or access to the Safari Books Online digital library, InformIT has a solution for you.

THE TRUSTED TECHNOLOGY LEARNING SOURCE

Addison-Wesley | Cisco Press | Exam Cram
IBM Press | Que | Prentice Hall | Sams

SAFARI BOOKS ONLINE

Microsoft .NET Development Series

Essential .NET
Volume 1
The Common Language Runtime

Don Box
with Chris Sells

978-0-201-73411-9

The .NET Developer's Guide to Windows Security

Keith Brown

978-0-321-22835-2

Framework Design Guidelines
Conventions, Idioms, and Patterns for Reusable .NET Libraries

Krzysztof Cwalina
Brad Abrams

978-0-321-54561-9

Concurrent Programming on Windows

Joe Duffy

978-0-321-43482-1

Effective Use of Microsoft Enterprise Library
Building Blocks for Creating Enterprise Applications and Services

Len Fenster

978-0-321-33421-3

Essential C# 3.0
For .NET Framework 3.5

Mark Michaelis

978-0-321-53392-0

The Common Language Infrastructure Annotated Standard

James S. Miller
Susann Ragsdale

978-0-321-15493-4

Enterprise Services with the .NET Framework
Developing Distributed Business Solutions with .NET Enterprise Services

Christian Nagel

978-0-321-24673-8

Data Binding with Windows Forms 2.0
Programming Smart Client Data Applications with .NET

Brian Noyes

978-0-321-26892-1

Designing Forms for Microsoft Office InfoPath and Forms Services 2007

Scott Roberts
Hagen Green

978-0-321-41059-7

eXtreme .NET
Introducing eXtreme Programming Techniques to .NET Developers

Dr. Neil Roodyn

978-0-321-30363-9

Windows Forms 2.0 Programming

Chris Sells
Michael Weinhardt

978-0-321-26796-2

Essential Windows Workflow Foundation

Dharma Shukla
Bob Schmidt

978-0-321-39983-0

The Visual Basic .NET Programming Language

Paul Vick

978-0-321-16951-8

.NET Compact Framework Programming with C#

Paul Yao
David Durant

978-0-321-17403-1

.NET Compact Framework Programming with Visual Basic .NET

Paul Yao
David Durant

978-0-321-17404-8

NORTHWEST CADENCE®

where technology meets teamwork

Are You Ready for Hands-On Training on Test Professional 2010?

Testing with Test Professional 2010 & Visual Studio 2010 Ultimate

A two-day Hands-On Training Course developed by author Jeff Levinson and Northwest Cadence based on published book *Software Testing with Visual Studio 2010*

Location: Learn in our classroom, at your facility, or remotely.

Audience: Testers, Test Managers and Development Managers

By the end of this course, testers will be able to:
Start testing software with Microsoft Test Manager and TFS. Test Managers will have enough knowledge to manage testing activities with MTM and TFS. All participants should understand the workflow between developers and testers and understand the benefits of MTM and TFS.

Register: For details and dates, email testing@nwcadence.com

RECEIVE A DISCOUNT ON THE COURSE! 20%

Mention **Discount Code: AlreadyOwnBook** at Time of Registration

---

At Northwest Cadence, we are technologists. We are the trusted experts and we believe our customers deserve that. When you need something to work and work well, you call in specialists. We consult, coach, and train organizations to perfect your software development.

For more information on our consulting services and other offerings, email info@nwcadence.com

FREE Online
Edition

Your purchase of **Software Testing with Visual Studio® 2010** includes access to a free online edition for 45 days through the Safari Books Online subscription service. Nearly every Addison-Wesley Professional book is available online through Safari Books Online, along with more than 5,000 other technical books and videos from publishers such as Cisco Press, Exam Cram, IBM Press, O'Reilly, Prentice Hall, Que, and Sams.

SAFARI BOOKS ONLINE allows you to search for a specific answer, cut and paste code, download chapters, and stay current with emerging technologies.

Activate your FREE Online Edition at
www.informit.com/safarifree

> **STEP 1:** Enter the coupon code: EHSKYFA.

> **STEP 2:** New Safari users, complete the brief registration form.
> Safari subscribers, just log in.

If you have difficulty registering on Safari or accessing the online edition, please e-mail customer-service@safaribooksonline.com